◉ 普通高校专业英语教程系列

U0365872

文秘英语

陈红美 司爱侠 编著

清华大学出版社
北京

内 容 简 介

本书是针对文秘专业学生和相关职场人士编写的专业英语教材，力求切实提高读者实际使用英语的能力。

本书的每一单元由以下几部分组成：对话——提供课文相关的对话场景；课文——包括工作描述、应用技巧、常用方法和新颖观念；单词——给出课文中出现的新词，读者可以积累专业基础词汇；词组——给出课文中的常用词组；缩略语——给出课文中出现的且业内人士必须掌握的缩略语；注释——讲解课文中出现的疑难句子，培养读者的阅读理解能力；习题——巩固所学知识；阅读材料——提供最新的行业资料，进一步扩大读者的视野。

本书既可作为高等院校文秘专业的英语教材，也可作为相关专业的培训教材，供文秘从业人员自学使用。

版权所有，侵权必究。举报：010-62782989，beiqinquan@tup.tsinghua.edu.cn。

图书在版编目（CIP）数据

文秘英语 / 陈红美，司爱侠编著. —北京：清华大学出版社，2016（2023.2 重印）
（普通高校专业英语教程系列）
ISBN 978-7-302-45689-6

Ⅰ. ①文…　Ⅱ. ①陈… ②司…　Ⅲ. ①秘书—英语—高等学校—教材　Ⅳ. ① C931.46

中国版本图书馆 CIP 数据核字（2016）第 277241 号

责任编辑：徐博文
封面设计：平　原
责任校对：王凤芝
责任印制：沈　露

出版发行：清华大学出版社
网　　址：http://www.tup.com.cn, http://www.wqbook.com
地　　址：北京清华大学学研大厦 A 座　　**邮　　编**：100084
社 总 机：010-83470000　　**邮　　购**：010-62786544
投稿与读者服务：010-62776969, c-service@tup.tsinghua.edu.cn
质量反馈：010-62772015, zhiliang@tup.tsinghua.edu.cn
印 装 者：北京鑫海金澳胶印有限公司
经　　销：全国新华书店
开　　本：185mm×260mm　　**印　　张**：18.25　　**字　　数**：427千字
版　　次：2016 年 11 月第 1 版　　**印　　次**：2023年 2 月第 5 次印刷
定　　价：68.00 元

产品编号：067922-02

普通高校专业英语教程系列

编　委　会

主　编　司爱侠

编　者　宋德富　姜彦君　张强华　吕淑文

马占青　古绪满　张美兰

前　言
Preface

随着我国改革开放的进一步发展，与国外的接触和交流日益频繁，社会越来越需要既熟悉日常文秘业务，又能熟练掌握英语的各类文秘人员。具备相关技能并精通外语的人员往往处于竞争的优势地位，成为不可或缺的核心人才。职场对从业人员专业英语水平要求的不断提高，有力地推动了从业人员学习专业英语的积极性。本书就是专门为文秘从业人员编写的行业英语教材。

本书结合不同的工作环境，根据实际工作需求，以秘书的日常工作环节为主线，选取大量真实、生动的素材，通过综合训练强化读者的听、说、读、写能力，使读者能够掌握工作所需的语言技能并在工作环节中熟练应用。本书的主要内容包括秘书工作介绍、办公室管理和办公自动化、文档管理、商务接待、商务信函、商务会议、商务礼仪、商务合同等。

本书以单元为单位，每一单元由以下几部分组成：对话——提供课文相关的对话场景；课文——包括工作描述、应用技巧、常用方法和新颖观念；单词——给出课文中出现的新词，读者可以积累专业基础词汇；词组——给出课文中的常用词组；缩略语——给出课文中出现的且业内人士必须掌握的缩略语；注释——讲解课文中出现的疑难句子，培养读者的阅读理解能力；习题——巩固所学知识；阅读材料——提供最新的行业资料，进一步扩大读者的视野。

读者在使用本书的过程中，如有任何问题都可以通过电子邮件与我们交流（邮箱地址：zqh3882355@163.com；cici12323@tom.com），也可通过出版社与我们联系，我们一定会给予答复。邮件标题请注明姓名及“文秘英语（清华大学出版社）”。

本书既可作为高等院校文秘专业的英语教材，也可作为相关专业的培训教材，供文秘从业人员自学使用。

由于时间仓促，编者水平有限，书中难免有疏漏和不足之处，恳请广大读者和同行提出宝贵意见，以便再版时进行修正。

编者

2016 年 6 月

目　录
Contents

Unit 1

Introduction to Secretarial Work

Part One Dialogues

Sample Dialogue 1

Situation ▶ Li Hua is being interviewed for a secretary post at Miss Brown's office.

(A—Li Hua, the interviewee; B—Mary Brown, the interviewer)

A: (Knocks at the door) May I come in?

B: Come in, please.

A: Good morning, Miss Brown! I'm Li Hua. I've come for an interview as requested.

B: Good morning, Miss Li! Please take a seat.

A: Thank you.

B: Well. Would you mind telling me about yourself?

A: Of course not. I come from Shanghai and study at Shanghai International Studies University as an English Major. I specialize in English Secretarial Studies. And I will graduate from Shanghai International Studies University this July.

B: Oh, I see. What courses have you taken in English Secretarial Studies?

A: I've taken such courses as secretarial principles, office administration, business English, public relations, etiquette study, psychology, computer programming, typing, stenography and file-keeping.

B: Oh, very good, very good. But how are your typing and shorthand skills?

A: Well. I am a good shorthand-typist. I can type 100 Chinese words a minute and take dictation in English at 150 words a minute.

B: Oh, fantastic! Can you operate computers skillfully?

A: Yes, I can. I have received some special training in computers. Besides I am good at operating common office machines, such as fax machines and duplicating machines.

B: Where did you learn to operate these machines?

A: At a Foreign Trade Corporation last summer. I worked there for nearly two months.

B: Oh, really? That must be very interesting experience. What did you do there?

A: Yes. Mostly typing and running errands.

B: Good. That experience will be very helpful to secretarial job. Ok, we'll be letting you know the result of the interview sometime next week. Thank you very much for coming.

A: Thank you very much for giving me the chance, Miss Brown.

B: You're quite welcome. Good-bye.

A: Good-bye.

Sample Dialogue 2

Situation ▶ Miss Brown invites Li Hua, the new secretary to have a cup of coffee with her at a cafe nearby. Now they are talking over coffee about qualities of a good secretary.

(A—Miss Brown; B—Li Hua, the new secretary)

A: Li Hua, how is your secretarial work going these days?

B: Um..., not bad. Miss Brown, could I ask you a few questions?

A: Yes, please!

B: What qualities would people like to find in his secretary?

A: Well. I think loyalty should be the first quality. If a man can't trust his secretary, whom he can trust?

B: Ah, I see! You mean a secretary is supposed to be loyal to his boss and his company and to be trustworthy. When making decisions and solving problems, he needs to keep the interests of the company in the forefront of his mind. What is the next, then?

A: Well, efficiency, I think. You know, a secretary needs to handle many repetitious and routine tasks and it's imperative for him to be able to complete a lengthy to-do list of tasks with a sense of urgency.

B: Right. Efficiency is essential to a qualified secretary. But do you think initiative is also one essential quality for a good secretary?

A: Of course it is. Although a good secretary should not exceed his duties and meddle in the boss' affairs, yet he needs to act for his boss in his absence. Surely, he needs to consult with his boss before he take the initiative to make any major decisions.

Therefore, it is crucial for secretaries to know when to act on your own and when to consult.

B: I agree with you. Well, what other qualities do you think a good secretary should have?

A: I have to admit that a good secretary should be tactful and charming. Secretarial work can be so tense and tedious that secretaries are very likely to loose their tempers. Thus, a good secretary should be tactful enough to avoid any friction and resolve any conflicts. Additionally, a good secretary is expected to be charming, which involves looking and sounding attractive. As the company's appearance symbol, a good secretary should have a professional demeanor, good dress sense and presentation.

B: Ah... It seems very difficult to be a good secretary. I bet he must be very lucky if an executive can recruit a secretary with all those qualities.

A: Yes, of course. I am sure you will be a good secretary.

B: Thank you. I will try my best!

Useful Expressions

1. I've come for an interview as requested.
   我是应邀来参加面试的。
2. I specialize in English Secretarial Studies.
   我专攻英语文秘。
3. Besides I am good at operating common office machines, such as fax machines and duplicating machines.
   另外，我还能熟练操作一般的办公设备，比如传真机和复印机。
4. Yes. Mostly typing and running errands.
   是的，大多是打打字，有时候跑跑外勤。
5. We'll be letting you know the result of the interview sometime next week.
   我们会在下周的某个时间通知你面试的结果。
6. Therefore, it is crucial for secretaries to know when to act on your own and when to consult.
   因此，对于秘书而言，知道什么时候该独自行动而什么时候该请示至关重要。
7. Secretarial work can be so tense and tedious that secretaries are very likely to loose their tempers.
   秘书工作可能会很紧张，很烦琐。秘书发脾气是很有可能的。
8. Thus, a good secretary should be tactful enough to avoid any friction and resolve any conflicts.
   因而，一个好的秘书应该要足够机智去化解摩擦，解决矛盾。

9. As the company's appearance symbol, a good secretary should have a professional demeanor, good dress sense and presentation.
作为公司形象的象征，一个好的秘书应该有专业的行为举止、良好的着装和仪表。
10. I bet he must be very lucky if an executive can recruit a secretary with all those qualities.
我肯定如果一位主管能找到具有上述品质的秘书，他一定很幸运。

Situational Dialogues

Using the Sample Dialogue as a model, try to create a new dialogue with your partner.

Situation 1 ▶ Wang Li, majoring in English for secretaries, is soon to graduate from Sichuan International Studies University. Now she is being interviewed on telephone for a secretary post in a Sina-foreign joint venture.

Situation 2 ▶ Lily, a secretary in a foreign trade company, is talking with her superior, Mary Brown, and she wants to know secretarial duties and responsibilities.

Part Two Text A

Secretarial Work

1. The Term "Secretary"

The term "secretary" is derived from the Latin word secernere, "to distinguish" or "to set apart," with the eventual connotation of something private or confidential, as with the English word secret. A secretarius was a person, therefore, overseeing business confidentially, usually for a powerful individual (a king, Pope, etc.). As the duties of a modern secretary often still include the handling of confidential information, the literal meaning of their title still holds true.

Since the Renaissance until the late 19th century, men involved in the daily correspondence and the activities of the mighty had assumed the title of secretary. With time, the term was applied to varied functions, producing compound titles to specify various secretarial work better, like General Secretary, Financial Secretary or Secretary of State. Just "secretary" remained in use for relatively modest positions such as administrative assistant of the officer(s) in charge. As such less influential posts became more feminine and common with the multiplication of bureaucracies in the public and private sectors, new words were also coined to describe them, such as personal assistant.

For a long time, the term "secretary" has come to be used for too loosely. Many junior typists, who are only beginning to acquire their secretarial skills, like to think of themselves as secretaries. However, the true secretary should have not only highly competent manual skills but also an understanding of organization and administration and a capacity for obtaining results through people on behalf of her manager or managers. This is a complex activity requiring knowledge, experience, and social skills.

2. Duties and Functions

A secretary is a person in charge of records, correspondence, and related affairs, as for a company; a person employed to do routine work in a business office, such as typing, filing, and answering phones; or a person employed to attend to the individual or confidential correspondence, scheduling, etc. of an executive, celebrity, or the like.

The duties of a secretary or administrative assistant vary by industry or employer, but some tasks are common to many work settings. In general, secretaries perform basic clerical, organizational and office responsibilities for an organization or department. Their basic duties and functions are:

2.1 Files

Secretaries often manage customer files and other records in an office. In a doctor's office, for instance, the secretary pulls each patient's file at the time of the appointment for the nurse or doctor. She replaces it when the appointment is over. Keeping files in alphabetical order and using a local filing system for easy storage and retrieval are keys to successful file organization.

2.2 Correspondence

Secretaries are the common liaison for incoming and outgoing phone and mail correspondence. They receive calls from clients, business partners, workers or community members, and either answer questions or forward the calls. They also make calls on behalf of managers to communicate information to customers, to schedule appointments or to follow up on inquiries. Taking notes from a manager, preparing a memo or letter, and screening mail are common written correspondence duties.

2.3 Documents

Secretaries are often tasked with copying documents for mailings or for internal distribution. They also must fax documents from the company to clients or customers, and receive incoming faxes to pass on to the appropriate person. Some secretaries use e-mail, Word and Excel to create spreadsheets or documents and pass them on to employees or customers. Proofreading documents before they are sent out of the office is another duty.

2.4 Office Tasks

Especially in small offices, a secretary may be asked to carry out routine clerical tasks and errands to assist others. This may include canceling or rescheduling appointments, ordering office supplies, taking notes during meetings, and getting drinks for the supervisor and guests.

2.5 Reception

In general office positions, secretaries commonly assist new employees and visitors in finding their way around. This includes directing visitors to the people they come to meet and showing new employees where to go on their first day. In general, the secretary projects the image of the business by offering a friendly and professional reception to people who come into the office.

Admittedly, specific duties and functions vary with different types of secretaries. Executive secretaries or executive assistant may handle some routine and complex responsibilities, including managing budgets, doing bookkeeping, attending telephone calls, handling visitors, maintaining websites, making travel arrangements, conducting research, preparing statistical reports, training employees, and supervising other clerical staff, and so on.

Some secretaries, such as legal and medical secretaries, perform highly specialized work requiring knowledge of technical terminology and procedure. For instance, Legal secretaries often prepare documents, including legal briefs, court summons, spreadsheets and other office-related letters. Many legal secretaries also maintain electronic-filing databases, help lawyers with research for cases, gather necessary documents for trials and submit paperwork to courthouse. Other duties may include scheduling client appointments, answering calls, taking notes during legal meetings and maintaining the firm's legal research references. Medical secretaries perform secretarial duties using specific knowledge of medical terminology and hospital, clinic, or laboratory procedures. Their duties may involve scheduling appointments, billing patients, and compiling and recording medical charts, reports, and correspondence.

Other technical secretaries who assist engineers or scientists may handle correspondence, maintain the technical library, and gather and edit materials for scientific papers.

3. *Outlook for Secretarial Work*

Since the 1970s, office automation has developed rapidly in the new wave of technological revolution and a number of high-tech have quickly entered the field of office automation. With the application of a large amount of advanced office automation equipment in secretarial work, the efficiency and the quality of the work have been greatly improved, but traditional secretarial work has been affected deeply and the content, methods, thinking and work site of the secretarial work have been changed. Hence, the work has converted from experienced management to high-level one which is more standard, automotive and efficient. Therefore, Those people who wish to continue on as secretaries will need to demonstrate ever more flexibility on the job and get ready for some new tasks.

New Words

distinguish [dis'tiŋgwiʃ] *vt.* 区别，辨认，使显著

eventual [i'ventjuəl] *adj.* 最终的，可能的

connotation [ˌkɔnəu'teiʃən] *n.* 含义，言外之意

confidential [kɔnfi'denʃəl] *adj.* 秘密的，机密的；表示信任的，获信赖的

oversee ['əuvə'siː] *vt.* 监督，监管，监视

Pope [pəup] *n.* 罗马教皇

literal ['litərəl] *adj.* 逐字的，字面上的，文字的

Renaissance [rə'neisəns] *n.* 文艺复兴，再生
correspondence [ˌkɔris'pɔndəns] *n.* 通信，信件，相符，一致
mighty ['maiti] *adj.* 强大的，巨大的
assume [ə'sjuːm] *vt.* 假定，设想，承担，（想当然地）认为，假装
varied ['vɛərid] *adj.* 各种各样的
compound ['kɔmpaund] *adj.*（词语等）复合的
specify ['spesifai] *v.* 详细说明，指定，阐述
secretarial [ˌsekrə'tɛəriəl] *adj.* 秘书的
relatively ['relətivli] *adv.* 相对地
modest ['mɔdist] *adj.* 谦虚的；适度的；有节制的
administrative [əd'ministrətiv] *adj.* 行政的，管理的
assistant [əsistənt] *n.* 助手，助理，助教
influential [ˌinflu'enʃəl] *adj.* 有影响的，有权势的
post [pəust] *n.* 职位；邮件；标杆
feminine ['feminin] *adj.* 女性的
multiplication [ˌmʌltipli'keiʃən] *n.* 增加，繁殖，乘法运算
bureaucracy [bjuə'rɔkrəsi] *n.* 官僚制度，官僚主义，官僚
sector ['sektə] *n.* 部门，部分，区域
coin [kɔin] *vt.* 制造硬币；杜撰，创造 *n.* 硬币
junior ['dʒuːnjə] *adj.* 资历较浅的，年少的，下级的
typist ['taipist] *n.* 打字员
competent ['kɔmpitənt] *adj.* 有能力的，足够的，胜任的
manual ['mænjuəl] *adj.* 手工的，体力的
administration [ədminis'treiʃən] *n.* 实施，管理，行政，任期
capacity [kə'pæsiti] *n.* 能力，才能
obtain [əb'tein] *vt.* 获得，得到
complex ['kɔmpleks] *adj.* 复杂的，合成的，复合的
social ['səuʃəl] *adj.* 社会的，社会阶层的，社交的
employ [im'plɔi] *v.* 雇佣，使用
routine [ruː'tiːn] *n.* 例行公事，常规，无聊　*adj.* 常规的，例行的，乏味的
filing ['failiŋ] *n.* 整理成档案，文件归档
individual [ˌindi'vidjuəl] *n.* 个人，个体 *adj.* 个人的，个别的，独特的
celebrity [si'lebriti] *n.* 名流，名声，名人，知名人士，名誉
vary ['vɛəri] *v.*（使）变化，（使）不同
perform [pə'fɔːm] *v.* 执行，履行，表演，扮演
clerical ['klerikəl] *adj.* 文书或办事员的
replace [ri'pleis] *vt.* 代替，替换，把……放回原位
retrieval [ri'triːvəl] *n.* 检索，找回
liaison [li'eizaːn] *n.* 联络，联络人
client ['klaiənt] *n.* 顾客；当事人，诉讼委托人
inquiry [in'kwaiəri] *n.* 探究，调查，审查，询问，质询
memo ['meməu] *n.* 备忘录，内部通知
screen [skriːn] *n.* 屏幕，银幕，屏风 *vt.* 掩藏，庇护，检查
internal [in'təːnl] *adj.* 内部的，国内的，体内的，内心的
distribution [ˌdistri'bjuːʃən] *n.* 分配，分布
fax [fæks] *n.&vt.* 传真

appropriate [ə'prəupriit] *adj.* 适当的，合适的，恰当的
spreadsheet [spredʃi:t] *n.* 电子表格程序
document ['dɔkjumənt] *n.* 公文，（计算机）文档
proofread ['pru:fri:d] *v.* 校对，校正，校勘
errand ['erənd] *n.* 差事，使命
supply [sə'plai] *n.* 供应，补给，日用（必需）品
supervisor ['sju:pəvaizə] *n.* 监督者，管理者
reception [ri'sepʃən] *n.* 接待，招待会，接待处
specific [spi'sifik] *adj.* 具体的，明确的
handle ['hændl] *v.* 操纵，处理，负责，管理
maintain [men'tein] *vt.* 维持，维修，保养
supervise ['sju:pəvaiz] *vt.* 监督，管理，指导
staff [stɑ:f] *n.* 员工，全体人员，全体职员
legal ['li:gəl] *adj.* 法定的，法律的，合法的
terminology [ˌtə:mi'nɔlədʒi] *n.* 术语，术语学
procedure [prə'si:dʒə] *n.* 程序，手续，步骤
trial ['traiəl] *n.* 试验，试用
submit [səb'mit] *vt.* 提交，递交，使服从，使屈服
compile [kəm'pail] *vt.* 编译，编制，编纂
automation [ɔ:tə'meiʃən] *n.* 自动化
revolution [ˌrevə'lu:ʃən] *n.* 革命，变革，重大改变
application [ˌæpli'keiʃən] *n.* 应用；申请；应用程序
advanced [əd'vɑ:nst] *adj.* 先进的，高级的
efficiency [i'fiʃənsi] *n.* 效率，功率
convert [kən'və:t] *v.*（使）转变，转化；兑换，换算
standard ['stændəd] *n.* 标准，规格，水准 *adj.* 标准的，普通的，规范的
automotive [ɔ:tə'məutiv] *adj.* 机动的；自驱推进的
flexibility [ˌfleksə'biliti] *n.* 灵活性，弹性，适应性，柔韧性

Phrases and Expressions

as with 与……一样
hold true 适用，有效
be involved in 涉及，与……有关联
apply to 应用于，适用于
General Secretary 秘书长
Financial Secretary 财务司司长
Secretary of State 国务卿
administrative assistant 行政助理
on behalf of 代表，为了……的利益
in charge of 负责，主管
as for 至于，关于
attend to 注意，专心于，照料，料理，处理

or the like 或其他同类的东西等，或诸如此类
in general 大体上，一般来说，通常
follow up 跟踪，重复补充，跟进，采取措施
pass... on to sb. 将……传递给某人
carry out 实现，执行，完成
vary with 随……而改变
do bookkeeping 做账，记账
make arrangements 安排，操办
court summons 法院传票
technological revolution 科技革命
a large amount of 大量的

Notes

1 A secretarius was a person, therefore, overseeing business confidentially, usually for a powerful individual (a king, Pope, etc.).

本句中，overseeing business confidentially 是一个现在分词短语作后置定语，修饰限定前面的 a person。

英语中，现在分词短语通常放在被修饰词的后面，作后置定语。请看下例：

This is a complex activity requiring knowledge, experience, and social skills.
这是一项需要知识、经验和社交技能的活动。

另外，therefore 意为"因此"，在本句中作插入语。请看下例：

Many fast food restaurants, therefore, have red furniture and walls.
因此，许多快餐店都有红色的家具和墙。

2 Since the Renaissance until the late 19th century, men involved in the daily correspondence and the activities of the mighty had assumed the title of secretary.

本句中，involved in the daily correspondence and the activities of the mighty 是一个过去分词短语作后置定语，修饰限定前面的 men。

英语中，过去分词短语通常放在被修饰词的后面，作后置定语。请看下例：

Most of the people invited to the conference were my old friends.
大多数被邀请参加会议的人是我的老友。

另外，since the Renaissance until the late 19th century 是由连词 since 引导的时间状语。请看下例：

She hasn't been out riding since the accident.
她自从出了事故以后，一直没有骑马外出过。

3 Medical secretaries perform secretarial duties using specific knowledge of medical terminology and hospital, clinic, or laboratory procedures.

本句中，using specific knowledge of medical terminology and hospital, clinic, or laboratory procedures 是现在分词短语作谓语 perform 的伴随状语，表示伴随状态。

英语中，分词或分词短语作状语时，可表示时间、原因、让步、条件、方式或伴随状态。请看下例：

All night long he lay awake, thinking of the problem.
他整夜躺在床上睡不着，思考着那个问题。
Confined to bed, she needed to be waited on in everything.
她卧病在床，什么事都需要人伺候。

4 Many junior typists, who are only beginning to acquire their secretarial skills, like to think of themselves as secretaries.

本句中，who are only beginning to acquire their secretarial skills 是由关系代词 who 引导的非限制性定语从句，补充说明 many junior typists。

英语中，非限制性定语从句和先行词之间有逗号分开，而且两者之间的关系比较松散，只起补充说明的作用。请看下例：

My brother, who works abroad, is coming back next week.
我哥哥在国外工作，他打算下周回来。

另外，think of... as... 意为“把……看作是；把……认为是”。

5 The true secretary should have not only highly competent manual skills but also an understanding of organization and administration and a capacity for obtaining results through people on behalf of her manager or managers.

本句中，句子的主体结构是 not only... but also... 引导三个名词词组 manual skills, an understanding 和 a capacity 并列的平行结构。

英语中，not only... but also... 是非常有用的关联连词，意为“不仅……而且……”。通常用于连接两个相同的句子成分，即所谓的“对称结构”。请看下例：

If this project fails, it will affect not only our department, but also the whole organization.
要是这个项目失败了，这将不仅影响到我们部门，还会影响到整个单位。

另外，on behalf of... 意为“代表，为了……的利益”。

Exercises

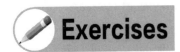

EX. 1 Answer the following questions.

1. Which word was the term “secretary” deprived from?
2. What were the titles produced to specify various secretarial work better as the term “secretary” was applied to varied functions?
3. According to this article, what should a true secretary have?
4. What are the keys to the successful file organization?
5. What are common written correspondence duties for secretaries?
6. What are secretaries obliged to do before the documents are sent out of office?
7. In small offices, what do the routine clerical tasks include?
8. How can a secretary project the image of the business?
9. What are the duties for medical secretaries?
10. What contributes to the improved efficiency and quality of office work?

EX. 2 **Complete the following sentences with appropriate words or expressions in the box.**

derive from	confidential	correspondence	routine	complex
on behalf of	efficiency	appropriate	administrative	in charge of

1. Secretaries perform a series of clerical and ________ duties needed to run an office.
2. Secretaries are often ________ mail and deliveries.
3. A secretary is a person employed to coordinate and maintain effective office procedures and ________ work flow.
4. The secretary was accused of leaking ________ information about her employer's private life.
5. A qualified secretary can handle not only routine tasks but also some ________ issues.
6. It is ________ for a secretary to display a positive image for the company.
7. As her private secretary he has access to all her ________.
8. ________ the company, the secretary extended a warm welcome to all the new employees.
9. As soon as she learns the office ________, she will be an excellent executive assistant.
10. The secretary's popularity ________ the fact that he was a person easy to get along with.

EX. 3 **Translate the following sentences into English.**

1. 秘书必须将准确的信息传递给职员和客户。(pass on to)
2. 另外，办公室自动化的广泛运用也有可能对秘书工作产生一些消极的影响。(office automation)
3. 一些行政秘书做一些枯燥的行政工作，如打出信件、文档整理。(administrative secretaries)
4. 随着更多的记录及文字处理工作由机器来完成，枯燥的秘书工作量将可能减少。(perform)
5. 除了接待来访者以外，秘书还应该承担一些复杂的职责，如进行研究以及监督其他员工。(supervise)
6. 行政助理或许还控制对经理的访问，成为有影响的、可信任的助手。(influential)
7. 高级专业秘书还包括医学秘书、法学秘书以及个人助理。(specialized)
8. 如果秘书以负面的形象示人，客户将会对这家公司形成不好的印象。(project)
9. 秘书具体的工作职责会随着他们的经验和头衔发生变化。(vary with)
10. 有能力的秘书把她的听写工具放在方便的桌子上，以便能马上拿作听写。(competent)

EX. 4 **Translate the following passage into Chinese.**

A secretary has many administrative duties. Traditionally, these duties were mostly related to correspondence, such as the typing out of letters, maintaining files of paper documents, etc. The advent of word processing has significantly reduced the time that such duties require, with the result that many new tasks have come under the purview of the secretary. The duties may vary according to the nature and size of organization. These might include managing budgets and doing bookkeeping, attending telephone calls, handling visitors, maintaining websites, and making travel arrangements. Secretaries might manage all the administrative details of running a high-level conference or arrange the catering for a typical lunch meeting. Often executives will ask their assistant to take the minutes at meetings and prepare meeting documents for review.

Part Three Text B

Executive Secretaries

An executive secretary is a person who works as an administrative assistant for a top executive. In most cases, the executive secretary is the right-hand man or woman to a top ranking executive in a business or establishment. This is generally not an entry-level secretarial position. Typically, this job will call for many years of experience as a secretary for predominantly high-ranking officials. The job duties of an executive secretary may extend those of a traditional secretary.

The executive secretary is quite often the driving force behind the scenes, ensuring that the business runs smoothly on a day-to-day basis. There are many tasks done by an executive assistant in this position, such as communicating important telephone and fax messages, maintaining a general filing system, documenting all the correspondence, planning and preparing meetings, organizing overseas conference calls, and providing word processing and secretarial support.

With the advent of office automation, a large amount of traditional secretarial work is being taken over by machines, some more complex duties comes to be under the purview of executive secretaries. They may conduct research on the Internet, manage projects and prepare reports. For example, they might study management methods and suggest ways to improve work flow or save money. They may even train and oversee office staff.

In some offices executive secretaries are called administrative assistants.

1. Primary Duties

Executive secretaries work directly for and provide close administrative support to an executive. Executives include those at the management level of an organization who have the authority to determine and implement policy. The extent of an executive secretary's own authority, along with his or her responsibilities and duties, often depends on the power exercised by the supervising executive. Whatever that may be, executive secretaries often have administrative and managerial duties, among other responsibilities.

Administrative duties include clerical and gate-keeping responsibilities typically associated with secretarial positions. Common administrative duties include the following:

- Taking dictation and writing correspondence.
- Reading and screening correspondence.
- Receiving and screening callers and visitors.
- Coordinating the executive's calendar, schedule, and itinerary.
- Making travel arrangements.
- Prioritizing and referring information appropriately.
- Producing documents, charts, and presentations.
- Editing documents and preparing them for executive approval.
- Maintaining records and files.
- Operating and maintaining office equipment.
- Monitoring office expenditures.

However, depending on the size of the office and the experience of the individual, an executive secretaries may be delegated supervisory responsibilities and they are expected to fulfill some managerial duties. The following list outlines various managerial duties:

- Hiring, assigning, and supervising office personnel.
- Writing, adjusting, and maintaining office procedures.
- Insuring compliance with organizational policies.
- Insuring compliance with federal, state, and local law.
- Planning and participating in meetings.
- Preparing budgets and reports.

2. *Skills*

Busy executives need competent secretaries to help them stay organized and take charge behind the scenes. The executive secretaries are often is responsible for managing the office and making sure the executive has everything he needs to function at full capacity. To be a qualified executive secretary, they are obliged to possess the following skills.

2.1 Communication Skills

An executive secretary must have strong communication skills to serve in this capacity. Most of the duties in this position require being able to effectively communicate with his boss as well as other executives inside and outside of the company. He often will be the first point of contact when people are trying to connect with his boss, and you will need to have a professional demeanor as well as have good customer service skills. Your boss may require that you screen all of his or her telephone calls as well as draft a considerable amount of his or her correspondence.

2.2 Technical Skills

An executive secretary needs to be proficient in utilizing office equipment, such as copiers, fax machines, transcription devices and personal computers. Many of the executive secretaries' duties are done on the computer, so he'll need to be competent with certain computer software programs, depending on the needs of his job and the executives. Additionally, his job may require his to produce certain reports, maintain a database and perform online research-all of which require some technical skill and computer use.

2.3 Management Skills

As an executive secretary, he will be responsible for managing certain aspects of the office. He may be responsible for scheduling conference calls and meetings for his boss. He will need to maintain the meeting or conference room schedules and put together any necessary materials for the attendees. He also may be responsible for managing relationships with outside vendors that his company works with on a regular basis.

Executive secretaries often manage other clerical staff in the office. If there are receptionists or other secretaries, he could be their immediate supervisor, so he should have the ability to train and direct their workloads. Consequently, he will need strong skills in multitasking as he manage he work while keeping your staff on task.

3. Qualities

Many aspects of an executive secretary job are covered in the preceding parts, but there are still some specific qualities which are essential if a person desires to become an executive secretary or personal assistant to a senior member of the management team. Some of these qualities are suggested below:

3.1 Goal Orientation

An executive secretary needs to have a nice balance of assertiveness and cautiousness. He should be comfortable working in a support capacity yet at ease taking initiative within the scope of her job description. The executive secretary should possess ambition but must not be too competitive. He should strive to better himself and continually learn, but may not have an opportunity to advance beyond the executive secretary role.

3.2 Pragmatism

An executive secretary needs to be a logical, practical thinker; he must assess situations objectively and solve problems critically. When communicating, he should keep conversations focused on the task at hand and share information succinctly. Some comfort for relationship-building is valuable, but it is more important that the executive secretary is professional than friendly. Additionally, he needs to possess a high level of discretion; he is privy to sensitive information as he transcribes and distributes executive documents, and he must keep it confidential.

3.3 Efficiency

Being able to move through a lengthy to-do list with a sense of urgency is imperative in the executive secretary role. The secretary needs to have a strong task focus and ease for handling repetitious and routine tasks. He should additionally possess strong organizational and prioritization skills, particularly if he handles administrative, scheduling and planning tasks for more than one busy executive.

3.4 Meticulousness

Errors committed by an executive secretary can be costly, so the individual needs to have a strong eye for detail and a deep commitment to quality. He should habitually check and recheck his work before deeming it complete, and he must be willing to accept constructive criticism.

He should also be respectful of protocol, procedures and rules as well as willing to follow his superior's lead.

3.5 Loyalty

An executive secretary should be dedicated to his superiors and his organization. He needs to work as a committed member of the team, which could include putting in extra hours to ensure a critical project is completed on time. When making decisions and solving problems, he needs to keep the interests of his company in the forefront of his mind.

3.6 Leadership

In some positions at this level, the executive secretary supervises other members of the administrative team. If leading others, he must be comfortable taking charge, providing direction, offering feedback and delegating work. He may need to diplomatically deal with conflict or assertively address poor performance, and he should be able to instill a sense of urgency in others.

Surely, there are still other vital qualities required for people working as executive secretaries, like dependability, confidentiality, initiative, ingenuity and so on. Besides, executive secretaries also need an abundance of knowledge to be qualified for this job. People in this career need to be familiar with general office work such as filing and recording information, to know well how to manage the operations of a business, company or group, and to have a good command of computer skills and foreign languages. With rich secretarial experience and strong abilities, executive secretaries may be promoted to positions with more responsibility, such as higher-level executives, office managers and the like.

New Words

establishment [is'tæbliʃmənt] *n.* 企业，机构；建立

entry-level ['entri-'lev(ə)l] *adj.* 入门水平的

predominantly [pri'dɔminənt] *adv.* 主要地，占优势地，压倒性地

high-ranking [hai-'ræŋkiŋ] *adj.* 高级的；级别高的，高层的；职位高的

smoothly ['smu:ðli] *adv.* 顺利地，流畅地，平滑地

conference ['kɔnfərəns] *n.* 会议，讨论会，协商会，会谈

purview ['pə:vju:] *n.* 范围

authority [ɔ:'θɔriti] *n.* 权力，官方，当局，权威

implement ['implimənt] *n.* 工具，器具，当工具的物品 *vt.* 实施，执行，向……提供工具

exercise ['eksəsaiz] *vt.* 行使，运用

managerial [ˌmænə'dʒiəriəl] *adj.* 管理的

prioritize [prai'ɔritaiz] *vt.* 把……区分优先次序

refer [ri'fə:] *vt.* 把……提交，把……归类

appropriately [ə'prəupriitli] *adv.* 适当地

edit ['edit] *vt.* 剪辑，编辑；校订
approval [ə'pru:vəl] *n.* 同意，批准，认可，赞同
monitor ['mɔnitə] *v.* 监视，监督，监听 *n.* 监视器；监听员；班长
expenditure [iks'penditʃə] *n.* 开支，消耗
personnel [ˌpə:sə'nel] *n.* 职员；人事部门
adjust [ə'dʒʌst] *v.* 调整，校准，调节，使适应
insure [in'ʃuə] *vt.* 保险，确保
compliance [kəm'plaiəns] *n.* 顺从，服从，遵守
possess [pə'zes] *vt.* 拥有，持有；支配
demeanor [di'mi:nə] *n.* 行为，风度，举止
considerable [kən'sidərəbl] *adj.* 相当大的，可观的；重要的
utilize [ju:'tilaiz] *vt.* 利用，使用
copier ['kɔpiə] *n.* 抄写员；复印机
database ['deitəbeis] *n.* 数据库
aspect ['æspekt] *n.* 方面，方位，外观
vendor ['vendɔ:] *n.* 卖方，供货商
workload ['wə:kləud] *n.* 工作量
multitask ['mʌltiˌtɑ:sk] *vt.* 多工化，多任务化，多任务处理 *n.* 多任务
preceding [pri(:)'si:diŋ] *adj.* 在前的，在先的
essential [i'senʃəl] *adj.* 本质的，必要的，重要的
orientation [ˌɔ(:)rien'teiʃən] *n.* 定位，定向，倾向
assertiveness [ə'sə:tivnes] *n.* 自信，果断
cautiousness ['kɔ:ʃəsnes] *n.* 谨慎，小心
ambition [æm'biʃən] *n.* 雄心，抱负，野心
competitive [kəm'petitiv] *adj.* 竞争的，有竞争力的
pragmatism ['prægmətizəm] *n.* 实用主义
assess [ə'ses] *v.* 评定，评估，估算
objectively [əb'dʒektivli] *adv.* 客观地
critically ['kritikəli] *adv.* 批评性地，爱挑剔地，危急地
succinctly [sək'siŋktli] *adv.* 简明地，简洁地
discretion [dis'kreʃən] *n.* 谨慎，慎重，自行决定
transcribe [træns'kraib] *v.* 抄写；用音标标出；转录
lengthy ['leŋθi] *adj.* 冗长的，漫长的
urgency [im'perətiv] *n.* 紧急（的事）
imperative [im'perətiv] *adj.* 紧要的，必要的
repetitious [ˌrepi'tiʃəs] *adj.* 多次反复的，反复性的
meticulousness [mi'tikjuləsnes] *n.* 小心，谨小慎微
commitment [kə'mitmənt] *n.* 承诺，保证，信奉，献身
habitually [hə'bitjuəli] *adv.* 日常地，习惯地
deem [di:m] *v.* 认为，视作
constructive [kən'strʌktiv] *adj.* 建设性的，构造上的
protocol ['prəutəkɔl] *n.* 草案，协议；外交礼仪
loyalty ['lɔiəlti] *n.* 忠诚，忠心，忠贞
forefront ['fɔ:frʌnt] *n.* 最前列，最前线
feedback ['fi:dbæk] *n.* 反馈，反馈意见
diplomatically [ˌdiplə'mætikəli] *adv.* 练达地，圆滑地

conflict [ˈkɔnflikt] *n.* 冲突，矛盾，斗争 *vi.* 冲突，抵触，争执
assertively [əˈsəːtivli] *adv.* 断言地
instill [inˈstil] *vt.* 逐渐灌输；滴注
dependability [deˌpendəˈbiliti] *n.* 可依赖性，可靠性
initiative [iˈniʃiətiv] *adj.* 自发的 *n.* 首创精神，主动权；倡议
ingenuity [ˌindʒiˈnjuːiti] *n.* 心灵手巧，独创性，精巧

Phrases and Expressions

work as 担当，充当
call for 需要，要求
driving force 驱动力
behind the scenes 在幕后，不公开的
with the advent of 随着……的到来，随着……的出现
take over 接收，接管，接任
under the purview of 在……的范围内
depend on 依赖，依靠，取决于，随……而定
take dictation 记录口述
participate in 参与，参加
take charge 负责，掌管
be responsible for 对……负责，对……有责任
be obliged to do sth. 必须或有义务做某事
connect with 连接，与……联系
be proficient in 熟练，精通
put together 合在一起，组装在一起
on a regular basis 定期地
at ease 不拘束，自在
be willing to 愿意，乐意
be respectful of 尊重，尊敬
be dedicated to 致力于，献身于
an abundance of 许多的，充裕的，丰富的
be familiar with 熟悉，通晓
have a good command of 掌握，精通

Exercises

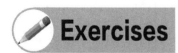

EX. 5 Answer the following questions.

1. What is the definition of an executive secretary?
2. What changes have taken place in the duties of executive secretaries with the advent of office automation?
3. What are the two major categories of the duties of executive secretaries?
4. Are executive secretaries expected to hire, assign and supervise office personnel?
5. According to Text B, what are the skills that executive secretaries are obliged to possess to be qualified for their jobs?
6. According to Text B, what are the office equipment that executive secretaries need to be

proficient in utilizing?

7. According to Text B, what are vital qualities required for people working as executive secretaries?
8. What can an executive secretary do to avoid committing errors?
9. When making decisions and solving problems, what does an executive secretary need to do to show her loyalty to her organization?
10. To what positions may executive secretaries be promoted if they have rich secretarial experience and strong abilities?

Part Four Extended Reading

Text	Notes
Company Secretary's Code[1] of Ethics[2]	[1] *n.* 密码，法规，准则
With the increasing complexity[3] of company laws and the continued rationalization[4] of business into larger groups of companies, the position of the company secretary in relation to the affairs of the company has evolved[5] from being a mere[6] servant to a much more important person in a company.	[2] *n.* 道德规范 [3] *n.* 复杂，复杂性 [4] *n.* 合理化 [5] *v.* 逐步演化，进化 [6] *adj.* 仅仅的，纯粹的
He is now, a recognized officer of the company with greater responsibility and authority[7] which demands ethical[8] conduct among company secretary at all times.	[7] *n.* 权力，当局，权威 [8] *adj.* 伦理的，道德的
The Code of Ethics may be broadly[9] understood as the application[10] of ethics to corporate affairs, is formulated[11] to enhance[12] the standard of corporate governance[13] and to instill[14] professionalism and effectiveness among the company secretaries.	[9] *adv.* 概括地，广泛地 [10] *n.* 应用，申请 [11] *v.* 规则，规划 [12] *vt.* 提高，加强 [13] *n.* 支配，管理 [14] *vt.* 逐渐灌输
This Code of Ethics should serve as[15] a code of human conduct and to deal with the question of what is morally right or wrong and what is morally good or evil[16].	[15] *vt.* 担任，充当 [16] *adj.* 邪恶的，有害的
Principles[17]	[17] *n.* 原理，原则，信念
The principles on which the code relies are those that concern[18] transparency[19], integrity[20], accountability[21] and corporate social responsibilities.	[18] *vt.* 涉及，影响 [19] *n.* 透明度 [20] *n.* 正直，诚实 [21] *n.* 有义务，有责任
Objectives[22]	[22] *n.* 目标，目的
The Code of Ethics is formulated to raise the standard of corporate governance and to inculcate[23] good corporate behavior[24] to achieve[25] the following objectives:	[23] *vt.* 谆谆教诲，教育 [24] *n.* 行为，举止，品行 [25] *vt.* 达到，实现
• To instill professionalism among company secretaries within the tenets[26] of morality[27], efficiency and administrative effectiveness; and	[26] *n.* 原则，宗旨 [27] *n.* 道德，美德

• To uphold[28] the spirit[29] of social responsibilities and accountability in line with[30] the legislation[31], regulations[32] and guidelines governing a company. **Code of Conduct** In the performance of his duties, a company secretary should always observe[33] the following codes: • Strive for[34] professional competency[35] and at all times exhibit[36] a high degree of skill and proficiency[37] in the performance of the duties of his office; • At all times exercise[38] the utmost[39] good faith[40] and act both responsibly and honestly with reasonable care and due[41] diligence[42] in the exercise of his powers and the discharge[43] of the duties of his office; • At all times strive to assist the company towards its proper[44] objectives within the tenets of moral responsibility, efficiency, and administrative effectiveness; • Have a clear understanding of the aims and objectives of the company, and of the powers and restrictions[45] as provided in the Memorandum[46] and Articles of Association of the company; • Be knowledgeable of law of meeting, meeting procedures[47], particularly quorum[48], requirements, voting procedures and proxy[49] provisions[50]and be responsible for the proper administration of meetings; • Neither direct for his own advantage any business opportunity that the company is pursuing, nor may be used or disclose[51] to any party any confidential[52] information obtained[53] by reason of his office for his own advantage or that of others; • Adopt an objective and positive[54] attitude and give full co-operation when dealing with governmental authorities and regulatory[55] bodies; • Disclose to the board of directors or an appropriate[56] public officer any information within his knowledge that he honestly believe suggests that a fraud[57] is being or is likely to be practiced by the company or by any of its directors[58] or employees; • Limit his secretary ship of companies to a number in which he can best and fully devote[59] his times and effectiveness; • Assist and advise the directors to ensure[60] at all times that the company maintains an effective system of internal[61] control, for keeping proper register[62] and accounting records; • Be impartial[63] in his dealings with shareholders[64], directors and without fear or favor, use his best endeavors to[65] ensure that the directors and the company comply with[66] the relevant legislations, contractual[67] obligations[68] and other relevant requirements;	[28] *v.* 支持，维持 [29] *n.* 精神，心灵 [30] 按照，与……一致 [31] *n.* 法律，立法 [32] *n.* 管理，规章 [33] *v.* 观察，遵守；注意到 [34] *vt.* 奋斗，争取 [35] *n.* 能力，胜任 [36] *v.* 展列，展示 [37] *n.* 熟练，精通 [38] *vt.* 运用 [39] *adj.* 极度的，最大限度的 [40] *n.* 信仰，信念 [41] *adj.* 应有的 [42] *n.* 勤奋 [43] *n.* 排除，释放，解除 [44] *adj.* 合适的，正当的 [45] *n.* 限制，约束 [46] *n.* 备忘录 [47] *n.* 程序，步骤 [48] *n.* 法定人数 [49] *n.* 代理权，委托书 [50] *n.* 规定，条款 [51] *vt.* 揭露，公开 [52] *adj.* 秘密的，机密的 [53] *vt.* 获得，得到 [54] *adj.* 积极的，正面的 [55] *adj.* 管理的，控制的 [56] *adj.* 适当的，相称的 [57] *n.* 欺骗，欺诈 [58] *n.* 董事，主管 [59] *vt.* 致力于，奉献给 [60] *vt.* 保证，确保 [61] *adj.* 国内的，内部的 [62] *n.* 登记簿，记录 [63] *adj.* 公正的 [64] *n.* 股东 [65] 争取，尽量 [66] 服从，遵守 [67] *adj.* 合同的，契约的 [68] *n.* 责任，义务

• Be present in person to ensure that in his absence[69] he is so represented at the company's registered office on the days and at the hours that the office is accessible[70] to the public; • Advise the board of directors that no policy is adopted by the company that will antagonize[71] or offend[72] any stakeholders of the company; • Be aware of[73] all reporting and other requirements imposed[73] by the statute[74] under which the company is incorporated[75]; and • Be present or represented at meeting and do not allow himself or his representative[76] to be excluded[77] or withdrawn[78] from those meetings in a way that prejudices[79] his professional responsibilities as secretary of company.	[69] 当某人不在的时候 [70] *adj.* 可得到的 [71] *vt.* 中和；和……对抗 [72] *vt.* 冒犯，犯罪 [73] *v.* 强加；征税 [74] *n.* 法令，法规，条例 [75] *v.* 合并，组成公司 [76] *n.* 代表 [77] *vt.* 排除，拒绝接受 [78] *vt.* 撤回，取回 [79] *vt.* 伤害，使……存偏见

参考译文

课文A 秘书工作

1. "秘书"一词

"秘书"一词来源于拉丁语 secernere，意为"区分"或"分开"，其最终的含义是指私人的或机密的东西，相当于英语中"秘密"一词。因此，一位 secretarius 指的是一个人。他通常为一个有权有势的个人(如国王、教皇等)秘密地管理业务。由于现代秘书的职责通常还包括处理机密信息，secretarius 这个头衔的原义仍然适用。

从文艺复兴到 19 世纪晚期，那些为权势人物处理日常信件和事务的男人们担任秘书这一角色。随着时间的推移，这个词被应用到各种各样的职务，并衍生出一些复合型头衔，以明确地阐述各种各样的秘书工作，如秘书长、财政司司长或国务卿。只有"秘书"一词仍被用来指那些相对来说不太重要的职务，如办公室主管的行政助理。由于公共和私营部门官僚机构的增加，这些不大重要的职位变得越来越女性化，越来越常见，因此，人们创造了一些新词语来形容它们，如私人助理。

长期以来，"秘书"一词被运用得极不严谨。许多初级打字员，才刚刚获得一些秘书技能，就喜欢把自己当作是秘书。然而，真正的秘书不仅需要高水平的操作技能，还需要熟悉机构和管理，并能够站在她的经理或经理们的立场，与他人沟通，取得工作成果。这是一项复杂的活动，需要知识、经验和社交技能。

2. 职责和职能

秘书是公司里负责记录、处理信件和相关事务的人；或是受聘在公司办公室做日常工作的职员，如打字、文件归档、接电话等的人；又或是被聘来处理某个行政主管或名人等的个人机密信件、负责调度等的人。

秘书或行政助理的职责因行业或雇主而不同，但有些任务在许多工作场景中都是常见的。总的来说，秘书在一个组织或一个部门中负责基本的文书工作、履行组织和办公职责。其基本职责和职能如下：

2.1 归档

秘书经常管理某一部门的客户文件和其他记录。例如，在一个医生那里，秘书将每个病人的档案按预约的时间取出来给护士或医生查阅。当就诊结束时她将病人的档案放回原处。成功编制文件的关键是按字母顺序保存文档，并使用本地归档系统，以方便存储和检索。

2.2 处理信件

秘书是电话联系和邮件通信的常用联络人。他们接听客户、商业伙伴、工人或社区成员打来的电话，或者直接回答对方的问题或者将电话转接给相关的人。他们也代表经理打电话，或向客户传达信息，或安排见面事宜或跟进调查。记笔记、准备一份备忘录或一封信件、筛查邮件等都是常见的处理信件职责。

2.3 传递文档

秘书通常负责复印文件，并邮寄或内部分发复印的文件。他们还必须将公司的文件传真给客户或顾客，接收传进来的传真，并把这些传真交给适当的人。一些秘书使用电子邮件、办公软件如 Word 和 Excel 来创建电子表格或文档，并将其传递给员工或客户。在送出办公室之前，校对这些文档是秘书的另一职责。

2.4 办公室工作

尤其在小型办公机构里，秘书可能被要求完成日常的文书工作，并做一些其他差事来协助他人。这些事可能包括取消或重新安排预约、订购办公用品、开会时记笔记以及为上司或客人取饮料。

2.5 接待

如果在总办事处任职，秘书通常要给新员工和来访者引路。这包括带来访者去见他们要见的人以及给第一天上班的新员工指路。总的来说，秘书需要友好地、专业地接待办公室来访者，从而树立公司的形象。

不可否认，不同类型的秘书其具体的职责和职能也不同。行政秘书或行政助理可以处理一些日常和复杂的事务，包括管理预算、记账、处理电话、接待访客、维护网站、安排旅行、进行研究、准备统计报告、培训员工以及监督其他职员等。

一些秘书，如法律和医学秘书，他们从事高度专业化的工作，需要具备技术术语和专业程序方面的知识。例如，法律秘书经常准备文件，包括法律摘要、法院传票、电子表格和其他办公相关的信件。许多法律秘书还要维护电子档案数据库，协助律师研究案情，收集审讯时必要的文件并向法院提交文书。其他职责可能包括安排客户预约、接听电话、在法定会议期间做记录并保存公司的法律研究参考资料。医学秘书运用医学术语和医院、诊所或实验室程序方面的相关专业知识来履行秘书职责。他们的职责包括安排预约、给病人计费，以及编辑和记录医学图表、报告和信件。

协助工程师或科学家的其他技术秘书可以处理信件、维护技术库，并收集和编辑科学论文的材料。

3. 展望秘书工作

自20世纪70年代以来，办公自动化在新一轮的技术革命浪潮中迅速发展起来，大量的高科技已迅速进入办公自动化领域。随着大量先进办公自动化设备在秘书工作中的应用，秘书工作的效率和质量得到了极大的提高，但是传统的秘书工作受到了极深的影响，秘书工作的内容、方法、思路以及工作场所发生了变化。因此，该工作已经从基于经验的管理模式转换为高层次的工作模式，即更标准、更自动化和更高效的工作模式。因此，那些希望继续担任秘书职位的人将需要在工作中展现出更多的灵活性，并随时准备承担一些新的任务。

课文B　行政秘书

行政秘书是一位高级行政主管的行政助理。在大多数情况下，行政秘书是企业或机构中高级行政主管的得力助手。这不是入门级的秘书职位。通常情况下，这项工作要求有多年的主要为高级官员担任秘书的工作经验。行政秘书的工作职责范围可能会远远大于传统秘书的工作职责。

行政秘书往往是幕后的驱动力，他们确保企业的业务每日顺利进行。担任该职位的行政助理需要做许多工作，如沟通重要的电话和传真信息、维护常规的文件系统、记录所有的信件、计划并准备会议、组织海外电话会议以及做一些文字处理工作和提供助理服务。

随着办公自动化的到来，大量的传统的秘书工作正在由机器来完成。一些更复杂的职责逐渐由行政秘书来履行。他们可以在互联网上进行调查研究、管理项目和准备报告。例如，他们可能会研究管理方法，并就如何改善工作流程或节省资金方面提供建议。他们甚至可以培训和监督办公室职员。

在某些办公机构中，行政秘书被称为行政助理。

1. 主要职责

行政秘书直接为行政主管工作，向其提供紧密的行政支持。行政主管包括机构管理层的那些有权决定和执行政策的人。行政秘书自身的权力范围，以及他或她的责任和义务，往往取决于行政主管行使的权力。无论是什么样的权力，行政秘书除了有其他责任以外，往往有行政和管理两方面职责。

行政职责包括与秘书职位密切相关的文书工作和把关责任。常见的行政职责如下：

- 记录口述和书写信函。
- 阅读和筛选信函。
- 接听电话和接待来访者。
- 协调行政主管的日程安排和旅程。
- 做旅行安排。
- 区分信息的轻重缓急和适当地归类信息。
- 提交文件，图表和报告。
- 编辑文档以备执行审批。
- 保存记录和文档。

- 操作和维护办公设备。
- 监控办公支出。

然而，根据办公室的规模和个人的经验，一位行政秘书可能会被委派监督职责，公司期望他们履行一些管理职责。其各种管理职责如下面的列表所示：

- 招聘，分配和监督办公室人员。
- 编写、调整和维护办公室章程。
- 确保符合组织政策。
- 确保遵守联邦、州和地方法律。
- 策划并参与会议。
- 准备预算和报告。

2. 技能

工作繁忙的行政主管需要有能力的秘书在幕后来帮助他们使其工作有序、管理有度。行政秘书经常负责管理办公室，确保行政主管能获得负荷工作所需要的一切。要成为合格的行政秘书，他们必须具备以下技能。

2.1 沟通技能

担任该职务，行政秘书必须有较强的沟通能力。在这个职位上，秘书的大部分职责都需要能够与他的老板以及公司内外的其他主管进行有效的沟通。当人们试图与他的上司联系时，他往往会成为第一个接触的人，因此他需要有专业的举止和良好的客户服务技巧。他的老板可能要求他筛选他或她的所有电话，以及草拟相当数量的信函。

2.2 技术技能

行政秘书需要熟练地使用办公设备，如复印机、传真机、转录设备和个人电脑。行政秘书的许多工作都是在电脑上完成的，所以他必须会运用某些计算机软件程序，具体的程序取决于他的工作和主管人员的需求。此外，他的工作可能需要他用电脑生成报告，维护数据库，并进行在线研究，所有这些工作都需要一些技术技能和计算机的使用。

2.3 管理技能

作为行政秘书，他将负责办公室的某些管理工作。他可能负责为老板安排电话会议和会面事宜。他需要确保会议或会议室的时间表可行，并为与会者整理提供任何必要的材料。他还需要负责维持与其公司有定期合作的外部供应商的关系。

行政秘书经常管理办公室的其他职员。如果有前台或其他秘书，他可能是他们的顶头上司，所以他应该具备培训他们和管理他们工作量的能力。因此，当他既要应付自己的工作又要确保他的员工能完成任务的时候，他将需要较强的同时能处理多项任务的能力。

3. 品质

行政秘书工作的许多方面在前文都有涉及，但是如果想成为管理层中的一位高级主管的行政秘书或私人秘书，他还需要具备一些特殊的品质。要求具备的品质如下：

3.1 目标定向

行政秘书需要将自信和谨慎两种意识很好地平衡起来。他应该乐于承担辅助性的工作，但是也需要在其职责允许的范围内轻松自在地发挥主动性。行政秘书应该具有自己的抱负，但不可以太好强。他应该努力完善自己，不断地学习，但不可以有超越行政秘书角色范围的行为。

3.2 务实

行政秘书必须是一个有逻辑的、务实的思想家；他必须客观地估计形势，并以挑剔的眼光来解决问题。交流的时候，他应该把对话集中在手头的任务上并和对方简要地互通信息。能在一定程度上令人感到舒适地建立关系是很重要的，但更重要的是，行政秘书是职业而非朋友。此外，他需要具备高水平的自由裁量权；由于负责行政文件的转录和发送，行政秘书还知晓一些敏感信息，因此他还必须保守机密。

3.3 效率

对行政秘书而言，能够带着紧迫感完成一堆繁杂的工作是非常必要的。秘书需要有很强的工作重心意识，并能轻松地处理好重复的常规工作。此外，他还应该具备很强的组织能力和按照优先顺序给工作排序的技能，特别是在他在为多个忙碌的主管处理行政事务、安排行程和规划任务的情况下。

3.4 谨慎

行政秘书犯下的错误可能会造成重大损失，所以行政秘书个人需要强烈关注细节并全身心致力于提高工作质量。他应该习惯性地反复检查自己的工作，直到他认为工作彻底完成了，而且他还必须愿意接受建设性的批评意见。他也应该尊重协议、程序和规则，并且愿意服从上司的领导。

3.5 忠诚

行政秘书应该对他的上级和组织具有敬业奉献精神。他需要做一名忠诚的团队成员，这可能要求他投入额外的时间，以确保一个重大的项目能按时完成。在制定决策和解决问题的时候，他需要把公司的利益放在第一位。

3.6 领导力

担任这一层次职位的一些行政秘书可监督管理团队的其他成员。如果领导别人的话，他必须乐于掌控事务，指明方向，提供反馈意见并分派工作。他可能需要圆滑地解决冲突或果断处理工作中的不良现象，因此，他应该要具备给他人施加紧迫感的能力。

当然，从事行政秘书工作的人还需要具备其他重要的品质，如可靠性、保密性、主动性、独创性等。此外，行政秘书还需要丰富的知识，以胜任这项工作。在这个职业生涯中，人们需要熟悉一般的办公室工作，如文件归档和记录信息，了解如何管理一个企业、公司或集团的业务，并拥有良好的计算机技能和外语能力。如果具有丰富的秘书经验和很强的能力，行政秘书可以被晋升担任更重要的职位，如高级管理人员、办公室经理之类。

Unit 2

Office Administration

Part One Dialogues

Sample Dialogue 1

Situation ▶ Mr. Brown wants to visit the branch companies, but he has another appointment. So he requests his secretary Li Hua to reschedule the date of his visit.

(A—Li Hua, the executive secretary; B—Mr. Brown, the general manager of Global Development Company Ltd.)

A: May I come in?

B: Yes, please. Come in, Li Hua. I'd like you to ask Mr. Smith if it's possible to reschedule another meeting on either Tuesday or Wednesday. You see, I have to fly to Germany on Monday to sign an important contract.

A: Yes. I'll go and handle it right away. When did Mr. Smith send us the provisional timetable?

B: I remember it's on November 3rd. Did you write a memo? It's very important. I wish you can check it.

A: Don't worry. I'll check it now. Oh yes, here it is. November 3rd. I've got the memo here.

B: Ah, very good. Thank you for your memo. Please send a copy of this memo to the sales department. It's very important for them to know that the meeting schedule has to be rearranged.

A: All right. I'll do it immediately. By the way, what's your contract in Germany about?

B: It's about a large-scale technology R&D project with Germany. I want you to go over the details of the content later.

A: You mean we will cooperate with Germany to research and develop a new technology?

B: Yes, absolutely! Germany has always had a good reputation for its excellence at developing new technologies, particularly in automobile industry. We should take this opportunity, or we'll regret it later.

A: I can't agree with you any more, Mr. Brown.

B: I'm planning to establish an office in Germany. Do you want to go there and take charge of the office work?

A: Yes. It'll be my great pleasure if I can work there.

B: Good. But one thing I worry about is that whether I can find such a good secretary as you if you go to work in Germany.

A: I bet you've no trouble in finding qualified secretaries since many employees would like to work for you.

Sample Dialogue 2

Situation ▶ Li Hua is receiving Black Smith who has an appointment with Mr. Brown.

(A—Li Hua, the executive secretary; B—Black Smith, a general manager of The General Export Company of Sweden)

A: Good morning. May I help you?

B: Yes. I have an appointment with Mr. Brown.

A: Are you Mr. Smith?

B: Yes. That's right.

A: I'm afraid Mr. Brown is not available at this moment and he is presiding an urgent meeting. Would you mind waiting for a while?

B: En... How long will that be?

A: About twenty minutes.

B: Oh, that is really too long. I have to attend an important meeting at 10:30.

A: Can your executive assistant deal with this?

B: No, I don't think so. I have discussed the details of the project with Mr. Brown on the telephone yesterday. And I don't think that anybody else would know about the project more than me.

A: If so. Perhaps you can make another appointment for some other time or just leave a message?

B: Well. Perhaps I can come here some other time. What about 9 o'clock tomorrow morning?

A: Oh, yes! Mr. Brown would be available until 11:00 tomorrow morning.

B: Oh, that's great! Here I'll leave my card in case he has lost the one I gave him.

A: Thank you, Mr. Smith. I am sorry about this.

B: That's all right. Thank you. Goodbye.

Useful Expressions

1. I'd like you to ask Mr. Smith if it's possible to reschedule another meeting on either Tuesday or Wednesday.
   我想你去问问史密斯先生可否在星期二或星期三重新安排一次会面。
2. I have to go to Germany on Monday to sign an important contract.
   我必须在星期一飞往德国签一份重要的合同。
3. When did Mr. Smith send us the provisional timetable?
   史密斯先生是什么时候将临时时间表发给我们的？
4. Please sent a copy of this memo to the sales department.
   请将备忘录的副本送一份到销售部。
5. Germany has always had a good reputation for its excellence at developing new technologies, particularly in automobile industry.
   德国在开发新技术方面一直享有美誉，尤其是汽车行业。
6. I'm afraid Mr. Brown is not available at this moment and he is presiding an urgent meeting.
   恐怕布朗先生现在没空，他正在召开一次紧急会议。
7. Can your executive assistant deal with this?
   你的行政助理可以处理这件事吗？
8. I have discussed the details of the project with Mr. Brown on the telephone yesterday.
   昨天，我已经就这个项目的细节和布朗先生在电话里讨论过了。
9. Perhaps you can make another appointment for some other time or just leave a message?
   或许你可以再约一个时间或是留个话？
10. I'll leave my card in case he has lost the one I gave him.
    我留一张名片，以免他找不到我上次给他的那张。

Situational Dialogues

Using the Sample Dialogue as a model, try to create a new dialogue with your partner.

Situation 1 ▶ Mr. Yu, the General Manager of Sandong Textile Export Company, will fly to Hong Kong to attend an important meeting and now he is asking his executive secretary Wang Li to reschedule the meeting with Black Brown.

Situation 2 ▶ Li Ping, a secretary in a company, is receiving Black Smith, the sales manager of Globe Export Company.

Part Two Text A

Office Automation

1. Overview

Office Automation is a general term that includes a wide range of applications of computer, communication and information technologies in office environments. Automation has altered not only our work environment, but our very concept of work.

The technology we see today had its start in the 1960s, when three clearly identifiable streams of development became evident. The first was computing, where the earliest applications were automated payroll and inventory-control systems. Other applications were also limited to the processing of data. These systems were usually operated only by programmers in the data-processing division of the organization. Nevertheless, the applications of computers in organizational settings grew to include more and more kinds of data processing.

The second stream of technological development was in the area of text processing. In the mid-1970s IBM introduced a product called the MCST—Magnetic Card Selectric Typewriter. This device had a box crammed with electronic equipment. The operator would insert a specially coated card into a slot on the top of the box and would type on the attached typewriter as usual. The card served as a memory device, on which the text would be written in a code based on magnetized spots. Once it was entered, the text could be edited and played back, causing a new copy to be typed out on the attached typewriter. Compared to current word-processing systems, this one was primitive, but it worked.

While the first two streams were centered around the processing of information in the office, the third, communications technology, focused on the movement of information from one place to another. The most dramatic shift for business in communications technology has been the Internet. Increasing use of the Internet in the form of e-mail and websites is transforming the work environment. The Internet has broken down traditional geographic barriers to communication, opened up markets, and created an environment of almost instant feedback. As the government policy of convergence makes high-speed Internet the norm, businesses will rely more and more on the Internet for their communication needs.

When the three technologies are incorporated into an office environment, many improvements become possible, but they are mostly improvements in the speed with which work is done rather than in the kind of work that is done. Office automation in the 1980s began a new trend—the integration of separate capabilities into single powerful "work stations." Even the most basic home office today contains, through the use of a single computer, the following capabilities and systems: word-processing and home publishing abilities; access to information previously stored on files at other locations; electronic messaging systems, including any combination of text, graphics and voice, connecting users to others on the same net or to people on different nets in other places; activity-management systems, including time management, project planning and scheduling; information management systems, including straightforward storage and retrieval systems, where the user does much of the work of storing and retrieving; decision-support systems incorporate sophisticated programs on large databases and allow the user to perform complex analyses so as to improve the speed and quality of decisions.

Today, we continue to see major developments in several areas. The power of the computers driving most technology continues to increase rapidly. Not only can computers process and hold more information, but they also process this information with greater efficiency and speed. More significantly, computers allow the individual to perform a multitude of tasks almost simultaneously. For example, on a single computer a worker can be connected to several websites at the same time, receive e-mail, and work on a number of different files.

2. The Impact of Office Automation

The computer is changing the office environment much like the automobile has changed the city. Effectively integrated office automation systems may result in the restructuring of entire organizations, with the emergence of new structural configurations and the elimination of departments or entire divisions. The new information technologies have led to a large reduction in the size of the average organization's middle ranks. Moreover, the workers who remain are no longer tied to a centrally located office: telecommuting has become a new trend in the business world. On the positive side, this trend enables individuals to work from the comfort of home; on the negative side, this lack of a common office environment may contribute to the erosion of the city core. The new technologies may also have the potential to strengthen the power of trans-national corporations in many countries, contributing to the erosion of national autonomy and displacing many people whose jobs will be automated. In most organizations office automation has been viewed as a means to computerize old procedures and to make employees more productive.

There is also a rising fear that new technologies will have negative impacts on job security and the privacy of the individual. There is also concern that the economy will suffer greatly if national organizations do not develop and adapt to the new technologies. Whether or not national industry will learn to use information technologies to their advantage in the increasingly competitive world system remains to be seen. It is safe to say, however, that the technologies will have a significant impact on people's working lives in the coming decades.

3. Office Automation Systems

Office Automation Systems (OAS) are configurations of networked computer hardware and software. A variety of office automation systems are now applied to business and communication functions that used to be performed manually or in multiple locations of a company, such as preparing written communications and strategic planning. In addition, with office automation systems, the expertise in typesetting, printing, or electronic recording can now be integrated into the everyday work of an organization, saving both time and money.

Types of functions integrated by office automation systems include (1) electronic publishing; (2) electronic communication; (3) electronic collaboration; (4) image processing; and (5) office management. At the heart of these systems is often a Local Area Network (LAN). The LAN allows users to transmit data, voice, mail, and images across the network to any destination, whether that destination is in the local office on the LAN, or in another country or continent, through a connecting network. An OAS makes office work more efficient and increases productivity.

New Words

alter ['ɔːltə] *v.* 改变，更改
concept ['kɔnsept] *n.* 观念，概念，想法
identifiable [ai'dentifaiəbl] *adj.* 可辨认的
evident ['evidənt] *adj.* 明白的，明显的
payroll ['peirəul] *n.* 工资单，工薪总额
inventory-control ['invəntri-kən'trol] *n.* 库存管理，库存控制
process [prə'ses] *n.* 工序，过程 *v.* 加工，处理，起诉，列队前进
division [di'viʒən] *n.* 划分，除法，部门
device [di'vais] *n.* 装置，设备，策略，设计
magnetic [mæg'netik] *adj.* 有磁性的，有吸引力的
insert [in'səːt] *vt.* 插入
slot [slɔt] *n.* 槽；狭缝；投币口
code [kəud] *n.* 密码；法规，准则
magnetize ['mægnitaiz] *vt.* 使磁化，吸引，诱惑
primitive ['primitiv] *adj.* 原始的，简陋的
dramatic [drə'mætik] *adj.* 戏剧性的，引人注目的，给人深刻印象的
shift [ʃift] *v.* 移动，改变；换挡，转换 *n.* 轮班，变化，移动，轮班职工
transform [træns'fɔːm] *v.* 改变，转换
barrier ['bæriə] *n.* 栅栏，障碍物，屏障
instant ['instənt] *n.* 瞬间，立即 *adj.* 立即的，即时的，速成的
convergence [kən'vəːdʒəns] *n.* 汇聚，汇合点，收敛
norm [nɔːm] *n.* 规范，标准
incorporate [in'kɔːpəreit] *v.* 合并，包含，组成公司
trend [trend] *n.* 趋势，倾向
integration [ˌinti'greiʃən] *n.* 集成，综合，同化
graphics ['græfiks] *n.*[语]书法，字体
straightforward [streit'fɔːwəd] *adj.* 易懂的，笔直的，坦率的
analyses ['ænəlaiz] *n.* 分解，分析(名词 analysis 的复数式)
significantly [sig'nifikəntli] *adv.* 意味深长地，意义深远地，重要地，较大地
simultaneously [siməl'teiniəsly] *adv.* 同时地
automobile ['ɔːtəməubiːl] *n.* 汽车 *adj.* 汽车的
restructure [ri'strʌktʃə] *vt.* 重建，重造，改组
entire [in'taiə] *adj.* 全部的，完整的，全面的

emergence [i'mə:dʒəns] *n.* 出现，浮现，露出

configuration [kənˌfigju'reiʃən] *n.* 结构，布局，形态；[计]配置

elimination [iˌlimi'neiʃən] *n.* 除去，消除；淘汰

telecommuting [ˌtelikə'mju:tiŋ] *n.* 远程联机，远程办公

erosion [i'rəuʒən] *n.* 腐蚀，侵蚀，减少，流失

core [kɔ:] *n.* 核心，果心；要点

potential [pə'tenʃəl] *adj.* 潜在的，可能的 *n.* 潜力，潜能

transnational [træns'næʃənl] *adj.* 跨国的

displace [dis'pleis] *v.* 取代，移置，替换

autonomy [ɔ:'tɔnəmi] *n.* 自治，自治权，自主

productive [prə'dʌktiv] *adj.* 生产的，有成效的，多产的

hardware ['hɑ:dwεə] *n.* 硬件

software ['sɔftwεə] *n.* 软件

multiple ['mʌltipl] *adj.* 多种多样的，许多的 *n.* 倍数，并联

strategic [strə'ti:dʒik] *adj.* 战略的，重要的，基本的

expertise [ˌekspə'ti:z] *n.* 专门知识，专门技术；专家的意见

typesetting ['taipˌsetiŋ] *n.* 排字，排版

collaboration [kəˌlæbə'reiʃən] *n.* 合作

transmit [trænz'mit] *vt.* 传达，传送，发送信号

image ['imidʒ] *n.* 印象，形象，影像，图像，肖像

destination [ˌdesti'neiʃən] *n.* 目的地，终点

continent ['kɔntinənt] *n.* 大陆，洲

productivity [ˌprɔdʌk'tiviti] *n.* 生产率，生产力

Phrases and Expressions

a wide range of 各式各样的

be limited to 局限于

be crammed with 塞满，填满

as usual 像往常一样，照例

serve as 担任，充当，起……的作用

be based on 根据，以……为基准

type out 打出，打字输出

compared to 与……相比

center around 围绕，以……为中心

focus on 集中在

communications technology 通信技术

break down 失败，划分，损坏，衰弱下来；中断

open up 打开，开发

rely on 依靠，信赖

be incorporated into 被收入，被并入

so as to 为的是，以便

a multitude of 许多，众多

connect to 连接，相连

work on 对……起作用，企图影响或说服，忙于

result in 导致，结果是

be tied to 被束缚着，被牵制着，与……有关系
on the positive side 从好的方面看
on the negative side 从坏的方面看
contribute to 是……的原因，有助于，为……做贡献
view as 视为，看作
adapt to 适应
to sb.'s advantage 对某人有利
It is safe to say. 可以肯定地说，完全可以这样说
have a significant impact on 对……有重大影响
a variety of 种种，多种多样的
in addition 另外，此外

Abbreviations

OAS (Office Automation System) 办公室自动化系统
IBM (International Business Machines) 国际商用机器公司
MCST (Magnetic Card Selectric Typewriter) 磁卡片自动排字机
LAN (Local Area Network) 局域网

Notes

1 The technology we see today had its start in the 1960s, when 3 clearly identifiable streams of development became evident.

本句中，when 引导了一个非限制性定语从句，补充说明主句中的时间状语 in the 1960s。

非限制性定语从句常用关系代词 who、which、whom, 关系副词 when、where 等引导。请看下例：

He will put off the picnic until May 1st, when he will be free.

他将把郊游推迟到 5 月 1 日，那时他有空。

My gardener，who is very pessimistic，says that there will be no apples this year.

我家的园丁非常悲观，他说今年不会结苹果了。

另外，we see today 是定语从句，修饰限定先行词 the technology, 其中关系代词 that 被省略。英语句子中，如果关系代词 that 在定语从句中做宾语，就可以省略。请看下例：

This is one of the most exciting football games (that) I have ever seen.

这是我见过的最激动人心的足球比赛之一。

2 Compared to current word-processing systems, this one was primitive, but it worked.

本句中，compared to current word-processing systems 是过去分词作条件状语，其逻

辑主语为 this one，相当于条件从句 If this one was compared to current word-processing systems。请看下例：

Given a few minutes, I'll finish it.

再过几分钟，我就完成了。

Compared with you, I still have a long way to go.

跟你比较起来，我还差得很远呢。

3 Not only can computers process and hold more information, but they also process this information with greater efficiency and speed.

本句中，主体结构为 not only... but also... 连接的两个句子。

英语中，当 not only... but also... 连接两个句子且放在句首时，not only 后面的句子要用部分倒装。请看下例：

Not only did they present a musical performance, but they also gave a brief introduction to the history of Western brass instruments.

他们不但做了音乐表演，而且简短地介绍了西方铜管乐器的历史。

另外，not only... but also 常用于连接两个表示并列关系的成分，着重强调后者，其意为“不仅……而且……”；其中的 also 有时可以省略。请看下例：

He not only writes his own plays, but he acts in them.

他不仅自编剧本，还饰演其中的角色。

4 The new technologies may also have the potential to strengthen the power of trans-national corporations in many countries, contributing to the erosion of national autonomy and displacing many people whose jobs will be automated.

本句中，contributing to the erosion of national autonomy and displacing many people whose jobs will be automated 是由 and 连接的两个现在分词短语并列作伴随状语。

英语中，现在分词短语作伴随状语，表达的动作或状态是伴随着句子谓语动词的动作而发生或存在的。请看下例：

Walking slowly across the grass, he pointed the gun at the lion and fired.

他慢慢地走过草地，把枪对准狮子就射击了。

另外，本句中 contribute to 意为“是……的原因；促成；引起”。请看下例：

Air pollution contributes to respiratory diseases.

空气污染可促使呼吸系统疾病发生。

5 Whether or not national industry will learn to use information technologies to their advantage in the increasingly competitive world system remains to be seen.

本句中，remains to be seen 是整个句子的谓语，Whether or not national industry will learn to use information technologies to their advantage in the increasingly competitive world system 是 whether 引导的从句作整个句子的主语，即主语从句。请看下例：

Whether we will go for an outing tomorrow remains unknown.

我们明天是否会远足目前还不清楚。

另外，whether or not 意为“无论是……或……；是否”。请看下例：

It's debatable whether or not the reforms have improved conditions.
改革是否改善了现状，这问题仍有争议。

Exercises

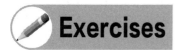

EX. 1 Answer the following questions.

1. What is office automation?
2. In terms of office automation technology, what did the three clearly identifiable streams of technological development refer to?
3. What systems were the earliest applications of computing technology?
4. What did communications technology focus on?
5. How is the Internet transforming the work environment?
6. What was the new trend that office automation began in the 1980s?
7. According to Text A, how powerful are today's computers?
8. As for the new technologies, what are people afraid of and concerned about?
9. What are office automation systems?
10. What types of functions are integrated by office automation systems?

EX. 2 Complete the following sentences with appropriate words or expressions in the box.

contribute to	alter	primitive	transform	incorporate
connect to	productivity	automation	transmit	apply to

1. Under certain conditions we can ________ the bad into the good.
2. The laws ________ everyone irrespective of race, creed or colour.
3. It allows users to effortlessly ________ Internet and network resources.
4. He will publish his observations on the social life of these ________ tribes.
5. We supply a wide range of office ________ devices.
6. Amity between the two nations will ________ the prosperity of the region.
7. A videophone can ________ and receive pictures as well as sound.
8. We should steadily ________ living allowances for laid-off workers from state-owned enterprises into the unemployment insurance.
9. No bidder shall be permitted to ________ his bid after the bid has been open.
10. There have been enormous increases in agricultural ________.

EX. 3 Translate the following sentences into English.

1. 办公自动化是计算机和通信技术在改善办事人员和管理人员的工作效率方面的一种应

用。(Office Automation)

2. 现代社会由于通信技术的发达，世界逐渐形成一个地球村。(communication technology)
3. 这样做将增加管理和集成的复杂度。(integration)
4. 激光器是一种用特殊材料制成的装置。(device)
5. 我需要一些灵活的人，能够适应新的制度和新的程序。(adapt to)
6. 销售经理想在远东开辟新市场。(open up)
7. 这位秘书目前的项目和兴趣集中于电子学习、内容管理、统计计算和数据库技术。(center around)
8. 经理们发现远距离工作为他们的技术注入了新的活力。(telecommuting)
9. 办公室自动化系统对秘书工作的效率有重大的影响。(have a significant impact on)
10. 作为他的私人行政助理，她能接触到他所有的信件。(have access to)

EX. 4 **Translate the following passage into Chinese.**

Office politics refers to the process and behavior in human interactions involving power and authority and it is the use of power and social networking within an organization to achieve changes that benefit the organization or individuals within it. Office politics may serve personal interests without regard to their effect on the organization itself. Some of the personal advantages may include access to tangible assets, or intangible benefits, such as status or authority that influences the behavior of others. On the other hand, office politics can increase efficiency, form interpersonal relationships, expedite change, and profit the organization and its members simultaneously.

Office politics differs from office gossip in that people participating in office politics do so with the objective of gaining advantage, whereas gossip can be a purely social activity. However, the two are somewhat related. Office gossip is often used by an individual to place themselves at a point where they can control the flow of information, and therefore gain maximum advantage. The secretive nature of office politics differentiates it from public gossip and thus, may be more harmful to the organization. Office politics also refers to the way co-workers act among each other. Employee interaction holds the potential to be either positive or negative.

Part Three Text B

Office Administration

Office administration is a set of day-to-day activities that are related to financial planning, record keeping and billing, personnel, physical distribution and logistics, within an organization. An employee that undertakes these activities is commonly called an office administrator or office manager, and plays a key role in any organizations infrastructure, regardless of the scale.

An office administrator has the responsibility of ensuring that the administrative activities within an organization run efficiently. These activities can range from being responsible for the management of human resources, budgets and records, to undertaking the role of supervising other employees. These responsibilities can vary depending on the employer and level of education. Many administrative positions require the candidate to have an advanced skill in the software applications Microsoft Word, Excel and Access.

1. Skill

The importance of an office administrator to an organization is substantial due to the duties that they are entrusted with, therefore specialized training is required in order for the employee to work efficiently and productively, these being:

- Payroll training that involves the responsibility in ensuring that all employees receive their pay slips on time.
- To have good communication skills in order to coordinate with other employees around the organization.
- The ability of being able to supervise support workers.
- The ability of adapting to changing environments and new technologies that could be implemented e.g. New software installation.
- To show good initiative.
- To be able to work under pressure when given a task that is of vital importance to the organization.

2. Office Roles and Duties

There are an extensive range of roles and duties that can be associated with an office administrator. They are as follows.

2.1 Receptionists

Receptionists play a key role in the organizations management, as they are entrusted with arranging and meeting the clients, suppliers and visitors directly via emails, phone calls or direct mail. The employee undertaking the role of a receptionist must show good organizational, communication and customer service skills in order to ensure efficiency within the organization. Other responsibilities that a receptionist is entrusted with are:

- To ensure that the outgoing and incoming mail is allocated to the right department within the organization.
- To organize and assist fellow employees with meetings, conferences and direct telephone calls when required.
- To communicate with members of the public when an inquiry is made.
- To manage and maintain the filing system that has been implemented into the organization e.g. information systems.
- Clerical duties that involve the ordering of equipment, office supplies and other inventories that

are required.

2.2 Personal Assistant

Personal Assistants are commonly associated with an office manager that help maintain the efficiency of their day-to-day work through providing secretarial support and assistance. Becoming a personal assistant requires the employee to have experience in previous administrative jobs, in which entailed the use of computers and information systems. Like any other role that is related to an office administrator, the job title of personal assistant requires the employee to be organized, show professionalism and the ability to work under pressure when given a task of vital importance. The duties that a personal assistant must carry out each day are the following:

- The task of inputting, filing and managing the data that is stored within the organization's office system.
- Personal assistants act as a first hand to the office manager so they must ensure that all contacts from third party individuals are processed through them.
- To arrange transportation and meetings that are of importance to the office manager.
- To ensure that documents, reports and presentations are set up prior to any meetings.
- To process emails and letters that are received in correspondent to the office manager.

2.3 Office Manager

An office manager has the responsibility in ensuring that an organization's office duties are completed efficiently and effectively, while allocated the task of supervising other member of staff. The role of an office manager requires the candidate to have a higher skill and qualification than other administrative vacancies. Such skills and qualifications include strong administrative experience, competency in human resources, reporting skills, delegation, managing processes and the ability to communicate to other members of the organization. Office managers are given many important duties daily that help the organization run effectively and efficiently, these being:

- Organizing the office's operations and procedures by undertaking several administrative tasks e.g. designing and implementing a new filing system.
- Assigning certain employees to undertake operational requirements, while following up on their progress.
- Recruiting, selecting and training new employees, while simultaneously maintaining the current employees through coaching ad counseling.
- Producing an annual budget that represents the organization's financial objectives (determines where expenditures need to be scheduled for the next financial year).
- Attending several workshops that will benefit and increase the knowledge of the office manager e.g. educational workshops and participating in professional societies.

3. Jobs Within Office Administration

There are many sectors within office administration that people can work under, office administrator and office manager being the most commonly associated roles. However there are hundreds of different roles and job vacancies that an employee can undertake within an organization, which fall under the category of office administration. Human resource administrators are the employees who are in charge of managing the organization's human capital. Payroll and benefits administration are the primary duties that an employee under human resources will carry out, while given the responsibility of recruiting new employees for the organization. An Executive secretary are entrusted with supporting their high-level executives with the production of statistical reports, scheduled meetings and written memorandums. Similarly, an executive secretary commonly share the same responsibilities as a personal assistant through daily tasks that benefit the organization or executive in an efficient and effective method. Their duties may include aiding their manager or superior with daily tasks, preparing correspondence and mail, managing their information systems and coordinating the office management effectively.

New Words

logistics [lə'dʒistiks] *n.* 物流，后勤学，运筹学

infrastructure ['infrə'strʌktʃə] *n.* 基础，基础设施

candidate ['kændidit] *n.* 候选人，应试者

substantial [səb'stænʃəl] *adj.* 大量的，实质的，可观的

installation [ˌinstə'leiʃən] *n.* 安装，装置；军事驻地

extensive [iks'tensiv] *adj.* 广泛的，广阔的，广大的

via ['vaiə] *prep.* 经由，通过

inventory ['invəntri] *n.* 详细目录，存货（清单） *vt.* 编制（详细目录）

previous ['pri:vjəs] *adj.* 以前的，先于，在……之前

entail [in'teil] *vt.* 使必需，带来，限定继承

input ['input] *n.* 投入，输入信息，输入数据 *v.* 输入

qualification [ˌkwɔlifi'keiʃən] *n.* 资格，资历；限制条件

vacancy ['veikənsi] *n.* 空缺，空白

competency ['kɔmpitənsi] *n.* 能力，胜任，技能

delegation [ˌdeli'geiʃən] *n.* 代表团，委派，授权，委托

recruit [ri'kru:t] *vt.* 吸收（新成员），征兵，招聘

counseling ['kaunsəliŋ] *n.* 顾问服务

annual ['ænjuəl] *adj.* 每年的，年度的，一年生的 *n.* 年刊，一年生植物

primary ['praiməri] *adj.* 首要的，主要的，初级的

statistical [stə'tistikəl] *adj.* 统计的，统计学的

Phrases and Expressions

play a key role in 起着举足轻重的作用	be allocated to 被分配给
regardless of 不管，不顾	prior to 在……之前
range from... to... 从……到……变动，范围从……到……	in correspondent to 与……一致的，相应的
due to 因为，由于	follow up on 追踪，进一步了解
entrust with 信托，委托	job vacancy 职务空缺
pay slip 工资单	fall under the category of 属于……的范畴
be associated with 与……相联系	aid with 用……帮助

Exercises

EX. 5 Answer the following questions.

1. What is office administration according to Text B?
2. What are the responsibilities of an office administrator?
3. Why does an office administrator need to take payroll training?
4. What skills is a receptionist supposed to have in order to ensure efficiency within the organization?
5. List at least two duties that a personal assistant must carry out each day.
6. What is the responsibility of an office manager?
7. What skills and qualifications do office managers need to have?
8. List at least two important daily duties of an office manager?
9. What is the job of human resource administrators?
10. What may the duties of executive secretaries include?

Part Four Extended Reading

Text	Notes
An Overview[1] to Office	[1] *n.* 概述
An office is generally a room or other area where administrative work is done, but may also denote[2] a position within an organization with specific[3] duties attached to it and as place, office	[2] *vt.* 表示，象征 [3] *adj.* 明确的，特殊的

originally[4] referred to the location of one's duty. In modern terms, an office usually refers to the location where white-collar workers are employed[5]. As per James Stephenson, "Office is that part of business enterprise[6] which is devoted to[7] the direction and co-ordination of its various[8] activities."

History of Office

The word "Office" stems from[9] the Latin officium. An officium was not necessarily[10] a place, but rather an often mobile "bureau[11]" in the sense of a human staff or even the abstract notion[12] of a formal position, such as a magistrature[13].

Offices in classical antiquity[14] were often part of a palace complex[15] or a large temple. There was usually a room where scrolls[16] were kept and scribes[17] did their work. These rooms are sometimes called "libraries" by some archaeologists[18] and the general press because one often associates scrolls with literature. In fact they were true offices since the scrolls were meant for record keeping and other management functions such as treaties[19] and edicts[20].

The High Middle Ages (1000—1300) saw the rise of the medieval[21] chancery[22], which was usually the place where most government letters were written and where laws were copied in the administration of a kingdom. The rooms of the chancery often had walls full of pigeonholes[23], constructed to hold rolled up pieces of parchment[24] for safekeeping or ready reference. Medieval illustrations[25] often show people in their private offices handling record-keeping books or writing on scrolls of parchment. All kinds of writings seemed to be mixed in these early forms of offices.

As mercantilism[26] became the dominant[27] economic theory of the Renaissance[28], merchants tended to conduct their business in the same buildings, which might include retail sales[29], warehousing and clerical work. During the 15th century, population density[30] in many cities reached the point where stand-alone[31] buildings were used by merchants to conduct their business, and there was a developing a distinction[32] between church, government/military and commerce uses for buildings.

Emergence[33] of the Modern Office

As the Industrial Revolution intensified[34] in the 18th and 19th centuries,the industries of banking, rail, insurance, retail,petroleum, and telegraphy[35] dramatically grew in size and complexity[36]. To transact[37] business, an increasing number of[38] clerks were needed to handle word-processing, accounting[39], and document filing, with increasingly specialized office space required to house these activities. Most of the desks of the era[40] were top heavy with paper

[4] *adv.* 原本，起初，独创地
[5] *v.* 雇佣，使用
[6] *n.* 企业，事业
[7] 把……献于
[8] *adj.* 各种各样的
[9] 源于，来自于
[10] 未必
[11] *n.* 局，办事处
[12] *n.* 观念，概念，想法，主张
[13] *n.* 长官的职位，地方行政长官
[14] *n.* 古代，古物
[15] *n.* 官邸群
[16] *n.* 卷轴；名册
[17] *n.* 抄写员，书记员
[18] *n.* 考古学家
[19] *n.* 条约
[20] *n.* 法令，布告
[21] *adj.* 中世纪的
[22] *n.* 大法官法庭；档案室
[23] *n.* 文件架的小间隔
[24] *n.* 羊皮纸
[25] *n.* 说明，插图
[26] *n.* 重商主义
[27] *adj.* 占优势的
[28] *n.* 文艺复兴，再生
[29] 零售
[30] *n.* 人口密度
[31] *adj.* 独立的
[32] *n.* 差别，区分
[33] *n.* 出现，浮现
[34] *v.* 增强，加剧
[35] *n.* 电报学，电报
[36] *n.* 复杂性
[37] *v.* 办理，交易
[38] 越来越多的
[39] *n.* 会计
[40] *n.* 时代，年代

storage bins extending above the desk-work area, giving the appearance of a cubicle[41] and offering the workers some degree of privacy. By the mid of the 20th century, it became apparent[42] that an efficient office required discretion[43] in the control of privacy, which is needed to combat tedium[44] linked to poor productivity, and to encourage creativity.	[41] *n.* 小室 [42] *adj.* 明显的 [43] *n.* 谨慎，慎重，自行决定 [44] *n.* 单调乏味，沉闷
Office Spaces The main purpose of an office environment is to support its occupants[45] in performing their job—preferably at minimum cost[46] and to maximum satisfaction[47]. With different people performing different tasks and activities, however, it is not always easy to select the right office spaces. To aid[48] decision-making in workplace and office design, one can distinguish[49] three different types of office spaces: work spaces, meeting spaces and support spaces. Work spaces in an office are typically[50] used for conventional[51] office activities such as reading, writing and computer work. Meeting spaces in an office are typically used interactive[52] processes, be it quick conversations or intensive brainstorm[53]. And support spaces in an office are typically used for secondary[54] activities such as filing documents or taking a break.	[45] *n.* 占有者，居住者 [46] 以最小的成本 [47] 最大程度的满足 [48] *v.* 辅助，援助 [49] *vt.* 区别，辨认 [50] *adv.* 典型地 [51] *adj.* 传统的，惯例的 [52] *adj.* 相互作用的，交互的 [53] *n.* 集思广益 [54] *adj.* 次要的，从属的
Office Environment Electronic technology changed not only the way work was formerly done in office but also the environment of the office itself. In general, modern office are quieter than those of previous[55] eras, because computers, laser printers[56], and other electronic equipment make much less noise than typewriters and other outmoded[57] office machines did. Electronic documents, such as e-mail and word processor documents, reduced the amount of paper used in offices, so modern offices are usually less cluttered[58] than offices of the past. In addition[59], today most business recognize that a pleasant working environment increases employee productivity[60], so the modern office is likely to be air-conditioned[61], carpeted, well lighted, and comfortable. Due to the health risks of secondhand smoke, most business now provide a smoke-free office environment.	[55] *adj.* 以前的，先于，在……之前 [56] *n.* 激光打印机 [57] *adj.* 过时的 [58] *adj.* 杂乱的 [59] 此外，另外 [60] *n.* 生产力 [61] *adj.* 备有空调装置的

参考译文

课文 A　办公自动化

1. 概述

办公自动化是一个通用术语，是指包括计算机、通信和信息技术在办公环境中的广泛应用。自动化不仅改变了我们的工作环境，而且改变了我们的工作理念。

我们今天看到的技术开始于20世纪60年代。当时有三股可清晰识别的发展潮流很明显。第一股潮流是计算领域。在该领域，最早的应用程序是自动化工资系统和库存控制系统。其他的应用程序也局限于数据处理。通常只有组织的数据处理部门的程序员才能操作这些系统。然而，计算机在组织环境中的应用越来越广泛，包括越来越多的数据处理。

技术发展的第二股潮流是文本处理领域。在20世纪70年代中期，IBM推出了名为MCST（磁卡片自动排字机）的产品。这个装置有一个配有电子设备的盒子。操作人员会在盒子顶部的槽中插入一个特制的涂层卡，并像往常一样在连接的打字机上打字。该卡用作存储设备，基于磁化点，文本将以代码的形式被写在该卡上。一旦输入，文本会被反复编辑，生成一个新的副本，并在所连接的打印机上打印出来。与现有的文字处理系统相比，这个系统是原始的，但它有作用。

虽然前两次技术发展主要是围绕办公室信息处理进行的，然而第三次发展潮流，即通信技术，却专注于如何将信息从一个地方传递到另一个地方。在通信技术中，最引人注目的转变是互联网。应用越来越广泛的互联网以电子邮件和网站的形式正在改变我们的工作环境。互联网打破了传统的交流地域障碍，开拓了市场，创造了一个几乎可以即时反馈的环境。由于政府的鼓励政策使高速互联网成为规范，企业将越来越多地依赖于互联网以实现通信需求。

当这三种技术被应用于办公环境中时，许多改进成为可能，但它们大多是提高工作速度，而不是需要完成的工作种类。20世纪80年代的办公自动化掀起了一个新的趋势，即将分别独立的功能整合成单个的功能强大的"工作站"。今天，通过使用一台计算机，即使是最基本的小型办公室也包括以下功能和系统：文字处理和首页发布功能；获取先前存储在其他位置的文件信息；电子传报系统，包括组合任何文本、图形和声音，连接同一网络中的用户或者其他地方不同网络中的用户；活动管理系统，包括时间管理、项目计划和调度；信息管理系统，包括简单的存储和检索系统，即用户主要完成存储和检索工作；决策支持系统整合了大数据库的复杂程序，并允许用户进行复杂的分析，以提高决策的速度和质量。

今天，我们将继续见证这几个领域的重大发展。电脑驱动技术的力量将继续快速增长。计算机不仅可以处理并容纳更多的信息，而且还可以更高效、更快速地处理这些信息。更重要的是，电脑让个人可以几乎同时执行多项任务。例如，在一台计算机上，一名员工可以同时连接好几个网站，接收电子邮件，并处理大量不同的文件。

2. 办公自动化的影响

正如汽车改变了城市一样，计算机正在改变办公室环境。有效地整合办公自动化系统可能会导致整个机构的重组。届时，将出现新型结构配置，一些部门或整个分部将消失。新的信息技术已经大幅减少了一般机构的中层人员。此外，留下的员工不再受限于位于市中心的办公室：远程办公已成为商界的一种新趋势。从好的方面看，这一趋势使个人能够舒适地在家里办公；从不好的方面看，缺少共同的办公环境可能会导致城市核心生活的没落。新技术还可能增强许多国家跨国公司的实力，导致国家自治权的丧失，并取代许多员工，因为他们的工作将自动化。在大多数机构中，办公自动化已被视为一种实现旧程序电脑化和提高员工生产力的方式。

人们也越来越担心新技术将会对工作安全和个人隐私产生负面的影响。他们也担心如果本国的组织不开发并适应新的技术，经济可能会遭受重大损失。在全球竞争日益激烈的情况下，民族工业是否会学着利用信息技术使自己占据优势还有待见证。但是，我们完全可以说，这些技术将对未来几十年里人们的职场生活产生巨大的影响。

3. 办公自动化系统

办公自动化系统（OAS）是网络化的计算机硬件和软件配置。各种办公自动化系统现已应用于商业和通信功能。在过去，诸如准备书面交流材料和战略规划等这些工作通常是人工完成的，或在一个公司的多个工作位置上完成的。此外，办公自动化系统的应用可以将排版、印刷或电子记录方面的专业知识整合到一个组织的日常工作中，从而节省时间和金钱。

由办公自动化系统整合的功能类型包括：（1）电子出版；（2）电子通信；（3）电子协作；（4）图像处理；（5）办公管理。这些系统的核心往往是局域网（LAN）。局域网允许用户在网络中通过连接网络的方式将数据、语音、邮件和图片传输到任何目的地，无论目的地是在局域网内的本地办事处，或在另一个国家或大陆。办公自动化系统提高了办公室工作效率和生产力。

课文B 办公室管理

办公室管理是与组织内财务规划，做账和计费，人员、物资调运和物流等相关的一套日常活动。从事这些活动的员工通常被称为办公室管理员或办公室经理。他们在任何组织基础设施中发挥着关键的作用，无论该组织的规模大小如何。

办公室管理员的责任是确保组织内的行政管理活动有效地运行。这些活动可以是负责人力资源管理的预算和记录，也可以是承担起监督其他员工的责任。其具体的责任可以根据雇主和教育程度的不同而有所变化。许多行政管理职位要求候选人有高级的技术知识，能运用微软 Word、Excel 和 Access 数据库等应用程序。

1. 技能

由于受托承担的职责，办公室管理员对一个组织是极为重要的。因此，为了让员工有效和高效地工作，专业的培训是必需的。这些培训包括：

- 发薪培训，即确保所有员工能按时领到他们的工资单。
- （使办公室管理者）具备良好的沟通能力，从而能够和组织的其他员工进行协调。
- （使办公室管理者）具备监督下属员工的能力。
- （使办公室管理者）具备适应不断变化的环境和可能被应用的新技术的能力，例如新软件的安装技术。
- （使办公室管理者）表现出良好的主动性。
- （使办公室管理者）在承担组织给予的重要任务时，能够在有压力的情况下工作。

2. 办公室角色及其职责

与办公室管理员有关的角色很多。这些角色及其职责如下所述。

2.1 接待员

接待员在组织管理中起着关键的作用，因为他们肩负直接通过电子邮件、电话或邮寄等方式安排并会见客户、供应商和访客的职责。担任接待员职位的员工必须表现出良好的组织、沟通和客服技巧，以确保组织运作的效率。接待员肩负的其他职责还有：

- 确保将发出和收到的邮件分配到组织内合适的部门。
- 组织和协助员工会议，并在需要的时候转接电话。
- 在有人咨询时，负责与公众沟通交流。
- 管理并维护组织应用的文件系统，如信息系统。
- 承担一些文员工作，包括订购设备、办公室用品以及其他所需货品。

2.2 个人助理

个人助理通常与办公室经理相类似。通过提供秘书性的支持和协助，他们协助保持办公室经理们日常工作的效率。要成为一名私人助理，就必须具有先前积累的行政工作经验，其中必须具备使用计算机和信息系统的经验。正如与办公室管理员相关的其他角色一样，个人助理的职位要求员工工作有条理，具有敬业精神，并且在完成重要任务时，能够在有压力的情况下工作。个人助理每天必须履行的职责如下：

- 输入数据、归档并管理存储在组织内办公系统中的数据。
- 个人助理直接协助办公室经理，所以他们必须确保和第三方人员的所有联系必须经由他们安排进行。
- 安排对办公室经理极为重要的出行及会面事宜。
- 确保在会议召开之前，将文件、报告、书面介绍等材料准备好。
- 处理办公室经理的往来邮件和信件。

2.3 办公室经理

办公室经理负责确保一个组织的工作得以高效地完成，同时还要承担监督其他职员的工作。与其他的行政管理职位相比，办公室经理职位要求应聘者具有较高的技能和资质。这些技能和资质包括丰富的行政管理经验、较强的人力资源管理能力、报告技能、知人善任的能力、管理工作流程的能力以及和组织其他成员沟通的能力。办公室经理每天需完成许多重要的工作，来协助组织有效和高效地运行。这些工作如下：

- 通过开展一些行政工作，安排办公室的工作及运行程序，例如设计并应用一个新的文件系统。
- 给某些员工分配工作任务，并同时跟踪他们的工作进展。
- 招聘、选拔和培训新员工，同时通过培训和辅导的方式培植现有的员工。
- 制定年度预算，阐明组织的财务目标（即确定安排下一个财政年度的支出方向）。
- 参加几个有利于增长办公室经理知识的研讨会，如参加教育研讨会和专业协会。

3. 办公室管理职位

在办公室，人们可以在许多办公室管理部门工作。办公室管理员和办公室经理是最常见的相关职位。然而，在一个组织内，员工可以担任数百个不同的角色和工作岗位，这些角色和岗位都属于行政管理工作的范畴。人力资源管理员负责管理组织的人力资本。另外，人力资源管理部的员工还主要负责管理工资和福利，同时也负责为组织招聘新员工。行政秘书肩负着协助高层管理人员工作的职责。他们制作数据报表、安排会议并撰写书面备忘录。同样，行政秘书还承担个人助理相同的工作，高效地完成有益于组织和有助于行政管理人员的日常工作。他们的职责可能包括协助经理或上司主管完成日常工作、准备信件和邮件、管理信息系统，并有效地协调办公室管理等。

File Management

Unit 3

Part One Dialogues

Sample Dialogue 1

Situation ▶ Sun Li is being asked about the filing work.

(A—Tom Brown, the General Manager of Far-East Textile Trade Company; B—Sun Li, the secretary)

A: Sun Li, do you know how to file the documents according to the "Filing Instruction" of our company?

B: Sorry, I don't know. Could you tell me about it?

A: Of course. There are four points you should keep in mind when you file documents.

B: What are the four points?

A: Well. The four points are: classify and keep the documents in each file; remove all the chips and pins; punch the documents evenly and place them squarely in the folder.

B: And what is the last point?

A: The last point is the most important filing principle — "One customer－one file".

B: Oh, I see. That principle is the essence of filing. But, Mr. Brown, how should our company's filing materials be sorted into order?

A: There are four basic methods of classifying materials for filing: alphabetical, dates, geographical, and by the subject. Are you clear about this?

B: Yes. I have got it. But I suppose a card index is also very useful in the filing work.

A: That's true. A card index is a most valuable friend to a secretary, so it must be kept handy and up to date.

B: Are there any other instructions on filing work?
A: En..., you also need to remember that prompt and careful filing contributes greatly to the efficiency of our office.
B: Thank you for your instructions. I'll do my best with the filling work in our office.

Sample Dialogue 2

Situation ▶ Sun Li is being asked to file some documents.

(A—Tom Brown, the General Manager of Far-East Textile Trade Company; B—Sun Li, the executive secretary)

A: Miss Sun, would you please fill all these documents for me?
B: Oh, yes. I'll list down all the documents.
A: Remember this: the rule of file-keeping is "one customer-one file." Do you know this rule?
B: Yes. That means bringing the documents together in a single folder or file all papers relating to a particular subject.
A: Yes, you are right. Besides, each file must be named clearly, either in block capitals or in jet-black typed capitals.
B: OK. Do you want me to file them according to dates?
A: No, please file them in alphabetical order.
B: Well. I think I'll make copies and file them both ways.
A: Great idea! You are an excellent secretary. By the way, have you found those files I requested yesterday?
B: I'm sorry. Mr. Brown. I couldn't find those files about that trade company, even though I checked all the cross-references. I don't think it's there.
A: I'm sure that those files were filed.
B: Maybe I should check again under a different heading?
A: Yes. Actually I believe I asked you to put it in Mr. White's file.

Useful Expressions

1. Sun Li, do you know how to file the documents according to the "Filing Instruction" of our company?
孙丽，你知道如何按照我们公司的"归档须知"进行归档吗？
2. The four points are: classify and keep the documents in each file; remove all the chips

and pins; punch the documents evenly and place them squarely in the folder.
这四点是：将文件分类并归档；去掉所有的回形针和大头针；将文件平放打孔，并把文件平整地放入文件夹。

3. There are four basic methods of classifying materials for filing: alphabetical, dates, geographical, and by the subject.
归档材料分类有四种基本方法：按字母顺序、按日期、按地理区域以及按主题。

4. A card index is a most valuable friend to a secretary, so it must be kept handy and up to date.
索引卡片是秘书最有用的朋友。因此索引卡片必须放在手边且及时更新。

5. En..., you also need to remember that prompt and careful filing contributes greatly to the efficiency of our office.
嗯……，你还要记住及时而细心的归档有助于极大地提高办公效率。

6. Remember this: the rule of file-keeping is "one customer-one file."
记住这一点：档案保存的原则是"一户一档"。

7. That means bringing the documents together in a single folder or file all papers relating to a particular subject.
那意味着将文档归入一个档案夹内或把所有的文件归入一个特定的主题目录中。

8. Besides, each file must be named clearly, either in block capitals or in jet-black typed capitals.
另外，每个档案都要命名清晰，或者用印刷体大写字母或者用黑体大写字母。

9. No, please file them in alphabetical order.
不，请按字母顺序归档。

10. I couldn't find those files about that trade company, even though I checked all the cross-references.
尽管查了全部的对照表，我还是未能找到有关那家贸易公司的资料。

Situational Dialogues

Using the Sample Dialogue as a model, try to create a new dialogue with your partner.

Situation 1 ▶ Ma Li, a new junior secretary, knows a little about the company's filing work and Mr. White, the general manager of Pacific Ocean Trade Company, is trying to get her to be familiar with the filing work.

Situation 2 ▶ Mr. Green, the general manager of Global Trade Company, is asking Wang Hong, a secretary in the company, to file some documents for him.

Part Two Text A

Filing System

1. Filing

Filing means keeping documents in a safe place and being able to find them easily and quickly. Filing is an essential and vital part of any business and it affects the whole organization.

In an organization or any business, we need to file documents that are sent to us by other people or organizations. We also file records of all our organizational activities. These can be letters, memos, reports, financial records, policy documents, etc.

In very busy organizations, filing is done at least every day and usually first thing in the morning. In a small or less busy office you could file once or twice a week. Therefore, when you file will depend on how busy your office is.

Nowadays, with the growing complexities of businesses, filing job has become increasingly elaborate and complicated. To complete filing work efficiently, you need to use the following filing equipment and employ some effective filing methods.

1.1 Equipment Used for Filing

Filing Cabinet — It is used to keep flat files and suspension or hanging files.

Steel Cabinet — It is used to keep big files that need to be locked up.

Date Stamp — It is used to date stamp documents that are received on daily basis so that they are filed in chronological order and so we have a record of when we received the document.

Register — It is used to record files taken out and files returned.

Filing shelves — It is used to file box files.

Box file — This is a big file that is used to keep big documents that cannot go into a filing cabinet. They are kept in shelves.

Clips —They are used for documents that need to be taken out very often; they hold documents tightly so that they do not fall out.

Folders — Paper or cardboard folders are used to keep loose documents together. The folders are placed inside suspension or box files.

Suspension file — The suspension files are used to keep documents in filing cabinets. The files are put into the drawers upright. The suspension files hangs down from the cradle. These files always remain in the cabinets but folders inside them can be taken out.

1.2 Methods of Filing

- Filing by Subject/Category.
- Filing in Alphabetical order.
- Filing by Numbers/Numerical order.
- Filing by Places/Geographical order.

• Filing by Dates/Chronological order.

These ways of filing is called classification and means organizing things that are alike, together. You can, however, combine some of these methods. For example, files that are kept together according to what they are about we say are subject filing but, inside each file the documents could be filed according to date order.

2. Filing System

A filing system refers to a system of classifying into files, usually arranged alphabetically and it is the central record-keeping system for an organization. It helps you to be organized, systematic, efficient and transparent. It also helps all people who should be able to access information to do so easily. Besides, documents that are cared for will not easily tear, get lost or dirty. The essential qualities of a filing system are reliability and accessibility. Therefore, a good filing system will have the following merits:

- It will be housed in suitable equipment, which needs to be neither costly nor elaborate.
- It will always be up to date. Each day's correspondence will be filed first next day and not left to accumulate.
- It will always be tidy. Each file will be clearly titled; if handwritten, in block letter; if typed, in jet-black capitals.
- It will always be easy to handle. The latest papers will be placed on top or, in vertical filing, in front. Non-current matter will be periodically removed and transferred to long-term storage files.
- It will be flexible. It will be capable of expansion or adaptation to suit changing circumstances.

Filing is in fact too important a job to be left entirely to the mercies of unsupervised juniors. It should be done only by the person or persons authorized to do it, and no document should be filed unless it has been marked by a responsible official for filing.

3. How to Set up a Filing System

Whether it is at home or at work, having a good filing system is the best way to keep track of the paper you accumulate. If the filing system is set up properly, you'll never have to hunt for hours for a report, bill or receipt. So how to set up a good filling system is of great important to an organization. Here are some rules and steps available for you to follow.

3.1 Filing Categories

To make a filing system more useful, you can group files into categories. When you file by categories, you try to file in a logical way; you put files together because they belong together; you don't put them together just because they start with the same letter.

For example, you could put all our files into correspondence, one category that takes up a whole drawer of our filing cabinet. Inside that drawer we could have sub-categories. Sub categories could be things like:

- Fund-raising correspondence.
- Correspondence with other organizations.
- Correspondence with members.
- Correspondence with members of the public.
- Correspondence with Board.
- ...and so on.

The way to form categories include:

- Sort all your documents out into piles that you think belong together.
- Give each pile a category name.
- Make a list of categories.
- Look at your list critically: Ask yourself: Can we combine any categories? Should we break up a category into two categories? What sub-categories do we need? Do we need to have alphabetical files within a category?

Make sure you don't have too many categories. It should not be difficult for anyone to decide in which category they are likely to find the information they need.

3.2 Filing Key

Once you have decided on your categories, you will have to draw up a filing index so that everyone can understand the system you use and find the information they want. This index is called a filing key.

Write up a filing key by listing all the categories and sub-categories in the order they are filed in. Make sure it is laid out so that everyone can understand it. Put it on the filing cabinet and also put a key for each drawer on the front of the drawers. Give everyone a copy of the whole filing key.

3.3 Filing Correspondence

All letters must be filed in two places:

Incoming mail

- The original letter together with a copy of your answer goes into the SUBJECT FILE.
- A second copy of the letter goes into the CORRESPONDENCE IN file.

Outgoing mail

- One copy of the letter goes into the SUBJECT FILE. Any letters in answer to your letter must go into this file; and all future correspondence about the subject.
- One copy goes into the CORRESPONDENCE OUT file.

3.4 Filing Rules

There are two basic rules underlying filing: ALPHABETICAL FILING — filing according to the letter of the alphabet; DATE FILING — most recent files on top. These rules are basic because they apply to all filing systems. When we file by name, subject and area we should always file alphabetically and by date.

Alphabetical filing rules can be listed as follows

Rule 1: File by name in terms of the first letter.

Rule 2: If the first letters are the same, file in terms of the second letter.

Rule 3: File in terms of surnames.

Rule 4: If surnames are the same, file in terms of the initial.

Rule 5: Some surnames have prefixes and are filed in terms of the first letter of the prefix.

Rule 6: When there are two surnames, file under the first surname.

Rule 7: Mac Mc & M' all files as Mac; St and Saint all filed as Saint.

Rule 8: When the file does not have the name of a person, file by the MOST IMPORTANT WORD or by the name of the PLACE.

4. Filing Procedure

4.1 Filing Procedure and Maintenance

Step 1: Receiving the document

If it is a letter or document that came through the mail, you record it in the "mail received" register and write the date received or date stamp it

Step 2: Action

Forward the letter/document to the person that has to deal with it.

Step 3: Follow up

Check that the letter has been dealt with.

Step 4: Collecting Documents to be filed

All documents and two copies of the replies must be collected in a filing tray.

Step 5: Filing

Choose a regular time to file every day so that you are never left with a huge pile of loose documents. Use a sorter to help you file and remember to file by date order.

4.2 Maintaining the Filing System

One of the most important reasons why file is to keep document safe. It is therefore very important to make sure that all papers and files are kept in good condition. Here are some ways that can help you do this:

- Keep documents that are waiting to be filed in trays, do not leave them lying about on desks or shelves.
- File documents away at least once a day, or if your organization is very small you can do it once a week.
- Do not put too much in files or folders
- Put new covers on old files which get a lot of use and have become worn or torn.
- Box files and lever arch files can hold more than simple folders.
- Never allow filing drawers or shelves to become too full. Acquire new filing cabinets when necessary.

New Words

file [fail] *n.* 档案，卷宗，文件
vt. 把……归档；提出(申请书、议案等)
financial [fai'nænʃəl] *adj.* 金融的，财政的
complexity [kəm'pleksiti] *n.* 复杂，复杂性；复杂的事物
elaborate [i'læbərət] [i'læbəreit] *adj.* 详尽的，复杂的，精心的，精美的
v. 详细地说明
complicated ['kɔmplikeitid] *adj.* 复杂难懂的，结构复杂的
efficiently [i'fiʃəntli] *adv.* 高效率地，有效地
effective [i'fektiv] *adj.* 有效的，生效的，实际的
suspension [səs'penʃən] *n.* 暂停，中止；悬挂
chronological [ˌkrɔnə'lɔdʒikəl] *adj.* 按时间顺序的
register ['redʒistə] *vt.* 登记，记录，注册；挂号 *n.* 登记簿；记录；暂存器
clip [klip] *vt.* 夹住 *n.* 夹子；回形针
folder ['fəuldə] *n.* 文件夹
alphabetical [ˌælfə'betikəl] *adj.* 按字母表顺序的
category ['kætigəri] *n.* 种类，类别，范畴
sub-category ['sʌb-'kætigəri] *n.* 子类，子范畴
geographical [ˌdʒiə'græfikəl] *adj.* 地理的；地理学的
classification [ˌklæsifi'keiʃən] *n.* 分类，类别
combine [kəm'bain] *vt.* 联合，使结合，结合
organized ['ɔ:gənaizd] *adj.* 有组织的
systematic [ˌsisti'mætik] *adj.* 有系统的，体系的，有条理的
transparent [træns'pɛərənt] *adj.* 透明的，明显的，清晰的
access ['ækses] *n.* 入口，通道；使用之权 *vt.* 进入，(电脑)存取
reliability [riˌlaiə'biliti] *n.* 可靠性
accessibility [ˌækəsesi'biliti] *n.* 可以得到，易接近
house [haus] *v.* 容纳，存储
merit ['merit] *n.* 优点；功绩；价值
accumulate [ə'kju:mjuleit] *v.* 积累，增加，聚集
tidy ['taidi] *adj.* 整齐的，整洁的，
jet-black [dʒet-blæk] *adj.* 漆黑的，乌黑发亮的
capital ['kæpitəl] *n.* 大写字母
vertical ['və:tikəl] *adj.* 垂直的，纵向的
remove [ri'mu:v] *v.* 消除，脱掉，免除，搬迁
transfer [træns'fə:] *v.* 转移；调任；转乘 *n.* 迁移，移动；换车
flexible ['fleksəbl] *adj.* 柔韧的，灵活的；易弯曲的
expansion [iks'pænʃən] *n.* 扩展，扩充
adaptation [ˌædæp'teiʃən] *n.* 适应
authorize ['ɔ:θəraiz] *vt.* 批准，委托，授权
receipt [ri'si:t] *n.* 收据，收条
logical ['lɔdʒikəl] *adj.* 符合逻辑的，逻辑上的，合理的

fund-raise [fʌnd-reiz] *v.* 筹集
board [bɔːd] *n.* 董事会
index ['indeks] *n.* 索引，指数
underlying [ˌʌndə'laiiŋ] *adj.* 潜在的，隐含的，在下面的
surname ['səːneim] *n.* 姓，绰号
initial [i'niʃəl] *n.*(词)首字母
prefix ['priːfiks] *n.* 前缀，(人名前的)称谓
action ['ækʃən] *n.* 行为，活动，措施
forward ['fɔːwəd] *v.* 促进，转交，发送
acquire [ə'kwaiə] *vt.* 获得，取得；学到

Phrases and Expressions

filing cabinet 档案柜
file box 文件盒
lock up 上锁，封锁
suspension file 悬挂式文件夹
date stamp 日戳，邮戳
on daily basis 每天，天天
in chronological order 按年代顺序，按时间顺序
fall out 松掉，散掉，散落，解散
in alphabetical order 按字母顺序
classify into 把……分类为
block letter 印刷体，铅字体，正楷字体
be capable of 有能力，能够
be left entirely to the mercy of 完全任由……支配
keep track of 跟上……的进展，记录
set up 建立，树立，创立
group into categories 划分为不同类别
take up 开始，从事，占去（空间或时间）
sort out 整理，选出，分类
break up into 分解为
draw up 拟定，起草，画出
make sure 弄明白，设法确保
lay out 设计；安排；陈列
incoming mail 寄来的邮件
outgoing mail 发送的或寄出的邮件
alphabetic filing 按字母顺序归档
date filing 按日期归档
as follows 如下
in terms of 就……而言，在……方面
deal with 讨论；处理，对付；涉及
a huge pile of 一大堆，许多
keep in good condition 完整保存，保持良好的状态
leave... lying about（将某物）乱放
file away 摆好放整齐，归档
wear and tear 磨损

Notes

1 Filing means keeping documents in a safe place and being able to find them easily and quickly.

本句中，means 为谓语动词，keeping documents in a safe place 和 being able to find them easily and quickly 是两个动名词短语并列构成宾语。mean 意为“意思是；意味着”，

后面常接名词，动名词或从句作宾语。请看下例：

This new order will mean (us) working overtime.

这一新订单意味着（我们）得加班加点。

The expansion of the factory will mean the employment of sixty extra workers.

工厂的扩展意味着将增雇六十名工人。

2 When you file will depend on how busy your office is.

本句中，depend on 是谓语动词，When you file 和 how busy your office is 是由 when 和 how 引导的名词性从句在句子中分别作主语和宾语。

在英语中，所有用来构成特殊疑问句的特殊疑问词，如 what、where、who、when、whose、which、why、whether 等，均可以用来引导名词性从句，意思也和特殊疑问词中的疑问词意思相同。请看下例：

Whether it will do us harm remains to be seen.

是否对我们有害还要看一看。

Why he did it will remain a puzzle forever.

他为什么这样做将永远是一个谜。

3 It is used to date stamp documents that are received on daily basis so that they are filed in chronological order and so we have a record of when we received the document.

本句中，that are received on daily basis 是由 that 引导的定语从句，修饰限定先行词 documents, so that 引导一个目的状语从句，意为“以便；为了”，相当于 in order that。请看下例：

Let's work harder so that we may fulfill our plan ahead of schedule.

让我们再加把劲以便能提前完成任务。

另外，when we received the document 是由特殊疑问词 when 引导的名词性从句在句中作介词 of 的宾语。请看下例：

I had no idea of when they broke up.

他们什么时候分手的，我完全不知道。

4 Filing is in fact too important a job to be left entirely to the mercies of unsupervised juniors.

本句中，too... to 是肯定形式的词组表达否定含义，意为“太……以致不能……”。

在英语中，这类词还有 hardly、seldom、few、little（几乎不）、rather than、instead of（而不是）等。请看下例：

They could scarcely complain after such good treatment.

在受到如此好的待遇后他们不会抱怨。

另外，词组 be left to the mercy of sb. 意为“听任某人粗暴对待；听任某人任意摆布”。请看下例：

I believe Mary was left to the tender mercies of her step-mother.

我相信玛丽受到了她的继母的虐待。

5 No document should be filed unless it has been marked by a responsible official for filing.

本句中，连词 unless 引导一个条件状语从句，意为“除非；如果不”。请看下例：

Talent is worthless unless you persevere in developing it.
除非你坚持不懈地发展天赋，否则它是没有价值的。

6 how to set up a good filling system is of great importance to an organization.

本句中，how to set up a good filing system 是由疑问词 how 加动词不定式构成的短语相当于一个名词，在句中做主语。

英语中，疑问词 what, which, who, when, where, how 及连接副词 whether 与不定式连用而形成一个短语，这个短语相当于一个名词，可在句中做句子的主语、宾语或表语等。请看下例：

How to begin is more difficult than where to stop.
如何开始比到哪里停止还困难。

She was worried about how to fill her leisure time.
她为如何打发她的闲暇时间而发愁。

另外，be of great importance 为“介词 of + 抽象名词”结构，相当于 very important。

英语中，介词 of + 抽象名词结构相当于该名词所对应的形容词。请看下例：

It is said Yogo is of great benefit to human health.
据说瑜伽对人体健康有极大好处。

Exercises

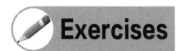

EX. 1 Answer the following questions.

1. What is filing according to Text A?
2. List some equipment used for filing.
3. What are the five methods of filing?
4. What are the essential qualities of a filing system?
5. List at least three merits of good filing systems.
6. What are the steps you should follow to form categories?
7. What's the purpose of drawing up a filing key?
8. What are the two basic rules underlying filing?
9. What steps do filing procedures involve?
10. How often should we file documents away according to Text A?

EX. 2 Complete the following sentences with appropriate words or expressions in the box.

transfer	in terms of	flexible	file away	accumulate
reliability	keep track of	systematic	apply to	complexity

1. Please ________ those letters in a drawer before you get off work.
2. This filing system increases the ________ of administration and integration.

3. An efficient executive secretary is typically Characterized by ordered and ________ habits or behavior.
4. We should not presume too much upon the ________ of such sources.
5. Dust and dirt soon ________ if a file cabinet is not cleaned regularly.
6. In some organizations, it is usually the secretary's job to data or programs to a central computer.
7. A qualified executive secretary is expected to be ________ , hardworking, loyal and responsible.
8. Most clerks tend to rely on a secretary to ________ what has been said in meetings.
9. Staying up late makes the secretary at her worst ________ physical situation.
10. The results of this research can be ________ new developments in filing systems.

EX. 3 Translate the following sentences into English.

1. 现将本公司目前所能提供的最低报价提供如下。(as follows)
2. 丰富的秘书工作经验使她能处理好各种各样的公共关系。(deal with)
3. 史密斯先生要求他的秘书负责建立并跟进生产所需的质量标准。(follow up)
4. 行政助理有必要整理些资料供上司参考。(sort out)
5. 报告是按年代日期顺序归档的。(in chronological order)
6. 秘书在完成多项任务的同时，还必须要能在压力条件下工作。(be capable of)
7. 您有权访问文档管理服务器。(have access to)
8. 请阁下附上名片或用正楷字体于下栏填写资料。(block letter)
9. 他整理并完整保存了前任总经理留下的资料。(keep in good condition)
10. 邮件可以分为两种类型：收到的邮件和发出的邮件。每一种都有它自己的一套步骤。(incoming mail; outgoing mail)

EX. 4 Translate the following passage into Chinese.

The first line of defense for document security is securing the business premises themselves. All businesses need to have security systems, such as alarm systems.They may also need or want to invest in other security devices, such as window bars/grilles, security cameras or patrol services.

General security procedures for electronic documents involve backing up documents regularly and keeping document backups somewhere other than the same hard drive where the original documents are located. Off-site is best to guard against having your business data wiped out by natural disasters.

Small businesses with colleagues or employees sharing the same computer network may also want to restrict some users' access so they can only use or see some of the network's resources. Even if a user is allowed to access a resource, such as a software program, particular documents can be password protected. Contents of documents can also be encrypted, making them accessible only to those who have the encryption key.

Part Three Text B

Document Management System

A Document Management System (DMS), based on computer programs in the case of the management of digital documents, is a system used to track, manage and store documents and reduce paper. Most are capable of keeping a record of the various versions created and modified by different users. It is often viewed as a component of enterprise content management (ECM) systems and related to digital asset management, document imaging, workflow systems and records management systems.

1. History

In the early 1980s, a number of vendors began developing software systems to manage paper-based documents. These systems dealt with paper documents, which included not only printed and published documents, but also photographs, prints, etc.

Later developers began to write a second type of system which could manage electronic documents, including all those documents, or files, created on computers, and often stored on users' local file-systems. The earliest Electronic Document Management (EDM) systems managed either proprietary file types, or a limited number of file formats. Many of these systems later became known as document imaging systems, because they focused on the capture, storage, indexing and retrieval of image file formats. EDM systems evolved to a point where systems could manage any type of file format that could be stored on the network. These systems enabled an organization to capture faxes and forms, to save copies of the documents as images, and to store the image files in the repository for security and quick retrieval.

2. Components

Document management systems commonly provide storage, versioning, metadata, security, as well as indexing and retrieval capabilities. Here is a description of these components:

2.1 Metadata

Metadata is typically stored for each document. Metadata may, for example, include the date the document will be stored and the identity of the user storing it. The DMS may also extract metadata from the document automatically or prompt the user to add metadata. Some systems also use optical character recognition on scanned images, or perform text extraction on electronic documents. The resulting extracted text can be used to assist users in locating documents by identifying probable keywords or providing for full text search capability.

2.2 Integration

Many document management systems attempt to integrate document management directly into other applications, so that users may retrieve existing documents directly from the document management system repository, make changes, and save the changed document back to the repository as a new version, all without leaving the application. Such integration is commonly available for office suites and e-mail or groupware software.

2.3 Capture

Capture primarily involves accepting and processing images of paper documents from scanners or multifunction printers. Optical Character Recognition (OCR) software is often used, whether integrated into the hardware or as stand-alone software, in order to convert digital images into machine readable text. Capture may also involve accepting electronic documents and other computer-based files.

2.4 Indexing

Indexing tracks electronic documents. Indexing may be as simple as keeping track of unique document identifiers; but often it takes a more complex form, providing classification through the documents' metadata or even through word indexes extracted from the documents' contents. Indexing exists mainly to support retrieval.

2.5 Storage

Store electronic documents. Storage of the documents often includes management of those same documents; where they are stored, for how long, migration of the documents from one storage media to another.

2.6 Retrieval

Retrieve the electronic documents from the storage. Although the notion of retrieving a particular document is simple, retrieval in the electronic context can be quite complex and powerful. Simple retrieval of individual documents can be supported by allowing the user to specify the unique document identifier, and having the system use the basic index to retrieve the document. More flexible retrieval allows the user to specify partial search terms involving the document identifier or parts of the expected metadata. This would typically return a list of documents which match the user's search terms. Some systems provide the capability to specify a Boolean expression containing multiple keywords or example phrases expected to exist within the documents' contents.

2.7 Distribution

A published document for distribution has to be in a format that can not be easily altered. As a common practice in law regulated industries, an original master copy of the document is usually never used for distribution other than filing. If a document is to be distributed electronically in a regulatory environment, then the equipment tasking the job has to be quality endorsed and validated.

2.8 Security

Document security is vital in many document management applications. Compliance requirements for certain documents can be quite complex depending on the type of documents. Some document management systems have a rights management module that allows an administrator to give access to documents based on type to only certain people or groups of people.

2.9 Workflow

Workflow is a complex process and some document management systems have a built-in workflow module. There are different types of workflow. Usage depends on the environment to which the Electronic Document Management System (EDMS) is applied. Manual workflow requires a user to view the document and decide whom to send it to. Rules-based workflow allows an administrator to create a rule that dictates the flow of the document through an organization: for instance, an invoice passes through an approval process and then is routed to the accounts-payable department. Advanced workflow mechanisms can manipulate content or signal external processes while these rules are in effect.

2.10 Collaboration

Collaboration should be inherent in an EDMS. In its basic form, collaborative EDMS should allow documents to be retrieved and worked on by an authorized user. Access should be blocked to other users while work is being performed on the document. Other advanced forms of collaboration act in real time, allowing multiple users to view and modify (or markup) documents at the same time. The resulting document is comprehensive, including all users additions.

2.11 Versioning

Versioning is a process by which documents are checked in or out of the document management system, allowing users to retrieve previous versions and to continue work from a selected point. Versioning is useful for documents that change over time and require updating, but it may be necessary to go back to or reference a previous copy.

2.12 Searching

Searching finds documents and folders using template attributes or full text search. Documents can be searched using various attributes and document content.

2.13 Publishing

Publishing a document involves the procedures of proofreading, peer or public reviewing, authorizing, printing and approving etc. Those steps ensure prudence and logical thinking. Any careless handling may result in the inaccuracy of the document and therefore mislead or upset its users and readers. The published document should be in a format that is not easily altered without a specific knowledge or tools, and yet it is read-only or portable.

New Words

track [træk] *v.* 追踪，跟踪　*n.* 踪迹；轨道；跑道；小路
store [stɔː] *vt.* 储存，贮藏，保存
version ['vəːʃən] *n.* 版本，说法；译本，形式
modify ['mɔdifai] *vt.* 修改，更改；修饰
asset ['æset] *n.* 资产；优点
workflow ['wəːkfləu] *n.* 工作流程
electronic [ilek'trɔnik] *adj.* 电子的，电子学的
proprietary [prə'praiətəri] *adj.* 专利的，所有权的　*n.* 所有权；所有人
capture ['kæptʃə] *vt.* 采集，捕获；占领　*n.* 捕获；战利品
indexing ['indeksiŋ] *n.* 索引
repository [ri'pɔzitəri] *n.* 仓库，贮藏室；容器
metadata [`metə'deitə] *n.* 元数据
prompt [prɔmpt] *vt.* 激起，促进，推动；提示　*adj.* 迅速的，敏捷的，立刻的
scan [skæn] *vt.* 扫描，浏览；审视，细看
extraction [iks'trækʃən] *n.* 抽出，拔出；抽出物；血统
groupware ['gruːpwɛə] *n.* 组件
scanner ['skænə] *n.* 扫描机，扫描仪
multifunction [ˌmʌlti'fʌŋkʃən] *n.* 多功能，多用途；一体机
identifier [ai'dentifaiə] *n.* 标识符；鉴定人
notion ['nəuʃən] *n.* 观念，概念，想法，主张
partial ['pɑːʃəl] *adj.* 不完全的，部分的；偏袒的，偏爱的
term [təːm] *n.* 学期；术语；条件；条款；期限　*vt.* 把……称为
original [ə'ridʒənəl] *adj.* 原始的，最初的；有独创性的
regulatory ['regjulətəri] *adj.* 管理的，控制的，调整的
endorse [in'dɔːs] *vt.* 赞同，支持；背书于
validate ['vælideit] *vt.* 使生效；证实，确认，验证
module ['mɔdjuːl] *n.* 组件；单元；模块
dictate [dik'teit] *vt.* 口授；规定；决定
invoice ['invɔis] *n.* 发货单；发票；货物
mechanism ['mekənizəm] *n.* 机制，原理
manipulate [mə'nipjuleit] *vt.* 操纵，操作，控制；利用
comprehensive [ˌkɔmpri'hensiv] *adj.* 全面的，广泛的，综合的
addition [ə'diʃən] *n.* 增加；加法；附加物
template ['templit] *n.* 模板，样板
prudence ['pruːdəns] *n.* 审慎，深谋远虑
inaccuracy [in'ækjurəsi] *n.* 不准确，错误
mislead [mis'liːd] *vt.* 误导，欺骗，使误入歧途
portable ['pɔːtəbl] *adj.* 轻便的；手提式的

Phrases and Expressions

based on 以……为基础，基于
in the case of 就……来说，在……的情况下
file format 文件格式
attempt to 企图，努力
so that 以至于，以便
be available for 对于……来说是可用的
office suites 办公用套装软件
integrate into 融入
give access to 准许出入；接见
pass through 穿过，透过，流过，经历
in effect 实际上；正在实行；有效
be inherent in 为……所固有
check in 登记，报到；记录

Abbreviations

DMS (Document Management System) 文件管理系统
ECM (Enterprise Content Management) 企业内容管理
OCR (Optical Character Recognition) 光字符识别
EDMS (Electronic Document Management System) 电子文件管理系统

Exercises

EX. 5 Answer the following questions.

1. What is a document management system based on Text B?
2. When did a number of vendors begin developing software systems to manage paper-based documents?
3. What capabilities do document management systems commonly provide?
4. What information may metadata include?
5. Why do many document management systems attempt to integrate document management directly into other applications?
6. What is the function of optical character recognition software?
7. How can the user retrieve the documents more flexibly according to Text B?
8. How does rules-based workflow work?
9. What is the definition of versioning?
10. What procedures does publishing a document involve?

Part Four Extended Reading

Text	Notes

File Management Tips for Digital[1] Files

Keeping track of your electronic documents can be quite a chore[2] in today's "wired[3]"world. In addition to storing documents locally on desktops, laptops or mobile devices, more and more businesses are using the cloud[4] for basic business applications and file storage.

Wherever the documents are stored it is important to keep them organized and up-to-date.The goal of electronic[5] file management is to ensure that you can find what you're looking for, even if you're looking for it years after its creation.These file management tips will help you keep your files accessible[6]:

1. Use the Default Installation Folders for Program Files

Use the default file locations[7] when installing[8] application programs. Under Windows[9], by convention[10] application program files reside under the (Drive Letter:)->Program Files directory[11]. Installing applications elsewhere is confusing and unnecessary.

2. One Place for All Documents

Place all documents under a single "root" folder[12]. For a single user in a Windows environment the default location is the My Documents folder.

In a file sharing environment try to do the same—created a single root folder and store all documents in subfolders[13] inside the root folder. Having a single location for all documents makes it easier to find things and to run backups[14] and archives[15].

3. Create Folders in a Logical Hierarchy[16]

These are the drawers of your computer's filing cabinet, so to speak. Use plain[17] language to name your folders; you don't want to be looking at this list of folders in the future and wondering what "TFK" or whatever other interesting abbreviation you invented means.

4. Nest[18] Folders Within Folders

Create other folders within these main folders as need arises[19]. For instance, a folder called "Invoices[20]" might contain folders called "2013", "2012" and "2011". A folder named for a client might include the folders "customer data" and "correspondence". The goal is to have every file in a folder rather than having a bunch of orphan[21] files listed.

[1] *adj.* 数字的，数码的
[2] *n.* 讨厌的工作，琐事，家务
[3] *adj.* 有线的
[4] *n.* 云
[5] *adj.* 电子的；电子学的
[6] *adj.* 可得到的；易接近的
[7] *n.* 默认的文件位置
[8] *vt.* 安装，安置
[9] *n.* Windows 操作系统
[10] *n.* 惯例，公约
[11] *n.* 目录
[12] *n.* 根文件夹
[13] *n.* 子文件夹
[14] *n.* 备份
[15] *n.* 文档；文档馆
[16] *n.* 等级制度
[17] *adj.* 清楚的，简单的
[18] *vt.* 嵌入
[19] *vi.* 出现，发生
[20] *n.* 发货单；发票
[21] *n.* 孤儿

5. Follow the File Naming Conventions

Some operating systems do not allow spaces[22] in file or folder names, so avoid this if your computing environment is mixed — instead use the underscores[23] as a delimiter[24] (e.g. Doe_John_Proposal.doc.) Other characters such as / ? < > \ : * | " ^ are also prohibited in file or folder names under Windows.

[22] *n.* 空格，空间
[23] *n.* 下划线
[24] *n.* 定界符，分隔符

Use descriptive file names for easy identification[25] and retrieval but don't go overboard[26] — file/path names have length limits which vary between operating systems. Under Windows the maximum full path length for a file (e.g. the drive letter + folder names + file name) is 260 characters. Use common abbreviations wherever possible.

[25] *n.* 确认，识别
[26] 过分爱好，狂热追求，爱走极端

6. Be Specific[27]

[27] *adj.* 明确的；特殊的

Give files logical, specific names and include dates in file names if possible. The goal when naming files is to be able to tell what the file is about without having to open it and look. So if the document is a letter to a customer reminding him that payment is overdue[28], call it something like "overdue_20120115"; rather than something like "letter". How will you know who the letter is to without opening it?

[28] *adj.* 过期的，未兑的

7. File as You Go

The best time to file a document is when you first create it. So get in the habit of using the "Save As" dialogue box to file your document as well as name it, putting it in the right place in the first place.

8. Order Your Files for Your Convenience[29]

[29] *n.* 便利，舒适

If there are folders or files that you use a lot, force them to the top of the file list by renaming them with a ! or an AA at the beginning of the file name.

9. Cull[30] Your Files Regularly

[30] *v.* 拣选，剔除

Sometimes what's old is obvious as in the example of the folder named "Invoices" above. If it's not, keep your folders uncluttered[31] by clearing out the old files.

[31] *adj.* 整齐的，整洁的

Do not delete[32] business related files unless you are absolutely certain that you will never need the file again. Instead, in your main collection of folders under your root folder, create a folder called "Old"or "Inactive[33]" and move old files into it when you come across them.

[32] *vt.* 删除
[33] *adj.* 不活动的，停用的

10. Back up Your Files Regularly

Whether you're copying your files onto another drive or onto tape, it's important to set up and follow a regular back up regimen[34].

[34] *n.* 生活规则；方案

11. Good File Management Makes Finding What You Want Easy Managing electronic documents should be part of an overall document management strategy for your business. A proper[35] document management plan should include all aspects of handling documents, including storage, retrieval, backups, and security. The search function is a wonderful thing but it will never match[36] the ease of being able to go directly to a folder or file. If you follow these file management tips consistently[37], even if you don't know where something is, you know where it should be — a huge advantage when it comes to[38] finding what you're looking for. Good file management practices will save your business time and money.	[35] *adj.* 合适的，正当的 [36] *v.* 相配，和……相配 [37] *adj.* 始终如一的，持续的 [38] 当涉及，当谈到

参考译文

课文A　归档系统

1. 归档

文件归档意味着将文件保存在一个安全的地方，并能够方便快捷地找到它们。文件归档是所有企业的重要组成部分，它影响整个组织。

在一个组织或任何企业，我们需要将其他人或组织发送给我们的文件进行归档。我们也需要将组织的所有有关活动记录进行归档。这些文档可能是信件、备忘录、报告、财务记录、政策文件等。

在非常忙碌的组织中，归档工作是每天至少要做的，而且通常是早上要做的第一件事。在一个小的或不太忙碌的办公室里，你可以一周做一次或两次归档工作。因此，你什么时候进行归档工作将取决于办公室工作忙碌的程度。

如今，随着企业的日益复杂化，档案工作变得越来越精细和复杂。要有效地完成文件归档工作，就需要使用以下的文件设备，并采用一些有效的归档方法。

1.1　用于归档的设备

文件柜——用来保存平面文件和悬挂式文档。

钢柜——用来保存需要被锁起来的大文件。

日戳——用来将每天接收的文件盖上邮戳，以便将它们按时间顺序进行归档，这样就能记录下文件接收的日期。

登记簿——用来记录文件的取出和归还情况。

文件架——用来存放档案盒。

文件盒——是一个大的档案盒，用来保存不能存放在档案柜里的大型文件。这些文件盒通常置于架子上。

回形针——用于经常需要被取出的文件；它们紧紧地别住文件，使文件不会散落。

文件夹——纸制的或纸板文件夹常用来保存零散文件。文件夹常被置于悬挂式文件夹或文件盒内。

悬挂式文件夹——悬挂式文件夹用于保存档案柜中的文档。文件竖着放置在抽屉里。悬挂式文件夹从支架上垂下来。这些文档总是留在档案柜里，档案柜里的文件夹是可以取出的。

1.2 归档方法

按主题 / 类别归档。

按字母顺序归档。

按数字 / 数字顺序归档。

按地方 / 地理位置顺序归档。

按日期 / 时间顺序归档。

这种归档叫作分类，意思是类似的文档组织在一起。然而，你可以将这些方法组合起来。例如，根据文件的内容将文件归档，我们说这是主题归档方法，但是，在每个文档中，又可以根据日期顺序归档文件。

2. 归档系统

归档系统是指将文档通常按字母顺序进行排列归类的系统，是一个组织主要的记录保存系统。该系统有助于使工作条理化、系统化、高效和思路清晰。它还有助于让所有有权检索信息的人轻松地获取信息。此外，该系统管理的文档不易撕毁、弄丢或弄脏。

归档系统的本质特性是可靠性和可访问性。因此，一个设置良好的归档系统将会有以下优点：

- 系统被安置在合适的设备中，该设备既不昂贵也不复杂。
- 系统将永远是最新的。每天的信件都会在第二天被归档，而不是任由其堆积。
- 系统将永远保持整洁。清楚地命名每一个文件。如果是手写的话，用正楷字体；如果印刷的话，用黑色大写字母。
- 系统将一直具有易操作性。最新的文件将被置于顶部，如果是垂直归档的话放在前面。非流通的材料会定期地被清理，移到长期存储文件的地方。
- 系统将具有灵活性。为适应变化的环境，系统将有扩展或适应的能力。

事实上，归档是极为重要的工作，不能完全由一些无人监督的初级职员来完成。它只能由被授权的某个人或某些人来做。除非负责人将某份文件标记为归档文件，否则这份文件不应被归档。

3. 如何建立归档系统

无论是在家还是在工作场所中，良好的文件归档系统是记录你所有文档的最好方式。如果档案系统设置合理正确，你便无须花数小时寻找某份报告、账单或收据。因此，如何建立一个良好的归档系统对一个组织而言是非常重要的。以下是一些可供遵循的规则和步骤。

3.1 归档类别

为了使文件归档系统更有用，你可以将文件分成几类。当按类别归档时，应尽力以一种合乎逻辑的方式给文件归档。将文件放在一起，因为它们是属于同一类；你不会仅仅因为它们都是以同一个字母开头就把它们放在一起。

例如，可以把所有的文件都归类为信件类别，这一类别的文件占了档案柜里其中一个抽屉。但是，在那个抽屉里，你可以设置子类。子类可以设置如下：

- 筹资信件。
- 与其他组织往来信件。
- 与成员往来信件。
- 与公共成员往来信件。
- 与董事会往来信件。

……

分类方法如下：

- 将所有的文件按照你认为的属性整理成堆。
- 给每个文件堆拟一个类别名称。
- 列一个类别列表。
- 挑剔地审视你的类别列表：问问自己这些问题：你能将某些类别进行组合吗？我们应该把某个类别分为两类吗？我们需要哪些子类？我们需要在一个类别内以字母顺序排列文件吗？

注意分成的类别不能太多，从而确保任何人都能较容易地判定他们可能要找的信息属于哪一类。

3.2 归档密钥

一旦决定了类别，你就必须制定一个归档索引，这样每个人都能理解你使用的系统，并找到他们想要的信息。这个索引被称为归档密钥。

详细写出归档密钥，以归档的顺序列出所有的类别和子类别，确保密钥的设置能让每个人都能理解。将归档密钥放在文件柜上，并把钥匙放在抽屉柜前面的每个抽屉里。此外，给每个人一份完整的归档密钥副本。

3.3 归档信件

所有信件必须归档在两个地方：

收到的信件。

- 原信连同回复的副本归入主题文件。
- 来信的副本归入信件接收文档。

发送的信件。

信件的一个副本归入主题文档。任何有关回复的信件都必须归入这个文档，以及以后的所有与该主题相关的信件也归入该文档。

- 复印件归入信件发出文档。

3.4 归档规则

归档工作隐含两条基本规则：按字母顺序归档，即按字母表中字母的顺序进行归档；按日期归档，即大多数最新的文件置于最上面。这些规则是基本的，因为它们适用于所有文件归档系统。当以人名、主题和地区对文件进行归档时，我们总是遵循字母顺序和日期两条基本规则归档文件。

按字母顺序归档的规则如下：

规则 1：以名字的第一个字母归档。

规则 2：如果第一个字母是相同的，按第二个字母归档。

规则 3：按姓氏归档。

规则 4：如果姓氏是相同的，按姓名首字母。

规则 5：一些姓氏有前缀，按姓氏前缀的第一个字母。

规则 6：当有两个姓氏时，按第一个姓氏。

规则 7：Mac Mc & M' 都归档为 Mac，St 和 Saint 都归档为 Saint。

规则 8：当文件没有人名时，按最重要的词或地方名归档。

4. 归档步骤和维护方法

4.1 归档步骤

步骤 1：接收文件

如果是通过邮件的方式收到的信或文件，你可以记录在"邮件接收"登记簿中，并写上接收日期或盖上日期戳。

步骤 2：行动

将信或文件转发给必须经办它的人。

步骤 3：跟进

检查一下信件是否被处理好。

步骤 4：收集需归档的文件

所有文件和回信的复印本两份都必须被收集在文件盒里。

步骤 5：归档

每天定期进行归档，这样你永远不会留下一大堆杂乱无章的文件。使用分类器来帮助自己，并切记按日期顺序归档。

4.2 维护档案系统

归档最重要的原因之一就是使文档安全。因此，确保完好地保存所有的文件和文档是非常重要的。这里有一些有用的方法：

- 将有待归档的文件保存在文件盒里，不要在桌子上或架子上到处乱放。
- 每天至少要归档一次。如果组织规模很小，可以每周做一次。
- 不要在文件夹中存放太多文件。
- 给那些经常被使用，而且已有磨损的旧文件装上新的封面。
- 文件盒和杠杆文件夹比简易文件夹能装下更多的文件。
- 绝不允许将文件柜或文件架塞得太满。必要时购置新的文件柜。

课文 B　文件管理系统

就管理数字文件来说，文档管理系统（DMS），是一个基于计算机程序的，用来跟踪、管理并存储文件从而减少纸张的系统。大多数系统都能够记录不同用户创建和修改的各种版本的文档。文档管理系统经常被视为企业内容管理（ECM）系统的组成部分，而且与数字资产管理、文档成像、工作流程和档案管理系统相关。

1. 历史

在20世纪80年代初，许多供应商开始开发软件系统来管理纸质文件。这些系统处理的纸质文件，不仅包括已印刷和公开发表的文献资料，还包括照片、印刷品等。

后来研发商开始创制另一类型的系统。这类系统可以管理电子文档，包括在计算机上创建的，而且经常存储在用户的本地文件系统中的所有文件或文档 。最早的电子文档管理（EDM）系统可管理专有的文件类型或有限的文件格式。后来，这些系统许多被称为文档影像系统，因为它们专注于采集、存储、索引和检索图像文件格式。如今，EDM系统已经发展到可以管理存储在网络上的任何文件格式的程度。这些系统使企业能够记录传真和表格，以图像的格式保存文件副本，并将图像文件保存在库里，以确保安全，方便检索。

2. 系统组件

文档管理系统通常提供存储、版本控制、元数据、安全，以及索引和检索功能。下面是对这些组件的描述。

2.1 元数据

通常每份文件的元数据都要存储。 例如，元数据可能包括文件存储日期以及文件存储用户的身份。DMS也可以从文档中自动提取元数据或提示用户添加元数据。有些系统还将光字符识别用于扫描的图像 ，或针对电子文档进行文本提取。由此产生的文本可以用来帮助用户通过识别可能的关键字或通过提供完整的文本搜索功能来定位文档。

2.2 集成

许多文档管理系统尝试将文档管理功能直接集成到其他应用程序中，这样用户就可以直接从文档管理系统库中检索现有文档，对文档进行更改，并将更改后的文档在该库内保存为一个新的版本。用户在完成所有这些操作时，都无须离开应用程序。这种集成化组件经常供办公套件和电子邮件或其他组件软件使用。

2.3 采集

采集主要涉及接收并处理由扫描仪或多功能打印机生成的纸质文档的图像。为了将数字图像转换成机器可读的文本，无论是集成到硬件设备上还是作为独立的软件，光字符识别（OCR）软件经常用于把数字图像转换为机器可读的文本。采集也可能涉及接收电子文件和其他计算机文件。

2.4 索引

索引跟踪电子文档。索引可能是简单地跟踪某个单独的文档标识符，但在通常情况下，索引呈现出更复杂的形式。它通过文档的元数据，甚至通过从文件内容中提取的文字索引来对电子文档进行分类。索引主要是为了支持检索。

2.5 存储

存储电子文档。文档的存储通常包括对那些相同文档的管理，即管理它们存储的位置、期限以及从一个存储介质转存到另一个存储介质的情况。

2.6 检索

即检索存储的电子文档。虽然检索一个特定文档这个概念是简单的，但是电子环境中的检索功能可能是相当复杂和强大的。简单检索个人文档可以通过允许用户指定唯一的文档标识符，让系统使用基本索引来检索文档的方法来完成。更灵活的检索允许用户指定部分搜索条件来完成。这些搜索条件涉及文档标识符或部分预期元数据。这样操作后，系统通常会返回一个与用户搜索条件匹配的文档列表。有些系统能够指定一个布尔表达式。这个表达式包含多个关键词或预期存在于文件内容中的例词。

2.7 发布

已公开的、供发布的文件必须以一种不易更改的格式呈现。在执法严格行业的普遍做法是文件的原版通常从不用于公开发布，而是用来归档。如果一个文件需要在监管的环境中通过电子手段进行发布的话，那么用于完成该任务的设备必须得到质量认可和验证。

2.8 安全

文档安全性在许多文档管理应用程序中非常重要。某些文件的合规性要求可能相当复杂，这取决于文件的类型。有些文件管理系统有一个权限管理模块。该模块允许管理员根据文件类型，只允许某些人或某些团体访问文件。

2.9 工作流程

工作流程是一个复杂的过程，而且有些文档管理系统有一个内置的工作流程模块。这里有不同类型的工作流程，其使用情况取决于电子文档管理系统（EDMS）应用的环境。手动工作流程需要用户查看文档并决定将它发送给谁。而基于规则的工作流程允许管理员创建一个能决定文件在组织内如何流动的规则。例如，一个发票先要经过批准，然后才能按规定流程发送到财务部门。当这些规则有效时，先进的工作流程机制可以操作控制内容或显示外在处理过程。

2.10 协作

协作性应该是 EDM 系统中所固有的。协作型 EDMS 的基本形式是允许被授权的用户对文件进行检索和加工，当文件正在被处理的时候，其他用户不能访问该文件。其他先进的协作形式应实时生效。它们允许多个用户同时查看并修改（或标记）文件。由此产生的文件是全面的，包括了所有用户对文件的添加。

2.11 版本控制

版本控制是指在文件被录入或提出文件管理系统的过程中，允许用户检索以前的版本并继续在选定的点对文件进行加工的过程。对于随时间推移而发生变化并且需要更新的文件来说，版本控制是有用，但它可能需要返回或参考以前的副本。

2.12 搜索

搜索是指使用模板属性或全文搜索查找文档和文件夹。它可以使用各种属性和文档内容搜索文档。

2.13 发布

发布一份文件包括校对、同行或公众审查、授权、印刷及审批等步骤。这些步骤一定要谨慎并运用逻辑思维。任何处理上的疏漏都可能导致文件的不准确，从而误导用户和读者，给他们带来麻烦。如果没有特定的专业知识或工具，已发布的文件格式应该是很难被改变的，但它是只读的或可移植的。

Unit 4

Daily Reception

Part One Dialogues

Sample Dialogue 1

Situation ▶ Wang Ping is receiving a visitor with no appointment.

(A—Wang Ping, the secretary of Rogers Household Electrical Appliance Co., Ltd.; B—John White, the visitor who has no appointment with Mr. Rogers, Wang Ping's executive)

A: Good morning, sir. Can I help you?

B: Yes. I'd like to see Mr. Rogers, please.

A: Do you have an appointment with Mr. Rogers?

B: No, I don't, but I'll take just a few minutes of his time.

A: Can I have your name, please?

B: My name is John White.

A: OK. Mr. White, could you tell me what company you are representing?

B: I am the sales manager of Sears Department Store.

A: OK. Please take a seat and wait for a moment, Mr. White! I'll go and see if he is available. (One minute later) Mr. White, I am afraid you can't see Mr. Rogers at this moment since he is in the middle of a meeting. Can I ask what you wish to see him about?

B: I'd prefer to explain that to him directly.

A: I'm sorry. I'm told to get that information from every caller. If you don't care to wait, I can arrange an appointment for you later today.

B: No, I'll take just a few minutes of Mr. Rogers' time.

A: Then, would you like to write a note? I can send it to Mr. Rogers and see if he can see you.

B: No, my business is personal.

A: I'm sorry. Mr. Rogers is occupied at the moment and can't spare any time for you. It would be a waste of your precious time if you keep waiting. Can your leave your name card so that I ask Mr. Rogers to contact you directly by phone?

B: No.

A: I'm awfully sorry. I couldn't be of any help.

Sample Dialogue 2

Situation ▶ Chen Bin is handling a caller, who is arriving at the office to make a complaint.

(A—Chen Bin, the secretary of Sales Department of Qihui Clothing Company; B—Jack Donald, the clothing dealer)

A: Good morning. Sales Department, what can I do for you?

B: Yes. I want to speak to whoever is in charge of orders.

A: May I have your name please?

B: Jack Donald, a clothing dealer of Xihua Department Store.

A: OK. Mr. Donald, what kind of order are you calling about?

B: It's an order for 100 boxes of sweaters. We've been waiting over 3 days for this order and you have promised us immediate delivery in the contract.

A: Well. Mr. Donald, I'm afraid our sales manager is not in at the moment. I am awfully sorry if it has caused you much inconvenience. But perhaps I can be of help for you. Now, could you just tell me again what the order was for?

B: 100 boxes of sweaters.

A: Have you got the order number handy?

B: Yes, here it is. It's 4846789.

A: Thank you. Now, I'll get the dispatcher to check our records and see if the goods are delivered.

B: That's right. Please see this matter immediately.

A: All right. How about calling you right back if I've spoken to the dispatcher?

B: Yes. My number is 010-88222732.

A: Well. I'll get back to you in a few minutes. Is there anything more you need us to do?

B: Yes. Is it possible that you could give me a 10% discount on the goods since the delivery is delayed?

A: Um...

Useful Expressions

1. Do you have an appointment with Mr. Rogers?
   您与罗杰斯先生有预约吗？
2. Mr. White, could you tell me what company you are representing?
   怀特先生，能告诉我您代表什么公司吗？
3. Mr. White, I am afraid you can't see Mr. Rogers at this moment since he is in the middle of a meeting.
   怀特先生，恐怕您现在不能见罗杰斯先生，因为他正在开会。
4. I'm told to get that information from every caller.
   我奉命询问每位来访者的来意。
5. No, I'll take just a few minutes of Mr. Rogers' time.
   不用，我只会占用罗杰斯先生几分钟的时间。
6. If you don't care to wait, I can arrange an appointment for you later today.
   如果您愿意等，我可以在今天晚些时候给您安排约见。
7. I want to speak to whoever is in charge of orders.
   我想找贵方负责订单的人，无论是谁。
8. We've been waiting over 3 days for this order, and you have promised us immediate delivery in the contract.
   三天来我们一直在等这批货，而且在合同中，贵方承诺会立即发货。
9. Please see this matter immediately.
   请立刻着手处理此事。
10. Is it possible that you could give me a 10% discount on the goods since the delivery is delayed?
    既然发货延误，贵方能否给我方 10% 的货价折扣？

Situational Dialogues

Using the Sample Dialogue as a model, try to create a new dialogue with your partner.

Situation 1 ▶ Li Fang, a secretary in Swan Sanitary Ware Co., Ltd., is dealing with John Smith, a visitor with no appointment with Li Fang's executive.

Situation 2 ▶ Li Yang, a secretary in Sunflowers Sewing Machine Industry Company, is handling the complaint from Thomas Johnson, a dealer from Sunshine Department Store.

Part Two Text A

Office Public Relations

Public Relations (PR) is the ongoing effort to create and maintain a positive image of your organization in the eyes of the public. It is important that the public thinks about you in a positive way because all organizations need to be trusted and supported by their target group or members.

People who use your services will expect you to be helpful, friendly, efficient and professional. Most people will contact you by visiting your office or by phoning you. This means that the phone and office are two of the most important areas where you should create a positive image.

If your interaction with the public is bad, it can have a devastating effect on your organization reputation. It is much easier to build a good public relations culture in your organization than it is to reverse a bad image once it exists.

Every person in your organization, including the secretary, should understand the importance of good public relations and know what role they should play in promoting a positive image.

1. Important Things to Know About Public Relations

Public Relations targets the people you see as the clients of your organization. Depending on the work you do, this could be your members, people from a specific target group (for example pensioners) or the general public. You can only develop a public relations strategy once you know who your clients are and what image or profile you want to project to them.

Try to match the image you project with the goals and work of your organization. The image projected by a business consultant office will be very different from that of a community advice office. You will have to answer the following questions:

- What does our organization stand for and what do we want people to know about it?
- What are the main services we provide and how do we make it accessible to people?
- What do we want people to feel when they come into our office or use our services?
- Who are our main clients and what will make them comfortable or uncomfortable?
- What is the first thing we want people to notice when they come into our office?

2. How to Make Your Office Welcoming for Visitors

The front office is the reception area. This is the area that every person who visits you will come to first before being seen by the relevant person. It is the public face of your organization and the place where people will form their first impression.

The front office serves the following functions:

- Receiving visitors. In most organizations, visitors will spend some time in the reception area before being seen by another person. It is very important that you receive people properly, make them feel comfortable and deal with them professionally.

• Giving out information. Not all visitors come for appointments with other staff. The reception staff often help people — give them information brochures or refer them somewhere else.
• Dealing with telephones. All of us have experienced the frustration of rude and incompetent telephone receptionists. It is very important to deal with telephone calls properly.

These functions are very important to the organization and everyone should be aware of it. Here are some tips that will help improve the way you run your reception area.

2.1 When a Visitor Arrives

The reception area is the first contact that people have with any office of an organization or institution. The work of the reception area differs from one organization to the other, depending on the type of service that is being offered by the organization. This should not create a problem, instead, a system to run the reception efficiently should be developed:

• Make sure every visitor feels welcome and is greeted at once on entering the reception area.
• Find out who she has come to see or what the purpose of the visit is.
• Find out if they made an appointment to see the person. You may find that the issue the visitor has come about does not need the person they have mentioned. You can just give the assistance and advice there and then.
• If you cannot help and the culture of the organization is that people are welcome to see visitors at any time, find out if the person they have come to see is available at that point in time. Make sure you do not just send visitors directly without notifying the person who you are sending them to.
• If the person who is being visited is not available, find out if there is anything you can do to help:

— You can ask the visitor to wait if it is worth waiting, offer them something to drink and read.

— Take the visitor's details and make sure you write them on a piece of paper, visible enough for the reader to see.

— Assure the visitor that the message will get to the right person.

— If you cannot give assistance, call a person who can.

— Never give false information or wrong advice. Always have next to you your organizational brochures, pamphlets and simple documents that will assist you in giving out the right information to the relevant people.

2.2 Staff Behavior

• Understand the work of the organization and know the answers to common questions.
• Be thirsty for information, attend staff meetings and learn from others. You should know everything that goes on in the organization.
• Always speak to people in a friendly, clear and pleasant manner.
• Always be polite, and never lose your temper.
• Make people feel special at all times.
• Be professional and if people will have to wait, tell them how long it will take before someone

will see them.

- Greet anyone who arrives immediately and ask how you can help them.
- If you are busy when someone arrives, do not just ignore them, smile and give them a sign, tell them someone will be with them soon.
- Do not talk to other staff members while someone is waiting to be greeted.
- Never get into arguments in front of people in the reception area or gossip about other staff members.
- Dress in the manner that is suitable for the people who visit you office.
- Never disclose information that is private and confidential.
- Never act offensively. Offensive behavior includes smoking in front of everyone, swearing, and making personal telephone calls, speaking very loudly, chewing, etc.
- Always keep your work station/office tidy so that you have a professional and efficient image.

2.3 Environment

- Put a sign outside your office so that it is easy to find
- Put a sign for reception or waiting rooms
- Put signs on all other office doors so that people can easily find the right place
- Make sure you have seats for people who have to wait
- Decorate the reception area so that it is comfortable and welcoming
- Put magazines, books or pamphlets in the waiting area for people to read.
- Offer people tea or coffee. If you can, afford it or put a jug with water and glasses in the area.

3. How to Deal with Telephone Calls

Deal with telephone calls in the same way as you deal with visitors.

3.1 What to Say When Answering the Phone

- The best way to answer the phone is "Name of organization, hello, how can I help you?"
- If you have to put someone through, say "Please hold, I am putting you through".
- If the line is engaged, say: "He or she is on a call, would you like to hold or can I take a message?"

3.2 Rules for Answering the Telephone

- Always be polite and welcoming.
- Keep your conversation as brief as possible without sounding rude or in a hurry.
- Make sure that you know your telephone system are able to use all the facilities.
- Do not allow the phone to ring more than three times, this may give an impression that you are not there.

3.3 Tips for Answering Telephones

- Get organized. Have everything like your pens, desk pads, message books, etc, handy. Know the dynamics of your job. If queries are always the same, make sure you have the information at hand.
- Decide as an organization whether you should ask "who may I say is calling?" It must be

discussed in the organization whether it is acceptable to ask the callers who they are or just to put the calls through. In some office this may be a problem. If you are expected to screen the calls, this should not be a problem at all.

- Ask the caller how you can help or what their problem is. Listen attentively and let the caller know this. Avoid interruptions while you are listening to someone on the phone.
- When transferring calls, never make the caller wait too long. If the recipient of the call is busy, go back to the caller and ask if you can take a message. Assure him or her that you will give the message to the person.
- When taking a message, always read it back to the caller to make sure that you have taken the right message, especially phone numbers. Thank the caller for calling. Never slam the receiver in the ears of the caller.
- Develop a proper system for passing on messages. If a message is not passed on and the call seems urgent, phone the caller back, explain and ask if you can help in any way.

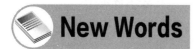

New Words

ongoing ['ɔŋgəuiŋ] *adj.* 不间断的，进行的，前进的

positive ['pɔzətiv] *adj.* 积极的，正面的，肯定的

trust [trʌst] *n.* 信任，信托 *vt.* 相信，委托

target ['tɑːgit] *n.* 目标，对象 *vt.* 把……作为目标，瞄准

interaction [ˌintər'ækʃən] *n.* 相互作用，相互影响，互动交流

devastating ['devəsteitiŋ] *adj.* 毁灭性的，破坏性的

reputation [ˌrepju'teiʃən] *n.* 声誉，名声，名气

reverse [ri'vəːs] *v.* 逆转，倒退 *adj.* 相反的，反面的，颠倒的

promote [prə'məut] *vt.* 促进，提升；促销，推销

project ['prɔdʒekt] *n.* 计划，工程，项目；课题 *v.* 计划，设计，投射，表达，突出

profile ['prəufail] *n.* 侧面，轮廓，形象，简介 *v.* 描绘……轮廓，评论人物

consultant [kən'sʌltənt] *n.* 顾问，咨询者

accessible [ək'sesəbl] *adj.* 可得到的，易接近的，可进入的

welcoming ['welkəmiŋ] *adj.* 受欢迎的

relevant ['relivənt] *adj.* 相关的；中肯的；有重大关系的

professionally [prə'feʃənli] *adv.* 职业上，专业地

brochure [brəu'ʃuə] *n.* 小册子，资料手册

refer [ri'fəː] *vt.* 把……提交给 *vi.* 参考；谈及；咨询

frustration [frʌs'treiʃən] *n.* 挫折，失败；令人沮丧的东西

incompetent [in'kɔmpitənt] *adj.* 无能力的，不称职的，不能胜任的

institution [ˌinsti'tjuːʃən] *n.* 制度，机构

greet [gri:t] *vt.* 迎接，问候，致敬
assistance [ə'sistəns] *n.* 援助，帮助
available [ə'veiləbl] *adj.* 可利用的，可得到的，有空的
notify ['nəutifai] *v.* 通知，通告
visible ['vizəbl] *adj.* 看得见的，可见的，显而易见的
assure [ə'ʃuə] *vt.* 使确信，使放心，确保
pamphlet ['pæmflit] *n.* 小册子
attend [ə'tend] *v.* 出席，参加，照料，注意，专注于
pleasant ['plezənt] *adj.* 令人愉快的，舒适的，宜人的
ignore [ig'nɔ:] *vt.* 忽视，不理，不顾
sign [sain] *n.* 手势，符号，迹象 *v.* 签，签名；做手势，做标记
gossip ['gɔsip] *n.* 流言蜚语，闲话 *vi.* 散播（流言蜚语）
disclose [dis'kləuz] *vt.* 揭露，使某物显露，公开
offensively [ə'fensivli] *adv.* 不愉快地，讨厌地
swear [swεə] *v.* 诅咒，咒骂；郑重承诺；发誓
chewing [tʃu: iŋ] *n.* 嚼，咀嚼，咬
decorate ['dekəreit] *v.* 装饰，布置
jug [dʒʌg] *n.* 水壶，罐
engaged [in'geidʒd] *adj.* 忙碌的，使用中的
brief [bri:f] *adj.* 短暂的，短期的，简短的，扼要的
facility [fə'siliti] *n.* 设施，设备，工具
impression [im'preʃən] *n.* 印象
handy ['hændi] *adj.* 方便的，手边的，灵巧的，现成的
dynamics [dai'næmiks] *n.* 活力，动力
query ['kwiəri] *n.* 疑问，质问，询问 *vt.* 质问，对……表示怀疑
acceptable [ək'septəbl] *adj.* 可接受的；合意的，受欢迎的
attentively [ə'tentivli] *adv.* 注意地，留意地
interruption [ˌintə'rʌpʃən] *n.* 打岔，中断
recipient [ri'sipiənt] *n.* 接受者，收信人
slam [slæm] *v.* 砰地关上，猛力抨击，冲击
urgent ['ə:dʒənt] *adj.* 紧急的，急迫的

Phrases and Expressions

office public relations 办公室公共关系
in the eyes of sb. 在某人的心目中，就某人的观点来看
in a positive way 以积极态度
have a devastating effect on 对……有毁灭性的影响
play a role in 在……方面起作用
see as 看作为，视为
project a profile to sb. 向某人表现出某种形象
match… with…（使）与……相配，与……一致
form the first impression 形成第一印象
give out 分发；公布
be aware of 意识到，了解
have contact with 接触到，和……有联系

there and then 当场，立即；当时当地
be thirsty for 渴望，渴求
lose one's temper 发脾气，发作
at all times 随时，每时每刻；总是，一直
get into arguments 进行辩论或争论
gossip about 说……的闲话
be suitable for 适于；合适的
in the same way as 以和……同样的方式
put sb. through 为某人接通电话
be on a call 在打电话
take a message 留言，留口信，捎口信
in a hurry 急急忙忙地，慌忙地
get organized 有条理
desk pad 桌垫
at hand 手头，在手边，在附近，即将来临
pass on message 传递消息

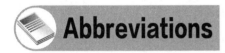

Abbreviations

PR (Public Relations) 公共关系

Notes

1 It is important that the public thinks about you in a positive way because all organizations need to be trusted and supported by their target group or members.

本句中，连词 because 引导原因状语从句，说明主句 It is important that the public thinks about you in a positive way 的原因。其中，主句为“It + be + 形容词 + 主语从句”句型，该句型中 it 是形式主语，真正的主语是主语从句。请看下例：

It is necessary that he should sort out the information for my reference.

他有必要整理些资料供我参考。

2 It is much easier to build a good public relations culture in your organization than it is to reverse a bad image once it exists.

本句中，连词 than 将不定式短语 to build a good public relations culture in your organization 和 to reverse a bad image once it exists 连接起来，形成比较结构。英语中，than 连接两个非谓语动词时，通常应使用一样的形式。请看下例：

It is better to express your anger than to bottle it up.

将闷气发泄出来比闷在肚内要好。

另外，本句中 it 是形式主语，真正的主语是动词不定式短语 to build a good... organization 和 to reverse a bad image... exists. 请看下例：

It is advisable to take an open-minded approach to new idea.

对新思想采取开明态度是明智的。

3 Make sure every visitor feels welcome and is greeted at once on entering the reception area.

本句中，on entering the reception area. 是“on + v.-ing”结构，常用来引导时间状语，意为“当……时；一……时，就……”。请看下例：

On hearing of the victory, the nation was transported with joy.

一听到胜利的消息，全国人民就欢腾起来了。

另外，本句中 make sure 是固定词组，意为“设法确保；确定”。请看下例：

To make sure that he was at home, I called him up in advance.

为了确定他在家，我事先打电话给他。

4 If you cannot help and the culture of the organization is that people are welcome to see visitors at any time, find out if the person they have come to see is available at that point in time.

本句中，if 引导的条件从句中包含两个分句，即 you cannot help 和 the culture of the organization... at any time，其中 that people are welcome to see visitors at any time. 是 that 引导的从句在第二个分句中作表语，构成表语从句。

另外，主句中 if the person... at that point in time 是 if 引导的从句作谓语动词 find out 的宾语，构成宾语从句。请看下例：

I am calling to see if you would like to have lunch tomorrow.

我打电话给你，是想知道明天一起吃顿中饭怎样？

5 It must be discussed in the organization whether it is acceptable to ask the callers who they are or just to put the calls through.

本句中，it 是形式主语，whether it is acceptable to ask... put the calls through 是由连词 whether 引导的从句在整句中作真正的主语，即构成主语从句。请看下例：

Whether it rains or not makes no difference to me.

下不下雨对我来说都一样。

另外，主语从句中 it 也是形式主语，而从句真正的主语是 to ask the callers who they are 和 just to put the calls through 两个动词不定式词组，其中 who they are 是由连词 who 引导的从句作动词 ask 的直接宾语，构成宾语从句。请看下例：

I asked him who you were the moment you buzzed in.

你一进来我就问他你是谁。

Exercises

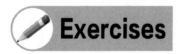

EX. 1 Answer the following questions.

1. What is the definition of public relations according to Text A?
2. Why is it important for an organization to be thought about by the public in a positive way?
3. Which is much easier for an organization to do? To build a good public relations culture or to reverse a bad image?
4. How important is the reception area in an organization?

5. What are the major functions the front office serve?
6. What can you do to help the visitor if the person who is being visited is not available?
7. What behaviors are offensive in front of the visitors?
8. List at least three things you can do to improve the environment of the reception area?
9. What should you say if the line is engaged when answering the phone?
10. What should you pay attention to when taking a message?

EX. 2 Complete the following sentences with appropriate words or expressions in the box.

target	stand for	visible	assist in	at hand
ignore	reverse	promote	image	maintain

1. Only by keeping down costs will this company ________ its competitive advantage over others.
2. Being always friendly, polite, cheerful and optimistic, the secretary has helped establish a strong corporate ________.
3. This makes organizational problems and challenges ________.
4. And, if time and situation allow, the secretary will be asked to ________ training her replacement.
5. Firms can't sacrifice environmental protection to ________ economic growth.
6. The company would be unwise to ________ the growing public dissatisfaction with its services
7. Having the right office equipment ________ be enormously helpful for secretarial work.
8. The executive assistant has become a ________ of public criticism and he is under attack on all sides.
9. Though good-tempered, the secretary can not ________ the visitor's rude behaviors any more.
10. A secretary's wrong attitude will have exactly the ________ effect while dealing with the visitors.

EX. 3 Translate the following sentences into English.

1. 公共关系经理和媒介经理负责此事宜。(public relations manager)
2. 秘书用积极的方式同访客交谈，这点十分重要。(in a positive way)
3. 秘书粗暴的态度可能对公司的形象产生毁灭性的影响。(have a devastating effect on)
4. 秘书还应该协助前台经理为客人提供服务。(front office manager)
5. 访客通常会基于他第一次被接待的情况对一家公司形成第一印象。(form the first impression)
6. 更重要的是，这位秘书开始接触到一些潜在的客户。(have contact with)
7. 秘书应当渴求知识，这样她才能给访客提供有价值的信息。(be thirsty for)

8. 那位主管人员告诫他的助理不要对客户发脾气。(lose one's temper with)
9. 秘书散播有关同事的丑闻谣言是极为不合适的。(spread gossip about)
10. 请您给您的销售经理捎个口信好吗？ (pass on the message to sb.)

EX. 4 **Translate the following passage into Chinese.**

Communication is a process where ideas, opinions, facts and emotions are exchanged between two or more people. Visitors who visit a business will have their first point of contact at the greeting area which is usually the reception. So being at reception one has to have good communication skills and has to communicate with the customers in appropriate ways.

Working at reception area, you represent the organization and any impression that you create with the client will have a lasting effect on the organization as a whole. So presenting yourself professionally and communicating professionally with the client is very important. Communication also helps you to better understand the needs and purpose of visit of the visitor and for the visitor to gain information that they require, which contributes a lot to mutual understanding. In brief, good communication leaves the visitor with a satisfaction, attracts more visitors, and boosts your organization's business.

Part Three Text B

Handling Visitors

One of the most important aspects of a secretary's work is the way in which she handles visitors. She is a reflection not only of the company's public relations image—as is the receptionist—but of her executive's personal image. She is a key figure in building good will both for him and for the company through her attitude of considerateness regardless of the relative importance of each visitor.

1. Smoking at the Desk

In most modem offices smoking at the desks is allowed. But because smoking is an objectionable habit to many people, if you do smoke, be discreet. When a visitor approaches your desk and you are smoking, either put out your cigarette or place it in an ash tray to one side of your desk while you are talking to the visitor. Do not smoke while you are conversing with him.

Never put lighted cigarettes any place but in an ash tray. If you rest them on the edges of desks and cabinets, unsightly burns can be the result.

2. Rising to Greet Guests

Unless your desk is hidden from view, there is a need for you, a secretary, to rise to greet guests and doing so is a mark of friendship or honor.

3. When the Visitor Has an Appointment

If the executive is free, the secretary can call on the intercom to say Mr. XX has arrived for his 10:30 appointment. However, if the executive is occupied with another visitor or is on the telephone, the secretary places a note before him explaining that Mr. XX has arrived and is waiting. If the person already in the executive's office is a co-worker, or a personal friend or relative, the secretary can announce the visitor on the intercom and need not use a note.

If he can't immediately wind up what he is doing, or has fallen behind schedule in his appointments, it is courteous for an executive to leave his office to greet the man who is waiting for his appointment and explain that he needs only a minute or two more to finish up what he is doing. If the executive does not or cannot perform this courtesy, the secretary can smilingly make the same explanation to the waiting visitor.

4. When the Executive Is Not in His Office

On occasion an executive will have been called out of his office just before a visitor arrives. When this happens the secretary should apologize for her executive and explain the circumstances.

You can say, "Good morning, Mr. Smythe. Mr. Rogers was called into the plant about ten minutes ago because of a production problem. He should be back any minute now. Do you mind waiting?"

If an unexpected emergency will keep the executive out of his office for more than a few moments, you might explain it this way:

"Good morning, Mr. Smythe. I'm so sorry, but Mr. Rogers was called to the office of the chairman of the board a little while ago. I'm not sure when he'll be back. I tried to reach you, but your office said you had already left. Can you wait?" The visitor can then decide whether to wait, come back later or make another appointment, or even see someone else—the executive's assistant, for instance, if he has one.

5. When the Visitor Has to Wait

If the visitor has to wait, the secretary invites him to be seated and gets on with her work. If the guest is particularly important, she may ask if there is anything she can do for him. She makes no effort to "entertain" waiting visitors, but responds pleasantly to their small talk, just as a receptionist does. If direct questions are put to her about the business, she avoids them adroitly, pretending complete ignorance of the topic, if need be, or changing the subject.

When the secretary tells a receptionist a visitor will have to wait, it is courteous for her to come out to the reception room and explain to the visitor the reason for the delay. If this is not possible—if she is taking dictation, for example—the receptionist will have to explain the delay. When the executive is ready to see the visitor, the secretary can either call the receptionist and tell her to send the visitor in, or she can go out to the reception room and escort him in herself.

6. Announcing a Visitor

If the secretary is told to send the guest right in, she may do one of two things. If the visitor is known to her employer, and has visited the office before, she may nod to him and say something to the effect that, "Mr. Michaels is free. Won't you go right in?" However, if it is the visitor's first visit, or he is an infrequent visitor, the secretary should accompany him to the door of her employer's office, open it if it is kept closed, step to one side and say, "Mr. Michaels, here is Mr. Rogers."

When older people or dignitaries or women are announced in a business office, it is considered proper to mention the guest's name first. For instance, should a church dignitary visit your executive, the polite announcement would be: "Bishop McLaughlin, Mr. Michaels."

Members of the executive's family are allowed to enter his office unannounced, unless there is a guest in the office. In this case, the secretary announces their arrival on the intercom right away.

7. Cancelling an Appointment

Occasionally there is reason for cancelling an appointment, but this should not be done lightly. Only a matter of absolute necessity makes the cancellation of an appointment excusable.

If an executive is called away and knows he will not be back in time to keep a scheduled appointment, his secretary should telephone the individual who is due for the appointment, explain the circumstances, and offer to make another appointment.

Should you have to call and change the time of an appointment for any reason, be as gracious as possible. Perhaps you could say, after introducing yourself: "I am sorry to have to ask this favor. But would it be possible for Mr. Springer to come to Mr. Michaels' office at three o'clock today instead of two o'clock? Mr. Michaels has been asked by the president of our company to attend a very important luncheon meeting which will probably last until well after two o'clock."

8. When the Executive Is Behind Schedule in His Appointments

If he is badly off schedule, it might be best to try and cancel one appointment, so he can catch up. The next best thing is to point out to him that he will have to make up time and ask him to cut short the next one or two appointments. If he is agreeable to this, you can let him know when the allotted time is up for each one.

9. Interrupting When a Visitor Is Present

Should your executive have on his schedule a meeting at a specific time and a visitor is in his office as the hour approaches, the secretary may enter the office, apologize for the interruption and remind him that an appointment is coming up. The time of the appointment should not be mentioned. A vocal reminder is better than a note because then the visitor is alerted to the fact that he should depart.

Allow enough time for your employer to end his talk with his visitor unhurriedly and still reach his appointment promptly.

10. When Your Executive Does Not Want to See the Visitor

When you are certain your executive is not interested in seeing a certain individual, be polite but definite in refusing him. You can say something like this:

"I wish I could be of help, Mr. Gray, but right now Mr. Michaels will see only those directly connected with a new project. He will be involved in this for some time, and I think the best way to reach him would be by letter."

Some people have a flair for turning people down in such a way that they feel they've been honored rather than refused. Try to cultivate this manner by treating even the unwanted guest solicitously. Never try to raise your own sense of self-importance by acting in an unpleasant, rude manner.

11. When the Visitors Are Office Personnel

Many executives today maintain an "open door" policy for members of their company. Naturally, executives on the same level are free to come and go as they please, unless the executive has a visitor from outside the company. When lower level personnel indicate that they'd like to see your executive, try to first find out why. You can sometimes prevent someone from going over his immediate superior's head and thereby causing ill feeling, or you can point out that your executive is not the right one with whom to discuss this matter. If you feel the problem merits your executive's attention, make an appointment for the employee and explain the problem to your executive so that he will have some idea of what to expect.

If the employee will not tell you his problem, do not refuse him an appointment as you might be an outsider. Set up an appointment for him and inform your executive that Charles Cole, the new young salesman, or John White in the mailroom, has asked to see him but is reluctant to tell you why.

The secretary will interrupt her executive whenever a company employee comes in with an emergency work situation.

12. When the Visitor Has No Appointment

In a majority of cases, it is left to the secretary to decide how the visitor without an appointment will be handled, since she knows her executive's business needs and his schedule. It is her job to protect him from unnecessary interruptions.

First she must find out what the visitor wants. If he doesn't volunteer the information, she must politely ask for it.

If she feels that her executive will want to see the visitor, she asks the visitor to wait and goes into her employer's office (unless he has told her to handle such situations over the phone or intercom). She gives the executive the visitor's card and states his reason for calling. When the executive is with someone, whether a company employee or another visitor, she does not interrupt him, but waits until he is free. The visitor without an appointment must, of course, expect to wait.

The executive may be free at the moment and consent to see the visitor, but if he has an imminent appointment, the secretary should remind him, saying, "You have ten minutes until Mr. Grant arrives for his three o'clock appointment." She lets her employer know the minute Mr. Grant comes in.

At times visitors without appointments refuse to state their business. The secretary then politely asks them to write for an appointment. She can say, "Unless I know what you wish to discuss with Mr. Michaels, I cannot announce you. This is a rule laid down by Mr. Michaels. I would suggest that you write him, telling him what you want to see him about and asking for an appointment." If the visitor is persistent, she should be firm but treat him courteously.

When her employer has an assistant, the secretary usually turns unknown and uninvited visitors over to him; or she may refer the visitor to another person in the firm.

She might say, "I think Mr. Gray in our Accounting Department would be more familiar with your problem than Mr. Michaels. Do you mind if I telephone Mr. Gray's secretary and find out if he can see you now?"

If she can arrange the meeting immediately, she should give explicit directions for reaching Mr. Gray's office, or she can accompany the visitor there. Should Mr. Gray be unable to see the visitor until another time, she passes that information on, telling him the date and time if a future appointment is arranged.

New Words

reflection [ri'flekʃən] *n.* 反射，反映，沉思，考虑

receptionist [ri'sepʃənist] *n.* 接待员；接线员

considerateness [kən'sidərit] *n.* 体贴，考虑周到

objectionable [əb'dʒekʃənəbl] *adj.* 该反对的，讨厌的，有异议的

discreet [dis'kri:t] *adj.* 小心的，谨慎的，慎重的

approach [ə'prəutʃ] *vt.* 接近，着手处理 *n.* 方法，途径，接近

unsightly [ʌn'saitli] *adj.* 不美观的，难看的

bum [bʌm] *n.* 流浪者；笨蛋；废物

honor ['ɔnə] *n.* 荣誉，尊敬，敬意 *vt.* 尊敬，给以荣誉

intercom ['intəkɔm] *n.* 对讲机，内部通话设备

courtesy ['kə:tisi] *n.* 谦恭有礼，礼貌

smilingly ['smailiŋli] *adv.* 笑眯眯地，微笑地

circumstance ['sə:kəmstəns] *n.* 环境，境遇

unexpected ['ʌniks'pektid] *adj.* 意外的，想不到的，料不到的

emergency [i'mə:dʒnsi] *n.* 紧急情况，突发事件 *adj.* 紧急的，应急的

adroitly [ə'drɔitli] *adv.* 熟练地，敏捷地

ignorance ['ignərəns] *n.* 不知，漠视，愚昧无知

escort [is'kɔ:t] *n.* 护送者 *vt.* 护送，护卫

infrequent [in'fri:kwənt] *adj.* 不频繁的，不经常的，不常见的

accompany [ə'kʌmpəni] *v.* 陪伴，陪同；附加，补充

dignitary ['dignitəri] *n.* 高官，显要人物 *adj.* 权贵的，高官的

Bishop ['biʃəp] *n.* 主教
absolute ['æbsəlu:t] *adj.* 绝对的，完全的，无条件的
excusable [iks'kju:zəbl] *adj.* 可原谅的，可免除的
due [dju:] *adj.* 到期的，适当的，预定的 *n.* 应有的权利，应得到的东西，应缴款
gracious ['greiʃəs] *adj.* 亲切的，和蔼的，有礼貌的
allot [ə'lɔt] *v.* 分配，拨给，摊派
depart [di'pɑ:t] *v.* 离开，出发，去世，离职
unhurriedly ['ʌn'hʌridli] *adv.* 不慌不忙地，从容不迫地
promptly ['prɔmptli] *adv.* 迅速地，立即地；敏捷地
definite ['definit] *adj.* 明确的，肯定的，有把握的
flair [flɛə] *n.* 天分，天资，眼光，鉴别力
cultivate ['kʌltiveit] *vt.* 教养，培养；改善；种植
solicitously [sə'lisitəsli] *adv.* 热心地，热切地
mailroom ['meilru:m] *n.* 邮件室，收发室
reluctant [ri'lʌktənt] *adj.* 不情愿的，勉强的
volunteer [vɔlən'tiə] *n.* 志愿者；志愿兵 *adj.* 自愿的 *vt.* 志愿提供
imminent ['iminənt] *adj.* 即将来临的，紧急的，迫近的
persistent [pə'sistənt] *adj.* 持续的，持久的，坚持不懈的
firm [fə:m] *adj.* 坚固的，坚定的，坚决的
explicit [iks'plisit] *adj.* 明确的，清楚的，详述的

Phrases and Expressions

build good will 增加善意或好感
an ash tray 烟灰缸
converse with 交谈
be occupied with 忙于
fall behind schedule 滞后于计划时间
on occasion 有时，偶尔
apologize for 为……道歉，替……道歉
get on with 继续（做某事）；与……相处
make an effort to do sth. 努力做某事
small talk 闲谈，聊天
if need be 如果需要的话
send sb. in 请进某人
nod to sb. 向某人点头打招呼或示意
to the effect that 其大意是
cancel an appointment 取消预约
keep a scheduled appointment 遵守预约
instead of 而不是
a luncheon meeting 一个午餐会
be off schedule 延期
catch up 追赶，跟上
cut short 打断，中断，缩短
be agreeable to 同意

on one's schedule 在某人的日程表上	prevent from 阻止，防止
at a specific time 在特定时间	immediate supervisor 直接领导，顶头上司
come up 发生	set up an appointment 安排见面时间
be alerted to 警惕，留意	it is left to sb. to do sth. 由某人做某事
turn down 拒绝，驳回	protect from 保护，保卫
a sense of self-importance 自负感，自我重要的感觉	be consent to 同意
in an unpleasant and rude manner 以一种不愉快和粗鲁的方式	lay down a rule 制定规则
office personnel 办公室人员	turn over to 移交给
	refer sb. to 把某人提交给或委托给

Exercises

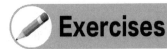

EX. 5 Answer the following questions.

1. Why is it important for a secretary to handle visitors according to Para.1?
2. How can the secretary remind him of a waiting visitor if her executive is occupied with another visitor or is on the telephone ?
3. What should the secretary do when her executive is called out of his office just before a visitor arrives?
4. What is the secretary supposed to do if the visitor put direct questions to her about the business?
5. How should the secretary send the visitor in if it is the visitor's first visit?
6. What should his secretary do if an executive is called away and will not be back in time to keep a scheduled appointment?
7. How should the secretary refuse the visitors whom her executive does not want to see?
8. Must the secretary stop the employee from seeing her executive if he does not want to tell her his problem ?
9. Why is it up to the secretary to decide how to handle the caller without an appointment in most cases?
10. What should she do if the secretary feels that her executive will want to see the visitor?

Part Four Extended Reading

Text

Complaints[1] Handling

In business, Customer complaints are inevitable[2], no matter how streamlined[3] your business is. A customer complaint can affect the reputation[4] of the business and needs to be acknowledged[5] and handled appropriately[6]. If you have several customers that have a bad experience and the business chooses to ignore[7] it or do nothing, you will not only lose that business, but also the business of everyone they know. By ignoring or dismissing[8] their complaints, you are effectively telling the customer that you don't value[9] their opinions.

As a secretary in a business, it is common to receive the customers' complaints where the customers are typically emotional and agitated[10]. Therefore, a secretary needs to be patient enough to communicate with the clients tactfully[11] so that the problems can be solved efficiently. Whatever the clients' complaints are and whenever receiving complaints calls, you have to remain calm and answer the complaint calls with great patience. Most importantly, being a secretary, you must be aware that customers' complaints do not imply they are dissatisfied with you, so do not get angry at the customers' rude attitude. Contrarily[12], what you need to do most is to listen patiently to the customers when they are making complaints and find the effective solutions[13] to those complaints. There is a process that can be used to ensure customer complaints are handled effectively. This creates a relationship where the customer feels valued and returns in future.

1. Taking the Complaint

- When a customer first makes a complaint, take a step back[14]. It can be difficult to remain impassive[15] in the face of criticism[16], but an emotional response will only serve to irritate[17] the customer further.
- Give the customer your full attention and listen to the whole problem before responding. Put yourself in their shoes[18] — if you had a problem, you would want someone to listen to you. Appearing disinterested[19], or attempting to argue back[20], will only exacerbate[21] the situation.

Notes

[1] *n.* 抱怨，控诉，投诉
[2] *adj.* 不可避免的
[3] *adj.* 流线型的，现代化的
[4] *n.* 名声，信誉，声望
[5] *vt.* 承认，鸣谢
[6] *adv.* 适当地
[7] *vt.* 忽视，不理睬
[8] *vt.* 不考虑，拒绝受理
[9] *v.* 重视；估价，评价
[10] *adj.* 激动的，不安的
[11] *adv.* 机智地，巧妙地
[12] *adv.* 相反地
[13] *n.* 解决方案
[14] 退一步
[15] *adj.* 无动于衷的，冷漠的
[16] *n.* 批评，批判
[17] *vt.* 刺激，使发怒
[18] 站在别人的立场设想
[19] *adj.* 不感兴趣的，不关心的
[20] 反驳
[21] *vt.* 激怒，使恶化，使加重

- Don't jump the gun[22]. You might deal with complaints on a regular basis, and may well have handled a similar situation before. However, for the customer, their complaint is unique[23] to them. Treat them as an important individual by listening to their problem in full[24].
- Try to understand. In the face of a complaint, it's easy to be defensive[25]—particularly if you don't believe you're at fault[26]. However, you have to put yourself in the customer's shoes. If you were on the receiving end of their experience, would you personally be satisfied?
- Always use your initiative[27] when dealing with complaints. If the blame lies with one particular member of staff, it is often best to remove the customer from their presence. This can defuse[28] tension[29] and emotion, and help the customer to reevaluate[30] their anger.
- However, never pass the customer around[31] from person to person. Each complaint should ideally be handled by one staff member. Therefore, you should always ensure that the person assigned to the case has the authority[32] to deal with the situation.

[22] 操之过急，行动过早
[23] *adj.* 唯一的，仅有的，独特的
[24] 全部，完全地
[25] *adj.* 防御用的，防守的，辩护的
[26] 有错，有责任，有过失
[27] *n.* 主动性，主动精神
[28] *vt.* 缓和
[29] *n.* 紧张，不安，紧张气氛
[30] *vt.* 再评估，再评价
[31] 传递，推诿
[32] *n.* 权力，权威

2. Finding a Solution

- Once the customer has aired their grievance[33], you should immediately give a sincere[34] apology. Any number of factors could have contributed to the issue, and you might not be at fault. However, you need to take responsibility for the problem. Sometimes, an apology is all it takes to placate[35] an angry customer.
- Customers never want to hear excuses. However, you are fully entitled[36] to briefly explain why they didn't receive the standard of service they expected. This should take place after you've listened to their complaint and made an apology.
- Sometimes, a complaint will be followed by a request for compensation[37] — typically a refund[38] or a voucher[39]. However, customers often haven't planned beyond making the initial[40] complaint. In these cases, ask the customer for their desired outcome. This makes them feel both involved and valued.

[33] *n.* 委屈，不满，牢骚
[34] *adj.* 诚挚的，真诚的
[35] *vt.* 安抚，抚慰，使平静
[36] *vt.* 使有资格，使有权
[37] *n.* 补偿，赔偿
[38] *n.* 退还，归还或偿还
[39] *n.* 优惠券，券
[40] *adj.* 最初的，开始的

3. Useful Tips for Dealing with Complaints

- Try to remain calm when dealing with a complaint — even if the customer becomes irate[41] or confrontational[42]. Your ultimate [43]aim is to turn their negative experience into a positive one, but arguing back will only make the situation worse.

[41] *adj.* 盛怒的
[42] *adj.* 对抗的，挑衅的
[43] *adj.* 最终的

- Complaints should always be resolved[44] as quickly as possible. The aim is to make the customer feel as though their problem is being treated as a priority[45], without being rushed.
- Keep comprehensive[46] records of all customer complaints, from the initial problem to the eventual[47] solution. You can then periodically assess[48] these records, identifying any common complaints, and taking steps to improve company processes.
- All customer-facing staff members should be trained to deal with complaints. If possible, give your employees some authority when it comes to issuing refunds or other consolatory[49] gestures. Forcing the customer to wait for a manager can make a bad situation worse.

Factually, businesses live or die by their reputations. Unfortunately, it's not always possible to prevent poor customer experiences. However, by handling any complaints quickly and effectively, it's possible to salvage[50] negative situations.

[44] *v.* 解决
[45] *n.* 优先，优先权
[46] *adj.* 综合的，广泛的
[47] *adj.* 最终发生的，结果的
[48] *vt.* 评定，估价
[49] *adj.* 慰问的，可慰藉的
[50] *vt.* 救援，补救

参考译文

课文 A　办公室公关

公共关系（PR）是指为了不断地创造并维护组织在公众心目中的正面形象而进行的一系列活动。公众对你组织持肯定态度，这一点很重要，因为所有组织都需要它们的目标群体或成员对其给予信任和支持。

接受你服务的客户期望你能提供有用的、友好的、高效的和专业的服务。大多数客户会通过到办公室来或打电话联系你。就意味着电话和办公室是两个你塑造积极形象的最重要的区域。

如果你与公众的互动交流不良，就可能对组织的声誉产生毁灭性的影响。在组织中建立良好的公共关系文化要比改变一个现存的糟糕形象容易得多。

组织中的每个人，包括秘书，都应该懂得良好公共关系的重要性，以及他们在提升组织正面形象所扮演的角色。

1. 了解公共关系相关的重要方面

公共关系的目标人群是你视其为该组织的客户的人。这个目标人群可能是组织成员，或某个特定目标群体（如领养老金者），又或是公众，具体视你承担的工作而定。只有当知道客户是谁以及你想对他们展现何种形象时，你才能制定公关策略。

尽力使你的形象与组织的目标和工作性质保持一致。商务顾问办公室展现出的形象将与社区咨询办公室的形象有很大区别。你将必须回答以下问题：

- 我们组织代表什么以及希望客户对本组织有何了解？

- 我们提供的主要服务是什么以及我们如何让客户能得到这些服务？
- 当客户走进我们的办公室或使用我们的服务时，我们想让他们有什么样的感受？
- 谁是我们的主要客户以及什么样的服务会使他们感到舒适或不舒适？
- 当客户走进我们的办公室时，我们想让他们第一眼注意到的是什么？

2. 如何使办公室受访客欢迎

前台是接待区。这是每个来访人员在被相关人员接见之前首先来到的地方。接待区是你所在组织的公众形象，也是客户形成他们第一印象的地方。

前台提供以下功能：

• 接待访客。在大多数组织中，访客在被其他相关人员接见之前，都会在接待区停留一会儿。这时，你以适当的、专业的方式接待他们，并使他们感到舒适。这很重要。

• 提供信息。并不是所有的来访者都是来和其他员工会面的。接待人员可经常给他们一些帮助，如给他们提供资料册，或是把他们带到别处。

• 处理电话。所有的人都经受过粗鲁和无能的电话接待员所带来的沮丧。所以，恰当地处理电话是非常重要的。

这些功能对组织而言非常重要，每个人都应该意识到这一点。以下是一些有助于提高接待区运行方式的建议。

2.1 当来访者到达时

接待区是他人与一个组织或机构的任何办公室接触的第一个地方。接待区的工作因组织机构而异，取决于该组织提供的服务类型。接待区不是制造麻烦的地方，相反，在这里应当制定一个制度，使工作高效运行，即：

- 确保每位来访者一进入接待区就能感受到颇受欢迎，受到迎接。
- 弄清他来约见的人是谁或他此次来这里的目的。
- 弄清他们是否和想找的人预约过。也许，你会发现来访者需解决的问题并不需要他们所提及的人来处理，这时，你当即可提供一些帮助和建议。
- 如果你无法提供帮助并且组织文化规定，组织成员可在任何时候自由接见访客，那么去弄清楚访客来见的人在这个时间点是否有空。确保你不能直接把访客带到他们要见的人那里，而是要事先告知一下，一定要避免直接将来访者带到当事人那里去的做法。
- 如果被访者正忙，你应当看看自己能否提供一些帮助，如：
  - —如果值得等，请访客在此等待，并给他们提供饮品和读物。
  - —记录访客的详细情况，并务必将其清晰地写在一张纸上，让读者易见。
  - —向访客保证一定会将信息转给适当的当事人。
  - —如果你无法给予帮助，则找一个能提供帮助的人来。
  - —绝不能提供虚假信息或错误建议。身边随时放几本你所在组织的宣传册、小册子和一些简单的文档，这样你就可以向相关的人提供正确的信息。

2.2 员工行为

- 了解组织的工作性质并且知道该如何回答常见问题。

- 积极获取信息，参加员工会议，向别人学习，这样你就能了解组织内进行的一切事务。
- 始终以友好的、清晰的、令人愉快的方式与人们交谈。
- 始终彬彬有礼，从不发脾气。
- 让他们随时感到他们自己与众不同。
- 要专业化。如果有人需要等，则告诉他们要等多久，才会有人见他们。
- 立即迎接来访者，并问你如何能帮助他们。
- 当有人来时，你恰好在忙，这时，不要忽视他们。相反，你应当微笑、示意，并告知有人很快会来接待他们。
- 当有人需要招呼时，不要其他员工交谈。
- 在接待区绝不能当着他人的面争论或谈论其他员工的流言蜚语。
- 着装方式要适合接待来访者的场合。
- 绝不透露私人和机密信息。
- 避免冒犯别人的举止。冒犯性的行为包括：当着所有人的面吸烟、说脏话、打个人电话、大声讲话以及咀嚼等。
- 始终保持你的工作台 / 办公室整洁，这样可以树立专业、高效的形象。

2.3　环境

- 在办公室外贴标牌，以方便他人找。
- 在接待室或等候室贴标牌。
- 在所有其他办公室的门上贴标牌，以便他人很容易地找到准确的位置。
- 确保你为需要等待的人放置了座椅。
- 装饰接待区，使其舒适和受欢迎。
- 放杂志、书籍或小册子于等候区以供人阅读。
- 给人们提供咖啡或茶。如果可以的话，提供这些饮品或在等候区放一壶水和水杯。

3. 如何处理电话

处理电话的方式与接待访客的方式一样。

3.1　接听电话时说什么

- 接听电话的最好方式是说：“您好，这里是 ×× 组织，我能为你做点什么吗？”
- 如果需要帮某人接通电话，则说：“请稍等，我正在帮你接通电话。”
- 如果占线，则说：“他或她正在通话，您愿意等一下呢还是要我捎个话呢？”

3.2　接听电话的规则

- 始终保持礼貌和热情的态度。
- 尽量使你的通话简短，而且听起来有礼有节，很从容。
- 务必要知道电话系统可以使用所有的设施。
- 不要让电话铃响超过三次，这可能会让人觉得你不在那里。

3.3　接听电话的技巧

- 有条理。随时把所有的东西放在身边，如笔、桌子垫、留言本等等。了解工作动态。如果询问的问题总是相同的，应确保手头有资料。

- 站在组织的角度，决定你是否应该问“请问您是哪位？”这样的问题。接听电话时是否可以询问对方的身份，或只是帮对方接通电话，组织内应该就这个问题加以讨论。在某些办公室里，这可能是一个问题。但如果你负责筛查电话的话，这便完全不是一个问题。
- 询问对方是否需要帮助或他们的来电事由。用心倾听，并让来电者意识到这一点。当你在电话中倾听他人时，不要打断他人讲话。
- 当转接电话时，不要让对方等太久。如果被叫者忙，则回到与来电者的通话状态，并问他是否要留言。向他或她保证你会将消息转给当事人。
- 留言时，记得每次将留言信息再读给来电者听，确保你已记录下正确的信息，特别是电话号码。感谢来电者。不要对着来电者的耳朵猛摔听筒。
- 设置合理的信息传递系统。如果一条消息没有传递成功，而来电好像又很急，那么给来电者打电话解释并问他你是否能提供一些帮助。

课文B　接待访客

如何接待访客是秘书工作中最重要的一个方面。她不仅像接待人员一样反映了公司的公共关系形象，还反映了主管的个人形象。无论访客的身份是否重要，她都以体贴周到的态度予以接待，从而秘书成了一个为主管和公司建立良好商誉的关键性人物。

1. 在办公桌前吸烟

大多数现代化办公室里是允许在办公桌前吸烟的。但由于吸烟是很多人反对的不良习惯，所以如果你吸烟，那么应当谨慎。当访客走近你的办公桌，而你却正在吸烟时，那么和访客交谈时，务必把香烟熄灭或放入你办公桌旁边的烟灰缸里。在你和访客谈话时，一定不要吸烟。

不要把点燃的香烟放在除烟灰缸以外的任何地方。如果你将香烟放在桌子和柜子的边上，其结果是留下难看的烧痕。

2. 站起来迎接访客

除非看不见你的办公桌，否则，作为秘书，你必须站起来迎接访客，这样做标志着友好和尊重。

3. 当访客有预约时

如果主管有空，秘书则可以通过对讲机说“某某先生已到，10:30 想见你”。然而，如果主管正在接待其他访客或正在打电话，秘书则需在他面前放一张纸条提示他，某某先生已经来了，正在等他。如果已在主管办公室的人是同事、私人朋友或亲戚，秘书则可以在对讲机上告知有访客来访，不需要使用纸条说明。

如果一位主管不能立即结束手头上的事情，或已延误了预约的会面时间，那么礼貌的做法是他应当走出办公室去招呼那个正等着他会面的人，并解释他只需要再用一两分钟就能完成手头上的事情。如果这位主管没有或不能执行这一礼节性的做法，秘书可以微笑地向等待的访客做出相同的解释。

4. 当主管不在办公室时

有时，主管正好在访客到来之前被叫走，离开了办公室。这时，秘书应该替她的主管向访客道歉，并解释情况。

你可以说："早上好，斯迈思先生。十分钟前，由于一个生产问题，罗杰斯先生去了工厂。他现在随时可能回来。您愿意等吗？"

如果由于意外紧急情况，主管不得不离开办公室较长时间，你可以这样解释：

"早上好，斯迈思先生。我很抱歉，但董事会主席的办公室打电话来叫走了罗杰斯先生。我不知道他什么时候回来。我想联系您，但您的办公室说您已经离开了。您愿意等吗？"然后，访客可以决定是否等待、稍后再来、另外预约，或者甚至与其他相关的人会面，如主管的助理（如果他有话）。

5. 当访客必须等时

如果访客必须等，秘书可先请他坐下，然后继续进行自己的工作。如果访客特别重要，秘书则可以问问如何能帮助他。但秘书不用努力去"招待"等待中的访客，只需要像接待人员那样和他们愉快地闲谈。如果访客向秘书直接提出有关业务方面的问题，她要巧妙地回避这些问题，装着对该话题一无所知，或转换谈话主题，如果需要的话。

当秘书告知前台接待员某位访客必须等时，她应该礼貌地走到接待室，向访客解释延误的原因。如果秘书做不到的话（例如她正忙于做口授记录），前台接待员将不得不解释延误情况。当主管准备好见访客时，秘书可以打电话给接待员，让她请访客进来，或者秘书自己去接待室，亲自护送访客过去。

6. 通报访客的到来

如果被告知即刻将访客请进去，秘书可以做两件中的任意一件事。如果访客是老板认识的人，而且他以前来过办公室，秘书可以向他点头示意，并说一些话，大意是，"迈克尔斯先生现在有空，您现在就去见他，好吗？"然而，如果访客第一次来，或者他不经常来，秘书应该陪他到老板办公室的门口，开门（如果门是关着的），让到一边，并说："迈克尔斯先生，罗杰斯先生来了。"

当在商务办公室通报老年人、贵宾或女士的到来时，被认为适当的方式是先提及访客的名字。比如，一位教会显要人物来访，礼貌的通报方式是："迈克尔斯先生，McLaughlin主教来了。"

主管的家属可以不用通报直接进办公室，除非有访客在办公室。在这种情况下，秘书可以立即用对讲机通报他们的到来。

7. 取消预约

有时也有理由取消预约，但不能轻率地取消预约。只有当一个绝对必要的问题需要处理时，预约取消才是情有可原的。

如果主管被叫走，并且他知道不能及时赴约，他的秘书应该致电给和主管预约好的那个人，向他说明情况，并主动安排另一次预约时间。

如果你需要打电话改变约定时间，应尽可能友好。自我介绍后，你或许可以说："很抱歉不得不请求您一件事情。Springer 先生可否今天下午三点而不是两点去迈克尔斯先生的办公室呢？我们公司的总裁已邀请迈克尔斯先生参加一个非常重要的午餐会，这个会可能会一直持续到下午两点以后。”

8. 当主管赴约晚点时

如果主管晚点太久，你最好试着取消他的另一个预约，这样他就能赶上。接下来，你最好向他说明，他必须弥补上晚点的时间，并让他缩短接下来的一两个约见时间。如果他同意，你就告诉他每个预约具体分配的时间。

9. 当访客在场需打断时

如果在某个特定的时间安排有一次会议，而会议时间就快到了，访客还在主管的办公室，这时秘书可以进办公室，为打断致歉，并提醒他即将还有另一个约见。约见的时间不必提及。口头提醒要比纸条提示更好，因为这时访客知道他应该告辞了。

留够时间让你的老板从容地结束他与访客的谈话，并能及时地赴约。

10. 当主管不想见这位访客时

当你确定主管对见某个人不感兴趣时，你需要礼貌但明确地拒绝访客。你可以这样说：

“格雷先生，我希望我能帮助您，但是现在迈克尔斯先生只见那些与新项目有直接关联的人员。他处理这些事务需要一段时间，我想你最好通过书信的方式联系他。”

有些人有天赋，他们能拒绝别人，但又能使被拒绝的人感到很荣幸，而不是被拒绝。试着通过热心地对待甚至讨厌的访客来培养这种接待方式。而不要试图用一种不愉快、粗鲁的方式来体现自己的优越。

11. 当访客是办公室人员时

现在许多主管坚守对公司员工“敞开大门”的政策。当然，同一级别的管理人员可以随意走动，除非这位主管有非公司成员的访客。当低级别的员工表明要见你的主管时，你要先弄清楚原因。有时你可以阻止某人绕过他的顶头上司直接去找你的主管，从而避免造成不良感觉，或者你可以向他说明你的主管并不是解决这个问题的适当人选。如果你觉得这个问题值得你的主管去关注，请为该员工预约，并向你的主管解释这个问题，这样他就会对可能要发生的事情有一些概念。

如果这名员工不愿告诉你他的问题，不要拒绝为他安排预约，因为你可能是一个局外人。为他安排预约并告知你的主管，新来的年轻推销员查尔斯•科尔，或者收发室的约翰•怀特请求见他，但不愿意告诉你事由。

公司员工无论什么时候来汇报紧急工作情况，秘书都可以打扰她的主管。

12. 当访客没有预约时

在大多数情况下，如何接待没有预约的访客都是由秘书来决定的，因为她知道主管的业务需要和他的日程表。秘书的工作就是保护她的主管不受不必要的干扰。

首先，秘书必须弄清楚访客的需求。如果他不主动说明来意的话，她必须有礼貌地提出要求。

如果觉得主管想接见访客，秘书可以让访客稍等，然后亲自去老板办公室（除非他已通过电话或对讲机告诉过她该如何处理这种情况）。她向主管递上访客的名片，陈述来访事由。如果主管那里有其他人，无论是公司的员工还是其他访客，她必须等到他空下来时才去打扰他。当然，没有预约的访客通常要等待。

主管或许现在有空，同意见访客，但如果他马上还有预约，秘书应该提醒他，说："十分钟后，格兰特先生三点钟有约。"这样，格兰特先生一到，她就告知老板。

当没有预约的访客拒绝表明他们的来意时，秘书可以礼貌地要求他们写信预约。她可以说："除非我知道你想跟迈克尔斯先生讨论的问题，否则我不能通告你的到来。这是迈克尔斯先生制定的一项规定。我建议你给他写信，告诉他你找他的事由，并请求预约。"如果对方坚持要见主管，秘书应该态度坚决但有礼貌地予以接待。

如果老板有助理，秘书通常将陌生的和不请自来的访客交由他接待；或者让访客去找公司里的另一个人。

她可能会说："我认为我们会计部的格雷先生会比迈克尔斯先生更熟悉你的问题。你介意我打电话给格雷先生的秘书，看看他现在能不能见你吗？"

如果能立即安排会面，她应该明确告诉访客到格雷先生办公室的路该怎样走，或者亲自陪访客到那里。如果格雷先生不能马上接见对方，需要另外安排时间，秘书会把这一信息传给他，并告诉他日期和时间。

Unit 5

Communication

Part One Dialogues

Sample Dialogue 1

Situation ▶ Chen Li is calling to confirm merchandise with Mr. Green.

(A—Chen Li, Mr. Black's secretary from Global Trade Company; B—Mr. Green, the supplier)

A: Good afternoon. May I speak to Mr. Green, please?

B: Yes. This is Mr. Green speaking.

A: Mr. Green, this is Chen Li, Mr. Black's secretary from Global Trade Company. Mr. Black asked me to call you confirming whether we can receive fifteen cartons of cotton tomorrow. He is on a business trip to Singapore now.

B: Surely. I've asked my secretary to send a fax message about this yesterday.

A: Oh, really? But I'm sorry, Mr. Green. We haven't received any fax messages about this issue up to now.

B: Oh, really? Please hold a moment! Let me check if the secretary has sent the fax message.

A: Ok, please.

B: Oh! My new secretary have sent the fax massage to another customer by mistake. I'm really sorry about that. But don't worry. I'll sent you a fax message about this issue right now.

A: OK. Thank you, Mr. Green.

B: Miss Chen, please tell Mr. Black that everything is on schedule. And I will visit your company some time next week and make an apology to him in person.

A: OK. I will tell him as soon as he gets back. Good-bye.

Sample Dialogue 2

Situation ▶ Chen Li is calling to cancel Mr. Black's appointment with Mr. Green.

(A—Chen Li, Mr. Black's secretary from Global Trade Company; B—Mr. Green, the supplier)

A: Good morning. May I speak to Mr. Green, please?

B: This is Mr. Green speaking. Who is that calling, please?

A: Hello, Mr. Green. This is Chen Li, Mr. Black's secretary. Mr. Black wanted me to tell you that he couldn't meet you on Tuesday. Because his wife is going to deliver a baby, he'll have to go to the hospital.

B: Oh, please sent my congratulations to him. Then, could I fix another appointment to meet him next week ?

A: I'll check Mr. Black's schedule and see if I could arrange another appointment for you. Hold on a minute, please. Yes, Mr. Black seems to have some time on Monday morning and Thursday afternoon.

B: Then, will he be free the coming Monday at 10 in the morning?

A: Would 10:30 be convenient for you?

B: Yes. That'll be okay.

A: Well. I'll make a note of that. I'll confirm with you again tomorrow.

B: Thank you, Miss Chen. Good-bye.

Useful Expressions

1. Good afternoon. May I speak to Mr. Green, please?
   下午好，我想与格林先生通话，可以吗?
2. Mr. Black asked me to call you confirming whether we can receive fifteen cartons of cotton tomorrow.
   布莱克先生要我打电话给你，想确定我们明天是否可以收到那 15 箱棉花。
3. He is on a business trip to Singapore now.
   他现在去新加坡出差了。
4. Surely. I've asked my secretary to send a fax message about this yesterday.
   当然，昨天我已经让秘书发传真告知他这件事了。
5. We haven't received any fax messages about this issue up to now.

到目前为止，我们并没有收到任何有关那批货的传真消息。

6. My new secretary have sent the fax massage to another customer by mistake.
   我的新秘书错误地将传真信息发给了另一位客户。
7. And I will visit your company some time next week and make an apology to him in person.
   我会在下周某个时候拜访贵公司，亲自向他道歉。
8. Then, could I fix another appointment to meet him next week ?
   那么，我可以再约他下周见面吗?
9. I'll check Mr. Black's schedule and see if I could arrange another appointment for you.
   我来查看一下布莱克先的日程安排，看看是否能再给你预约。
10. I'll confirm with you again tomorrow.
    我明天会再打电话与你确认。

Situational Dialogues

Using the Sample Dialogue as a model, try to create a new dialogue with your partner.

Situation 1 ▶ Chen Hong, a secretary in a company, is calling to Mr. Brown, a supplier, confirming whether her company can receive 20 cartons of merchandise.

Situation 2 ▶ Mary, a secretary in a company, is calling to Mr. David, a supplier, canceling her boss' appointment with Mr. David.

Part Two Text A

Telephone Communication

The telephone supports business operation, socialization and global interaction by offering a way for business to communicate without delays between messages. The invention of the telephone offered an instantaneous form of communication that spawned other valuable communication tools, such as the Internet and cellular phones. The telephone is important for its ability to reduce the distance users need to communicate.

In any business or company, the telephone is its most important link with its customers. A telephone call is very often the first contact a potential customer has with a business; the attitude that the caller takes toward the company is often directly related to the tone of a first phone call. The telephone is also used for the day-to-day running of virtually every business, and during its periodic rush season, there are days when the telephone rings insistently. Orders are taken, progress is checked, suppliers are contracted, advice is requested and given, and complaints are heard-all over the telephone.

Compared with writing letters, using the telephone for company business has two advantages: the telephone is less expensive, and the telephone projects a live voice, a real person, who can both listen and respond to a situation.

1. Importance of Telephone Communication

Although today's businesses have other options, such as digital communication through e-mail, texting and social media and telephone communication may be slower than its new-media counterparts, it still has benefits in an increasingly impersonal world. The business call is still an important business component.

1.1 Personal and Immediate

Short of talking with someone face-to-face, a phone call is the best way to get a personal response. If the person you called is available, you can take care of business on the spot. With other forms of communication, such as texting or e-mail, you leave a message and hope for a quick response. Phone calls have a vocal backup in the form of voice mail. The caller can leave a detailed voice message, without the restriction of a certain number of characters or typing a text message on a tiny cell-phone keypad.

1.2 Effective

Dr. Albert Mehrabian's 1967 study, "Inference of Attitudes from Nonverbal Communication in Two Channels," named three components of effective communications: body language accounts for 55 percent, voice tone for 38 percent and spoken words for 7 percent. On the telephone, voice tone give dimension and emotion to words, increasing the effectiveness of the communication. Certain body language, such as smiling and standing while talking, may come through in the conversation. Texting and emails are simply words open to interpretation by the receiver, without the benefit of voice tone or body language.

1.3 Interactive

Teleconferencing calls bring people together from all over the organization at a fraction of the cost of travel and meeting facilities. Attendees can phone in using a toll-free number and access code to join a virtual conference room where members can interact with the moderator and other members. Conference calls can be used in conjunction with video conferencing to view presentations, ask questions via the Internet and discuss answers with all attendees.

1.4 Confidential

Some communications, such as condolences, disciplinary issues, sensitive and confidential issues, should be handled with a personal phone call. Taking the time to make a phone call carries more weight than an impersonal text or e-mail. Without the opportunity for two-way communication, sensitive issues may be misinterpreted. Text messages and emails become legal documents and can be retrieved as evidence long after deletion. Some businesses monitor and record phone conversations between employees and customers for training purposes. Deleted voice-mail messages may not be retrieved and do not leave a record of the conversation.

1.5 Safe

Making phone calls while driving may be hazardous, but Bluetooth technology makes hands-free dialing and conversation safe—freeing up travel time to provide availability for business calls. Texting and emailing while driving are hazardous and, in some states, illegal.

2. Making Business Call

While it may be more convenient to contact someone by using more modern technology, such as e-mail or text messaging, the telephone is still a more personal means of communication. Although the other party can't see your face, your voice can still convey a sense of professionalism and authority. To help you make the most effective business call possible, following a few basic steps can be of help.

2.1 Prepare

Take a moment to prepare before you pick up the phone. Write down the key points you need to cover during the conversation, as well as any questions you need to ask. This will also serve as an outline to help guide you through the call while maintaining control of the conversation. If possible, be close to a computer with Internet connection so that you can access your company's website or locate information quickly.

2.2 Identify Yourself

Always identify yourself to the party that answers the phone. To sound as professional as possible, give your first and last name as well as your title if applicable. If your call will be lengthy and you sense that the person you're calling is pressed for time or otherwise distracted, try to set a better time when you can call back.

2.3 Identify Purpose

You can exchange pleasantries, such as a brief "How are you today?" but don't get involved in an extended conversation about sports or the weather, as this can serve as a distraction from the purpose of your call. State the purpose politely and directly, such as, "I received your e-mail this morning and I'm calling to follow up."

2.4 Take Time to Listen

While you may be intent on achieving the purpose of your call, be sure that you engage in a two-sided conversation. Give the other party time to respond to your points and ask any questions they may have. Be careful not to interrupt unless you discover that the other party is drifting from the topic at hand. If this occurs, interrupt politely by saying, "I'm sorry to interrupt, but another question just popped into my mind and I want to ask it before I forget."

2.5 Review Call

Before hanging up, review what was accomplished during the call with the other party and be sure you both agree on what should happen next. If additional communication is required, set up a specific day and time for a follow-up phone call or other method of communication such as e-mail. Always part on a pleasant note, even if the end result of the call is that a business relationship won't occur or continue at present. You may want to revisit the relationship at some point in the future.

3. Answering incoming business calls

There are a few vital points which need to be paid attention to when you are answering incoming business calls.

3.1 Screening Calls

Most executive appreciate having their secretaries screen calls. Quite often you can take care of the matter and save your boss' time. An excellent technique is to ask, in a friendly and polite voice, "May I tell Mr. XX who is calling?" Most callers will give you their name as well as the reason for the call. If a person is calling to make an appointment for a personal interview, it is particularly important to learn the purpose or business to be transacted.

3.2 Taking Messages

In the age of cell phones, knowing how to take messages is still useful when you're working in an office or taking calls for your boss who will not always be in the office. The person on the other end asks for your immediate supervisor or co-worker who is not at his/her desk. The first thing you should do is to say, "He/she isn't here at the moment. Can I take a message?" Assuming they say yes, you are supposed to write down everything they say. You may not think what they say is important but the person you are writing the message for might think it counts. Finally, give the message to the person as soon as possible or leave it somewhere they will find it.

It's worth noting that you should have a standardized form for these messages, preferably printed on colored paper so they will be eye-catching. Your company may have constructed such a form for its particular purpose; if not, there are generally forms of this type available in any good office supply or stationery store.

3.3 Transferring Calls

You will often need to transfer a phone call to another extension in the company for very legitimate reasons. This procedure calls for tact and competence, or the caller might get the impression that he is getting the "run-around". First tell the caller why you must transfer the call-perhaps the matter is taken care of in another department, or during your boss's absence, someone else is going to be transferred to, so that he will not think he is being cut off.

To signal your switchboard operator, press the receiver button firmly and slowly so that the operator will be sure to get the signal. When she answers, ask her to transfer the call, and give either the name of the person, the department, or the extension number desired.

3.4 Handling Simultaneous Calls

Occasionally you may find yourself in a "double or nothing" situation-where you have two or sometimes three phone extensions to take care of by yourself. You are talking on the phone, and one of the other extensions rings. The most courteous procedure is to permit the person to whom you are speaking to finish his sentence and then ask if he would object to holding the line for a minute while you answer another extension. Press your "hold" button and answer the second call with some comment which is similar to : "Mr. XX's office. I have a caller on another extension, please hold the line a minute." When you return to the first caller you may find that he will speed up the completion of his business call since he is aware of the "busy" situation in your office.

New Words

socialization [ˌsəuʃəlaiˈzeiʃən] *n.* 适应社会生活，社会化，社交，交际
delay [diˈlei] *vt.&n.* 耽搁，推迟，延误
spawn [spɔːn] *vt.* 产生，造成
tone [təun] *n.* 语气，音调，调子，色调
virtually [ˈvəːtjuəli] *adv.* 实际上，几乎
insistently [inˈsistəntli] *adv.* 坚持地
contract [ˈkɔntrækt] *n.* 合同，合约，契约 *v.* 订合同；缩短
complaint [kəmˈpleint] *n.* 抱怨，疾病，诉苦，控告，投诉
option [ˈɔpʃən] *n.* 选择权，可选物
digital [ˈdidʒitl] *adj.* 数字的，数码的
text [tekst] *vt.* 发送短信息
counterpart [ˈkauntəpɑːt] *n.* 职务相当的人；对应物
impersonal [imˈpəːsənl] *adj.* 不受个人感情影响的，冷淡的，没有人情味的
component [kəmˈpəunənt] *n.* 零部件，元件，组成部分，成分
personal [ˈpəːsənl] *adj.* 私人的，个人的
immediate [iˈmiːdjət] *adj.* 直接的，立即的，目前的
response [risˈpɔns] *n.* 反应，回答，响应，答复
restriction [risˈtrikʃən] *n.* 限制，约束
tiny [ˈtaini] *adj.* 极小的，微小的
keypad [ˈkiːpæd] *n.*［计算机］小键盘
nonverbal [ˈnɔnˈvəːbəl] *adj.* 非言语的，不用语言的
dimension [diˈmenʃən] *n.* 尺寸，维度，范围，方面
teleconference [ˈtelikɔnfərəns] *n.* 电话会议
attendee [ætenˈdiː] *n.* 出席者，在场者
toll-free [təul-friː] *adj.* 免电话费的
virtual [ˈvəːtjuəl] *adj.* 实质的；［计］虚拟的
condolences [kənˈdəuləns] *n.* 哀悼，吊唁，慰问
disciplinary [ˈdisiplinəri] *adj.* 规律的，训诫的，惩戒的，纪律的
sensitive [ˈsensitiv] *adj.* 灵敏的，敏感的；易受伤害的
misinterpret [ˈmisinˈtəːprit] *v.* 误解
retrieve [riˈtriːv] *vt.* 恢复，挽回，取回
deletion [diˈliːʃən] *n.* 删除
hazardous [ˈhæzədəs] *adj.* 危险的，冒险的，碰运气的
convey [kənˈvei] *vt.* 表达，传达，运输，转移
professionalism [prəˈfeʃənəˌlizəm] *n.* 职业水准或特性，职业化
authority [ɔːˈθɔriti] *n.* 权力，官方，当局，职权，权威
connection [kəˈnekʃən] *n.* 联系，关系，连接，亲戚
identify [aiˈdentifai] *vt.* 鉴定，识别，辨认出
applicable [ˈæplikəbl] *adj.* 合适的，适用的，可应用的
distract [disˈtrækt] *vt.* 分散，转移，分心，困扰
pleasantries [ˈplezəntri] *n.* 幽默，开玩笑，客气话
interrupt [ˌintəˈrʌpt] *v.* 打断，打扰，中断，阻碍
drift [drift] *v.* 漂流，漂移，偏离
accomplish [əˈkɔmpliʃ] *vt.* 完成，实现

occur [ə'kəː] *vi.* 发生，存在，出现，想到
appreciate [ə'priːʃieit] *vt.* 欣赏,赏识，感激，领会，意识到
transact [træn'zækt] *v.* 办理，交易，谈判，进行
eye-catching [ai-'kætʃiŋ] *adj.* 引人注目的，耀眼的
particular [pə'tikjulə] *adj.* 特定的；特别的，挑剔的
extension [iks'tenʃən] *n.* 电话分机
legitimate [li'dʒitimit] *adj.* 合法的，正当的，合理的
tact [tækt] *n.* 机智，手法
competence ['kɔmpətəns] *n.* 能力，胜任，管辖权
run-around [rʌn-ə'raund] *n.* 遁词，借口
signal ['signl] *v.*(发信号)通知，表示
switchboard ['switʃˌbɔːd] *n.* 电话总机
simultaneous [ˌsiməl'teinjəs] *adj.* 同时发生的，同步的
courteous ['kəːtjəs] *adj.* 有礼貌的，客气的，谦恭的
completion [kəm'pliːʃən] *n.* 完成，结束

Phrases and Expressions

global interaction 全球性互动
cellular phone 便携式电话，手机
communication tool 通信工具
have contact with 接触到，和……有联系
take an attitude 采取一种态度
be related to 与……有关
rush season 旺季，忙季
compared with 与……比较
respond to 响应，对……起反应
digital communication 数字通信系统
social media 社交媒体
be short of 除……之外；缺少，不够
on the spot 当场，在现场；马上
leave a message 留个口信
vocal backup 声音备份
voice mail 语音邮件
voice message 语音信息
be open to 对……开放的，易受……的
a fraction of 一小部分，少许
in conjunction with 连同，共同，与……协力
carry weight 有分量，有影响
bluetooth technology 蓝牙技术
be pressed for time 时间紧迫
call back 回电话
get involved in 参与，被卷入
be intent on 对……一心一意
achieve the purpose 达到目的
pop into mind 突然出现在头脑里
hang up 挂断，悬挂，搁置
agree on 对……意见一致
at some point 在某一时刻，在某一点上
incoming call 来电
make an appointment 预约，约会
take message 记录留言
be supposed to 应该
object to 反对
speed up 加快速度

Notes

1 The attitude that the caller takes toward the company is often directly related to the tone of a first phone call.

本句中，that the caller takes toward the company 是由关系连词 that 引导的定语从句，修饰限定先行词 the attitude。短语 take the attitude of 的意思是"采取……态度"。请看下例：

On the question of anti-corruption, we take the attitude of making firm and unremitting effort.

我们在反腐败问题上的态度是：坚定不移，坚持不懈。

另外，句中短语 be related to 意为"与……有关的"。请看下例：

Human biological rhythms are related to the natural cycle of day and night.

人的生物节奏与昼夜的自然循环有关。

2 Compared with writing letters, using the telephone for company business has two advantages.

本句中，compared with writing letters 是过去分词短语，在整句中作状语，逻辑主语是 using the telephone。

英语中，动词过去分词作状语可表示原因、时间、条件、方式或伴随。请看下例：

Filled with hopes and fears, he dived deep into the ocean.

心中充满了希望与恐惧，他跳进了深海里。

另外，句中 using the telephone 是动名词短语在全句中作主语。请看下例：

Driving a car during the rush hour is tiring.

在高峰时刻开车令人厌烦。

3 Attendees can phone in using a toll-free number and access code to join a virtual conference room where members can interact with the moderator and other members.

本句中，using a toll-free number and access code 是现在分词短语作谓语动词 phone in 的方式状语。where members can interact with the moderator and other members 是关系副词 where 引导的定语从句，修饰限定先行词 conference room。

英语中，where 既可以引导定语从句，也可以引导地点状语从句。请看下例：

Where there is a will, there is a way.（地点状语从句）

［谚语］有志者事竟成。

The bookshop where I bought this book is not far from here.（定语从句）

我买书的那家书店离这儿不远。

4 To sound as professional as possible, give your first and last name as well as your title if applicable.

本句中，if applicable 是 if it is applicable 的省略表达，表示"如果合适的话"。

英语中，类似的省略语表达有 if necessary（如果必要的话）；if possible（如果可能的话）等。请看下例：

If necessary they will go to the authorities themselves to press the demand.

如果必要，他们将自己去找当局，敦促他们接受这项要求。

另外，句中 as... as possible 为固定表达，意为"尽可能……的"。请看下例：

We should avoid confrontation as much as possible.

我们应该尽量避免正面冲突。

5 Before hanging up, review what was accomplished during the call with the other party and be sure you both agree on what should happen next.

本句中，what was accomplished 和 what should happen next 均为 what 引导的名词性从句在句中分别作 review 和 agree on 的宾语。请看下例：

He gave a description of what he had seen.

他描述了他所见到的一切。

另外，本句中 before 一词被用作介词，和动名词 hanging up 一起构成时间状语。请看下例：

The clerk marked up his daybook before going home.

办事员在回家前记好当天的日记账。

6 Assuming they say yes, you are supposed to write down everything they say.

本句中，assuming they say yes 是 assuming 引导的条件状语从句，其中省略了 that, assuming that... 意为"假定；如果；假设"。请看下例：

Assuming that he is innocent, he must be set free.

假使他是无罪的，就应当释放他。

Exercises

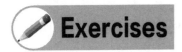

EX. 1 Answer the following questions.

1. How does the telephone support business operation, socialization and global interaction ?
2. Compared with writing letters, what are the two advantages of using the telephone for company business?
3. Why is a phone call personal and immediate according to Text A?
4. How can a phone call increase the effectiveness of the communication?
5. What kind of issues should be handled with a personal phone call?
6. How should you identify yourself to the party that answers the phone?
7. How are you supposed to review the call before hanging up?
8. What is worth noting if you are taking messages?
9. If you have no tact and competence in transferring calls, what impression might the caller get?
10. What are the most courteous procedure of handling simultaneous calls?

EX. 2 Complete the following sentences with appropriate words or expressions in the box.

contract	virtual	courteous	complaint	component
potential	pop into mind	applicable	assume	account for

1. The sales manager was in arrogance to ________ she would win every time.

2. Western notions of human rights are not necessarily ________ in other societies.
3. Petrochemicals today ________ one fourth of all the chemicals made, in ten years this amount is expected to double.
4. No doubt this is a side effect of using the disk as a ________ memory.
5. Salesmen should seize every opportunity to make contact with ________ customers.
6. The processing and assembling business is a ________ part of our foreign trade.
7. In case you do not carry out the ________, we'll have to cancel it.
8. The policeman was suspended while the ________ against him was investigated.
9. When you hear the term, "computer geek," what image immediately ________?
10. As a level-headed ambassador for her organization, a secretary must be ________ to all visitors, of whatever age.

EX. 3 **Translate the following sentences into English.**

1. 我公司的行政秘书已经通过电话联系了贵公司的代表。（have contact with）
2. 我们的价格和国际市场的价格相比还是合理的。（compared with）
3. 用社交媒体来宣传的目的是让你的生意人性化并与粉丝们建立情感联系。（social media）
4. 如果我不在，请在答录机中留言。（leave a message）
5. 无法否认那位主管与贪污案件有牵连这一事实。（get involved in）
6. 他一心一意想得到晋升，谁也阻止不了他成为一名行政助理。（be intent on）
7. 新研制的计算机和数字化通信技术能够使任何人都能够自由通信联络。（digital communication）
8. 我想预约贵公司的总经理商量事情。（make an appointment）
9. 秘书需要操作总机，接听公司来电，记录留言。（take messages）
10. 考虑到我们的长期业务关系，我们不反对再次与贵方洽谈。（object to）

EX. 4 **Translate the following passage into Chinese.**

A good secretary is the hub of the office that keeps all of the spokes in place and everything moving forward on the right path. Organization skills, attention to detail and computer and office equipment proficiency are important abilities. However, being able to communicate in writing, speech, and face-to-face situations is critical for being a successful secretary.

Secretaries are often the first point of contact for their departments, and commonly play the role of gatekeeper. As a secretary, you must be polite and discern the nature of each call or request so it gets routed to the proper person. This requires tact and proficiency, as you may need to solicit information to help a caller or visitor properly. Furthermore, as a level-headed ambassador, a secretary needs to be able to act with diplomacy and get along with diverse individuals. You will be building relationships with other departments and people from all levels—from board chairpersons to cleaning staff. You need to be prepared to bear the brunt of frustrations from irate callers, or an unsatisfied customer or investor, while maintaining a professional demeanor.

Part Three Text B

Telephone Skills

1. Importance of Telephone Skills

Telephones are the core of interpersonal business communications. Every day, telephones are used to confirm orders, schedule meetings, answer questions, and discuss various business issues. Therefore, good telephone skills are essential for employees and managers at every level of an organization.

1.1 Telephone Skills Affect the Company Image

An individual who answers a business telephone reflects the image of the company. Outside parties, such as customers and vendors, develop their first impression of the organization within seconds of a call being answered.

This first impression will influence a caller's attitude toward the entire company and set the tone for all future interactions. Therefore, a company's image is enhanced by the professional telephone skills of its employees.

1.2 Telephone Skills Help Provide Efficient Service

Customers expect efficient service and will take their business to a competitor if they are not satisfied. Questions need to be answered in a timely manner, messages must be taken properly, and calls must be forwarded to the correct department in order to provide quality service.

Only by using good telephone skills will you be able to provide customers with the quality of service they expect and deserve.

1.3 Telephone Skills Affect Time Management

In order to be effective, you must first be efficient. Therefore, you need to plan and organize your time so that you make high priority calls before calls of lesser importance. An example of a high priority call is one that authorizes others to begin a task.

By using effective telephone skills, you will be able to avoid spending more time than needed handling calls, and will therefore be able to use your time as productively as possible.

2. Basic Telephone Skills

Presenting a professional image, both in person and on the telephone, is very important in the Office Skills profession. Taking care of your customers over the telephone and making them feel well informed and appreciated is essential. Whether you are the front office receptionist or an executive secretary, the following telephone skills should always be followed.

2.1 Display a Professional Attitude

You enhance your professionalism when you display the following four characteristics during telephone calls:

- Assertiveness

An individual with an assertive attitude is firm but not demanding. They are clear and direct when communicating and assume they will be shown respect. You are more likely to have your request fulfilled when you state it in an assertive manner.

- Confidence

Your self-confidence will help reassure the other party that you and the information you are providing are reliable and can be trusted.

- Calmness

It is important to remain calm, regardless of the demeanor of the other party. Remaining calm allows you to think rationally and respond appropriately in all circumstances.

- Accuracy

The accuracy of the information you provide others influences your credibility, as well as that of your company. You should strive to confirm all information you receive or provide so that you have confidence in its accuracy.

2.2 Project a Positive Image to the Caller

Three basic factors affect the image you project on the telephone. You should strive to keep these in mind:

- Use clear diction, proper volume, and appropriate speed

Your words must be clear, distinct, and spoken at an appropriate volume and speed. Taking the time to enunciate your words clearly is more efficient and professional sounding than having to repeat yourself for the caller.

- Remember your posture

Posture is an important factor in telephone communication, even though the parties do not physically see each other. An individual who is sitting up straight will tend to sound businesslike and professional. However, a person slouched in a chair is more likely to project a careless demeanor.

- Never eat, drink, or chew gum

You should never eat, drink, or chew gum while you are using the telephone. These activities are rude, usually obvious to the other party, and give an unprofessional impression of you and your company.

2.3 Establish Rapport

Building rapport is the process of determining and building on what you have in common with the caller. There are three ways to build rapport with a caller:

- Use the caller's name

Occasionally, you should use the name of the caller during the conversation. Personalizing the call builds rapport and increases the caller's confidence in your desire to help them.

• Find common ground

When you are able to find common ground with the caller, you are more likely to build rapport with them. These small connections will demonstrate that you are working toward mutual goals.

• Match the caller's speaking rate

Matching the speaking rate of your caller is a subtle way of gaining and focusing the attention of the caller in order to build rapport. A person with a naturally slow rate of speech will tend to be suspicious of a fast speaking rate, and callers who speak more quickly can become very frustrated by a slow rate of speech.

2.4 Making a Good Impression

Callers appreciate a courteous response. The following four behaviors will enhance your ability to project a courteous image when you receive telephone calls:

• Answering promptly

All calls should be answered by the third ring. If you are unable to answer the telephone in this amount of time, your first words to the caller should be an apology. The caller does not always hear the same number of rings you do, so they may have heard five rings when you heard only four.

• Using appropriate identification

Answer all calls with the appropriate identification. If the only calls you receive are from within the company, you need to identify your department first and then yourself.

However, if you receive calls from customers, vendors, or other outside parties, you should begin your introduction by identifying the company first, and then the department and yourself.

• Using positive language

In general, positive words and messages are easy to understand and convey a strong image. They imply action and results, and instill confidence in the other party. A phrase such as, "She's away from her desk," is stronger than the negative, "She's not here." Negative phrases are more likely to be misunderstood.

• Being helpful

When you take a call for someone who is not available, offer the caller alternatives, such as holding, leaving a message, or calling back. Both the caller and the individual they are trying to reach will benefit when you are helpful, and the caller will appreciate your concern.

New Words

interpersonal [ˌintəˈpəːsənl] *adj.* 人与人之间的，人际关系的

schedule [ˈʃedjuːl] *vt.* 预定，安排，编制目录

reflect [riˈflekt] *v.* 反映，反射，反省，显示

enhance [inˈhaːns] *vt.* 提高，增加，加强

professional [prəˈfeʃənl] *adj.* 职业的，专业的，专门的
competitor [kəmˈpetitə] *n.* 竞争者，对手
deserve [diˈzəːv] *vt.* 应受，值得
assertive [əˈsəːtiv] *adj.* 断定的，自信的
demanding [diˈmaːndiŋ] *adj.* 要求多的，吃力的
fulfill [fulˈfil] *vt.* 完成，履行，执行，满足
reassure [riːəˈʃuə] *vt.* 使……安心，再保证；重拾（信心等）
rationally [ˈræʃənli] *adv.* 理性地
credibility [ˌkrediˈbiliti] *n.* 可信，确实性，可靠
diction [ˈdikʃən] *n.* 措辞；发音
posture [ˈpɔstʃə] *n.* 姿势，态度，情形
distinct [disˈtiŋkt] *adj.* 明显的，不同的，独特的
enunciate [iˈnʌnsieit] *v.* 清晰地发音，（清楚地）表达，阐述
businesslike [ˈbiznislaik] *adj.* 事务性的，公事公办的，有条理的，有效率的
slouch [slautʃ] *vi.* 懒散
personalize [ˈpəːsənəlaiz] *vt.* 个人化，私人化
subtle [ˈsʌtl] *adj.* 微妙的，敏锐的，不明显的
frustrate [frʌsˈtreit] *vt.* 挫败，击败，使沮丧，使灰心
identification [aiˌdentifiˈkeiʃən] *n.* 确认，鉴定，识别，身份的证明
apology [əˈpɔlədʒi] *n.* 道歉；辩解
negative [ˈnegətiv] *adj.* 否定的，消极的，负面的，负的
alternative [ɔːlˈtəːnətiv] *n.* 二者择一，供替代的选择
benefit [ˈbenifit] *n.* 利益；津贴；保险金；借助 *vt.* 有益于，得益
concern [kənˈsəːn] *n.* 关心，关心的事；忧虑，担心 *vt.* 涉及；影响；关心，（使）担心

Phrases and Expressions

set the tone 定基调
in a timely manner 及时地，按时地
present a professional image 展现出专业的形象
in person 亲自地
front office receptionist 前台接待员
display a professional attitude 显示出专业的态度
fulfill one's request 满足或实现某人的请求或要求
in all circumstances 在任何情况下
remain calm 保持沉着、冷静
project a positive image 树立一个正面形象
chew gum 咀嚼口香糖
at an appropriate speed 以适当的速度
even though 即使，尽管
tend to 倾向，易于
sit up straight 端坐，坐直
common ground 一致之处，共同点

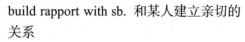

build rapport with sb. 和某人建立亲切的关系 mutual goal 共同的目标	be suspicious of 对……怀疑的 instill into 灌输

Exercises

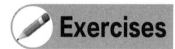

EX. 5 Answer the following questions.

1. What skills of the employees can enhance a company's image?
2. What will the customers do if they are not satisfied with a company's service?
3. Why do you need to plan and organize your time while handling telephones?
4. Why is self-confidence vital for a person to communicate by telephone?
5. Why do you need to remain calm while handling telephone calls?
6. How should you use your words in business calls ?
7. What are the ways to build rapport with a caller?
8. How should you begin your introduction if you receive calls from outside parties?
9. Why is it necessary to use positive words and messages in telephone communications?
10. What should you do if you take a call for someone who is not available?

Part Four Extended Reading

Text	Notes
Handling Difficult Callers	
You will likely encounter[1] situations in which communicating with the person on the other end of the line is somewhat challenging[2]. Being aware of the different types of difficult callers you may encounter will help you be prepared for such situations.	[1] *v.* 遭遇，遇到 [2] *adj.* 挑战性的，有吸引力的
1.Talkative[3] Callers Talkative callers tend to get off the subject and talk about irrelevant[4] issues. Although they can be enjoyable to speak with, these callers can waste time that could be spent more productively. You need to control conversations with talkative callers in order to prevent wasted time by following three steps:	[3] *adj.* 喜欢说话的，健谈的，多嘴的 [4] *adj.* 不恰当的，无关系的，不相干的
(1) Ask closed-ended[5] questions. Closed-ended questions which require, "yes" or "no" responses prevent the caller from providing you with more information than you need.	[5] *adj.* 有底的，封闭

(2) Keep your responses short. By limiting the length of your own responses, you will decrease the amount of unrelated discussion and keep the conversation directed toward the business at hand.

(3) Speed up your responses. Speaking slightly more quickly will help you shorten the amount of time between your responses and, therefore, give the caller less time to interrupt[6].

2. Indecisive[7] Callers

Sometimes you will encounter a caller who is not sure which department or individual they need to speak to, what information they need, or how to ask for a specific[8] service. Helping indecisive callers determine what they need is not only courteous, but saves the time that could be wasted waiting for them to make a decision. Follow four steps to guide indecisive callers:

(1) Listen to the caller. Being attentive[9] to the caller allows you to identify their needs.

(2) Ask specific questions. Ask the caller specific questions that will help pinpoint[10] their exact needs.

(3) Offer the caller options[11] . After you have identified the specific needs of the caller, offer them appropriate[12]options. However, do not offer more than two or three, or the caller will feel overwhelmed[13] with the choices.

(4) Recommend the best option. Help the caller choose the best option based on their needs by making a recommendation[14].

3. Demanding[15] Callers

Demanding callers are driven individuals who want results and do not care about the details of a situation. They focus on the bottom line and usually get to the point quickly. In order to handle demanding callers successfully, follow these guidelines:

(1) Be direct in your responses and use a strong and confident tone of voice.

(2) Interact[16] in a fast-paced manner to match the caller's need for quick results.

(3) Avoid engaging in non-business discussion, but remain friendly and courteous.

4. Callers Who Are Fast Talkers

When faced with a fast talker, wait for the caller to pause or take a breath. When they do, interject[17] by letting the caller know that you are having some difficulty understanding them. It is important not to use accusing[18] language, but instead approach[19] the situation by letting the caller know that in order to meet their needs, you need them to slow down.

[6] *v.* 打断，打扰，中断，阻碍

[7] *adj.* 犹豫不决的，非决定性的

[8] *adj.* 明确的，特殊的，具体的

[9] *adj.* 注意的，留意的

[10] *vt.* 精确地找到；使突出

[11] *n.* 选择权，可选物

[12] *adj.* 适当的，恰当的

[13] *vt.* 打击，压倒，淹没，打败

[14] 推荐

[15] *adj.* 要求多的，吃力的

[16] *v.* 相互作用，相互联系，相互影响，互动

[17] *v.* 插话，突然插入

[18] *adj.* 责难的，问罪的，归罪的

[19] *v.* 靠近，接近，接洽，要求，达到，动手处理

For example, avoid phrases such as, "Steve, slow down—I can't understand anything you're saying!" Use language that demonstrates[20] your desire to help the caller, such as, "Steve, I'm afraid I'm having some difficulty understanding you. Could you slow down just a bit so I can make sure I know what information you need?"	[20] *vt.* 证明，演示，示范
The same principle applies to[21] callers who speak softly and are difficult to hear. Politely let the caller know that you need them to speak up so you can understand them better. It is important that the caller not feel responsible for any communication problem.	[21] 适用于，运用于
5. Callers Who Are Slow Talkers	
Slow talkers are often indecisive individuals, so the most effective way to address[22] a slow talker is to guide the conversation by asking them what they need.	[22] *vt.* 处理
By asking a slow talker questions, you can speed up the conversation by prompting[23] them to provide you with the information you need to help them. Offering the slow talker a variety of options encourages them to make decisions and quickens the pace of[24] the conversation.	[23] *vt.* 激起，促进，推动，提示 [24] 加快步伐
For example, if a caller is slowly trying to tell you who they need to speak with, you can speed the conversation by asking a question that offers them options, such as, "Do you need to speak with our customer service department, or are you calling to place an order[25]?"	[25] 订货，定购
In addition, you may also want to take notes while speaking with a slow talker. Taking notes can help improve your concentration[26] during the conversation.	[26] *n.* 集中，专心，浓度
6. Callers with Foreign Accents[27]	[27] *n.* 口音
Given the diverse[28] nature of our society, you are likely to encounter a caller who speaks with a heavy foreign accent that may impair[29] your ability to understand them. To professionally handle these situations , follow these guidelines:	[28] *adj.* 不同的，多种多样的 [29] *vt.* 损害，削弱
Be patient. It is important not to rush through these calls. You will need to listen extra carefully to callers with foreign accents in order to identify what they need.	
Be honest. Don't pretend to understand the caller if you are not clear about something they said. Let the caller know that in order to help them you need them to slow down or repeat what they said.	
Be polite. When asking the caller to slow down or repeat what they said, do so in a tactful[30] and courteous manner.	[30] *adj.* 机智的，老练的
Be resourceful. If a caller's accent is so heavy that you know you cannot assist them, determine if a co-worker or supervisor is bilingual[31] in the caller's language and ask for their assistance.	[31] *adj.* 双语的

7. Callers Who Are Angry

A caller's anger represents an emotional response to a particular situation. You top priority[32] when faced with such situation is to stay calm while determining the real source of anger. There are five steps you should take when handling a situation with an angry caller.

[32] *n.* 优先权，优先，优先顺序

Step 1. Remain calm

You should always be patient and remain calm when dealing with an angry caller. Regardless of[33] how hot-tempered[34] or rude a caller becomes, you must stay relaxed and even-tempered[35].

A good way to maintain a friendly and professional attitude is by focusing on the positive aspects of the situation and telling the caller what you can do for them.

[33] 不管，不顾

[34] *adj.* 性急的，易怒的，暴躁的

[35] *adj.* 性情平和的，不易生气的

Step 2. Let the caller vent[36]

When the caller has a problem and is upset, he wants to express their feelings about the issue.

When a caller is venting, do not interrupt no matter how badly you may want to. Breaking in while the caller is venting will do nothing but further anger them. Allowing a caller to vent shows that you acknowledge[37] that there is a problem.

[36] *v.* 发泄，表达，排放

[37] *vt.* 承认，公认

Step 3. Express empathy[38]

Once you give the caller a chance to vent, you can begin to participate[39] more actively in the conversation. Sincerely expression your empathy about the caller's problem is the best way to calm them down. That does not mean that you have to agree with the caller, but appreciate[40] and understand their feelings.

[38] *n.* 移情作用，共鸣，[心]神入

[39] *v.* 参加，参与

[40] *vt.* 欣赏，赏识，感激

Step 4. Identify[41] what went wrong

Expressing understanding without developing a solution[42] is ineffective. After you empathize with[43] the caller, you should begin actively solving their problem by identifying what went wrong.

Ask questions that will help you clarify[44] the cause of the problem. Actively listen to the caller's answers and confirm that you understand them correctly by repeating the information back to them.

Repeating what the caller tells you allows you to double check the facts, verify[45] your understanding of the situation, and make sure you have adequate[46] information to solve the problem.

[41] *vt.* 鉴定，识别，辨认出，认出

[42] 找出解决办法

[43] 理解，同情

[44] *vt.* 澄清，阐明，净化

[45] *vt.* 核实，证明

[46] *adj.* 足够的，充足的

Step 5. Develop a solution

When you feel you have all of the facts surrounding[47] the situation , help the caller find a solution to their problem. Offer the individual a variety of options that will address their problem, and determine what option will give the caller the most satisfaction[48].

[47] *vt.* 包围，环绕

[48] *n.* 满意

参考译文

课文A 电话沟通

电话提供了一种信息不会延迟的沟通方式。它对业务运营、社交和全球互动起着支持性的作用。电话的发明提供了一种即时通信方式。这种通信方式还衍生了其他有价值的通信工具，如互联网和手机。所以，电话很重要，因为它能缩短沟通者的距离。

在任何企业或公司，电话都是与客户联系的最重要的环节。打电话通常是潜在客户与一家企业的第一次接触。打电话的人对这家公司的态度往往与第一次打电话的基调有直接的关系。电话也可以用于几乎所有的日常业务活动，在其周期性的旺季期间，有好多天电话都会一直响个不停。接订单、检查进展情况、和供应商签订合同、征求或给出意见、倾听投诉等所有业务都可通过电话完成。

与写信相比，使用电话处理公司业务有两个好处：电话比较便宜；电话能表现出真实的声音以及一个能听并能对某种情况做出反应的真实的人。

1. 电话沟通的重要性

虽然今天的企业有其他的沟通选择，如通过电子邮件、发送短消息和社交媒体进行沟通的数字通信方式，而且电话通信可能比新媒体慢，但它在一个越来越无人情味的客观世界中仍然大有好处。商务电话仍然是一项重要的业务内容。

1.1 人际性和即时性

除了面对面交谈以外，打电话是得到一个人亲自回复的最好方式。如果你呼叫的人有空，就可以马上处理业务。然而，如果用其他形式的沟通方式，如发送短消息或用电子邮件，则需要留下一个信息，并希望对方快速回复。电话中以语音信箱的形式可以对声音备份。打电话的人可以留一条详细的语音信息，不受字数的限制，并且无须在极小的手机键盘上编写短信。

1.2 有效性

Albert Mehrabian 博士在 1967 年的“根据两通道非言语交际进行态度推断”研究中将有效沟通的三个组成部分命名为：肢体语言（占 55%）、语音语调（占 38%）和口语语言（占 7%）。在电话中，语音语调赋予了话语的维度和情感，增加了沟通的有效性。某些肢体语言，如交谈时的微笑和站立，可能会体现在对话中。短信和电子邮件仅仅是一些可由接收者进行理解的简单话语，没有声音语调或肢体语言的好处。

1.3 交互性

电话会议以极少旅行费和会议设施费便可将组织的成员召集在一起。与会者可以拨打免费电话号码和接入编码加入一个虚拟会议室。在这里与会成员可以与会议主持人和其他成员进行互动。电话会议可以与视频会议结合使用，以便观看演示，通过互联网提出问题，并与所有与会者讨论解决问题的方案。

1.4 机密性

一些沟通，如吊唁慰问、纪律问题、敏感和机密问题，应该用个人电话来进行。花时间打电话比发一个没有人情味的短信或写一封电子邮件更有分量。没有机会进行双向沟通，敏感的问题可能会被误解。文本消息和电子邮件成为法律文件，即使被删除很久以后，也可以被检索成为证据。为了培训需要，一些企业监控和记录员工和客户之间的电话对话。被删除的语音邮件可能不会被检索，而且不会留下有关谈话的记录。

1.5 安全性

开车的时候打电话可能是危险的，但蓝牙技术提供了免提拨号和通话安全的技术支持，利用这些技术可以腾出旅行时间拨打商务电话。但是，开车的时候发短信和邮件是很危险的，而且在一些国家是非法的。

2. 打商务电话

虽然使用如电子邮件或发送短信等更为现代的技术，联系人可能会更方便，但是电话仍然是一个更具有人情味的通信手段。虽然对方看不见你的脸，但你的声音仍然可以传达专业性和权威性。为了让你能进行最有效的商务电话沟通，现提供以下几个可能有用的基本步骤。

2.1 准备工作

在你拿起电话之前花一些时间做准备工作。写下你在交谈中需要谈及的关键点，以及你需要问的问题。这些将作为大纲指导你完成整个通话，并掌控整个谈话。如果可能，靠近一台联网的电脑，这样你就可以快速访问你公司的网站或找到信息。

2.2 表明身份

总是把自己的身份告知接电话的人。为了听起来尽可能的专业，你需要介绍你的姓和名，以及你的头衔（如果有头衔的话）。如果你的电话可能持续很长时间，你感觉到对方时间紧迫或因为其他事务注意力分散，那么你要尽量确定更好的回拨时间。

2.3 明确目的

可以说一些客气话，如简短的问候“你今天好吗？”但是不要谈有关运动或天气这类广泛性话题，因为这样做可能会分散你的注意力，偏离打电话的目的。你应该直接礼貌地说出你的目的，如“今天上午我收到了你的电子邮件，我打电话来是想做进一步了解”。

2.4 花时间听

虽然你可能一心想达到打电话的目的，但是请注意你参与的是双边谈话。你应该给对方时间回答你的问题，并且如果他们有疑问就提出来。注意不要打断对方，除非你发现对方的谈话正在偏离当前的话题。如果发生这种情况，请礼貌地打断并说：“我很抱歉打断一下，但是有个问题刚刚突然出现在我脑海里，我想先问一下以免忘记。”

2.5 回顾电话内容

在挂电话之前，先回顾一下和对方的通话内容，确保双方就下一步该怎么做达成了一致意见。如果需要进一步的沟通，可设定特定的日期和时间、进行后续性的电话沟通或其他沟通方式，如电子邮件。注意每次结束电话时，尽量使用愉快的口气，即使这次电话沟通目前并没有使双方建立或推进业务关系。你可能想在将来的某个时候恢复这层关系。

3. 接听来电

在接听来电时，有几个关键点需要注意。

3.1 筛查来电

大多数行政人员喜欢让他们的秘书来筛查电话。通常，你可以处理这件事并节约你老板的时间。一个非常好的技巧是以友好且礼貌的声音问来电方，“我可以告诉X先生是谁打电话找他吗？”大多数用户会告诉你他们的名字，以及打电话的事由。如果有人打电话来预约面谈事宜的话，了解面谈的目的或洽谈的业务尤为重要。

3.2 记录留言

即使在手机时代，当你在办公室工作或替经常不在办公室的上司接电话时，知道该如何记录留言仍然是有用的。电话线另一端的人要求和你的直接主管或同事通电话，而他或她刚好没在办公。这时，你应该做的第一件事就是说，“他或她现在不在这里。我能替他或她捎个信吗？”如果他们说可以，你应该写下他们说的全部内容。你可能认为他们所说的内容并不重要，但最终接收消息的人可能会认为它非常重要。最后，将信息尽快给当事人或留在他们能找到的地方。

值得注意的是，记录留言时，你应该使用标准化的表格，最好打印在彩色纸上，这样它们比较醒目。公司可能已经编制了这种用于特殊目的的表格；如果没有的话，一般在好的办公用品店或文具店中都可以买到这种类型的表格。

3.3 转接电话

在公司里，你经常需要以非常合理的理由将一个电话转接到另一个分机上。这个程序需要机智和能力来完成，否则来电者可能会认为他被推诿了。首先，你应该告诉来电者你必须转接电话的原因——或许是因为这件事情是由另一个部门负责处理的，或许是因为你老板不在的情况下，电话需要转接到另一个人那里——这样打电话的人就不会认为他正在被断联。

要发送信号通知总机接线员，请稳稳地缓慢地按下“接收”按钮，这样接线员肯定能收到信号。当她接听时，请她转接电话，并给她提供相关的人名、部门名称和分机号。

3.4 处理同时来电

偶尔，你会发现你处于“来电数量翻倍或完全没有来电”的情形中。这种情形之下，你需要负责接听两个或有时三个电话分机。你正在打电话，而另一个分机又响了。这时，最有礼貌的做法是让那个正在和你通话的人说完他的话，然后问他是否愿意在你接听另一个分机的时候稍等一会儿。按下“稍候”按钮，然后接听第二个来电，并说一些类似的话：“这里是X先生的办公室。在另一个分机上，我还有个电话需要接听，请稍等一会儿。”当你返回去接听第一个来电时，你会发现对方会加速打完电话，因为他知道你办公室很忙。

课文B　电话沟通技巧

1. 电话沟通技巧的重要性

电话是人际关系商务沟通的核心。电话每天都用来确认订单、安排会议、回答问题、讨论各种业务问题。因此，掌握良好的电话沟通技巧对于组织各个级别的员工和管理人员都必不可少。

1.1　电话沟通技巧影响公司形象

接听商务电话的人能反映出公司的形象。公司外的人，如客户和供应商，在电话被接听的几秒钟内就可以对该公司形成第一印象。

这种第一印象会影响到来电者对整个公司的态度，并确定了以后相互交往的基调。因此，员工专业的电话沟通技巧可以提高公司的形象。

1.2　电话技巧有助于提供有效的服务

客户期望得到高效的服务，如果对服务不满意，他们会找别的公司做生意。为了提供优质服务，要做到及时回答问题，正确地记录留言，并将电话转接到合适的部门。

只有通过运用良好的电话沟通技巧，你才能够为客户提供他们想要的并且应该得到的优质服务。

1.3　电话沟通技巧影响时间管理

为了有效果，你必须首先有效率。因此，你需要计划和安排时间，这样你就能在打次要电话之前，先打重要电话，比如授权他人开始工作的电话便是应该先打的重要电话。

通过运用有效的电话沟通技巧，你能避免花更多不必要的时间来处理电话，从而可以尽可能高效地使用你的时间。

2. 基本的电话沟通技巧

个人自身和电话沟通都能呈现出专业的形象，这一点在办公室技能职业中非常重要。通过电话与客户交谈，让他们了解情况并感觉很受重视是必要的。无论你是前台接待员还是执行秘书，都应该遵循以下的电话沟通技巧。

2.1　展现专业态度

在通话过程中，当你表现出以下四个特点的时候，你就提高了你的专业水平：

• 果断

一个有主见的人坚定而不苛求。他们以明确直接的方式进行沟通，并且认为他们会受到尊重。当你以一种果断的方式来提出要求时，你更有可能使你的要求得到满足。

• 信心

你的自信将有助于向对方保证你本人以及你所提供的信息是可靠的、值得信赖的。

• 冷静

不管对方的行为如何，自己保持冷静是很重要的。保持冷静可以让你在任何情况下理性地思考并适当地做出反应。

• 准确

你提供给他人的信息是否准确影响到你和你公司的信誉。你应该设法确认你收到的或提供的所有信息，这样你就能对它的准确性充满信心。

2.2 给来电者呈现积极正面的形象

三个基本因素影响你在电话上的形象。你应该努力牢记这三点：

• 使用清晰的措辞，适当的音量以及适中的语速

你的话必须明确、清楚，并且讲话时音量要适当，语速要适中。相较于不得不给对方再次复述内容而言，花点时间把要说的内容清楚地表达出来会更高效，听起来也更专业。

• 注意你的姿势

在电话沟通中，姿势是一个重要因素，即使双方实际上看不到对方。一个端坐着的人说话往往听起来比较专业。然而，一个没精打采地坐在椅子上的人很有可能呈现出粗心的行为态度。

• 从不吃、喝或嚼口香糖

当你打电话的时候，绝对不应该吃喝东西或嚼口香糖。这些行为很粗鲁，通常易于被对方察觉，并且给对方留下你本人及你公司不专业的印象。

2.3 建立融洽关系

建立融洽关系是确定你和对方有哪些共同点并基于这些共同点建立良好关系的过程。和来电者建立融洽关系有三种方法：

• 使用来电者的名字

偶尔，你应该在谈话中使用来电者的名字。使打电话行为私人化有助于建立融洽关系并增加来电者的信任，他们更相信你愿意帮助他们。

• 找到共同点

当你能够找到与来电者的共同点时，你就更有可能与他们建立融洽的关系。这些小的连接点将证明你们双方都是朝着共同的目标而努力的。

• 与来电者的语速保持一致

与对方的语速保持一致是获得对方关注并关注对方，以便建立起融洽关系的巧妙方式。一个天生说话缓慢的人往往会怀疑语速快的动机，而语速较快的来电者则对语速较慢的通话感到很懊恼。

2.4 给人留下好印象

来电者欣赏有礼貌的回应。以下四个行为将提高你的能力，使你在接听电话的时候，表现出有礼貌的形象：

• 及时回答

所有的电话都应该在电话铃声响起第三声的时间内被接听。如果你无法在这一时间内接听电话，你的第一句话应该是向对方道歉。打电话的人听到的电话铃响起的次数并不总是和你听到的一样，所以他们可能已经听到了五次铃声，而你却只听到了四次。

• 适当地表明身份

接听来电时，应适当地表明身份。如果你接听的电话都来自公司内部，你需要先说出你部门的名称，接着表明自己的身份。

然而，如果你接听的是客户、供应商或其他外部人员打来的电话，你应该首先介绍公司，然后介绍部门和你自己。

• 用积极肯定的语言

在一般情况下，积极肯定的话语和信息易于被理解而且能传达出强有力的形象。这些话和信息暗示行为和结果，并给对方注入信心。例如，“她离开了她的办公桌”，这句肯定式表达的话语强于“她不在这里”这句否定式表达的句子。消极否定的话语更可能被误解。

• 乐于助人

当来电要找的人正忙时，你可以给来电者提供多种解决办法，比如稍等一会儿、请留个信息或者再打过来。当你愿意提供帮助时，无论是来电者还是来电要找的人都会从中受益，而且对方会感谢你。

Business Correspondence

Unit 6

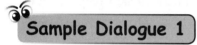

Part One Dialogues

Sample Dialogue 1

Situation ▶ Li Fang is being offered some suggestions by her general manager on how to handle e-mails.

(A—Mr. Frank, the genera manager of the Steel Trade Company; B—Li Fang, the newly hired secretary of Mr. Frank)

A: Good morning, Li Fang. How do you feel about today's work?

B: Good morning, Sir! Not bad.

A: Well. Have you checked the e-mails and put them into different folders this morning?

B: Yes. I have done that. Just as you've told me earlier, every morning what I should do first is to handle e-mails.

A: Good. You know, it is extremely important for you to organize them in various folders and then forward them to appropriate people since every day our company will receive quite a lot of e-mails.

B: Yes. I'll keep that in mind. But now I have another question.

A: Go ahead, please.

B: Well. You know we have a few thousands e-mail messages inside Microsoft outlook. What should I do if the computer crashes or something has gone wrong with the computer?

A: Good question. Although e-mail enables us to send or receive a variety of information and documents such as letters, papers, video and audio files to anyone, yet it'll be disastrous if a hardware or software fails. Therefore, it is important to make regular backups of e-mails.

B: Could you tell me how to make regular backups?

A: You can export all the e-mails to a mobile disk or to a webmail service.

B: Ah, it sounds a little complicated. Please tell me more about exporting e-mails to a webmail service.

A: It's a bit technical. You can read this tutorial. And the advantage of webmail service is that you will be able to access e-mails from any computer.

B: Thank you for your advice. I'll try that. Is there anything else I can do for you, Sir?

A: Oh, yes. Will you send an e-mail to ABC Toy Company and let them know what our terms of payment are?

B: OK. I'll do it right away.

Sample Dialogue 2

Situation ▶ Li Hua is talking with a secretary of Collier International Company on the phone, informing her of a fax.

(A—Li Hua, a secretary of IBM Company; B—Mary Green, a secretary of Collier International Company)

A: Good morning. May I speak to Miss Green, please?

B: Yes. This is Miss Green speaking.

A: This is Li Hua, from IBM Company.

B: Good morning, Li Hua.

A: Good morning, Miss Green. I'm calling to inquire you about your offer for your products. You know, since we have make an inquiry for your products, please make us an offer within this month.

B: OK. No problem. Would you like us to send you an e-mail or fax the details to you?

A: What about a fax?

B: OK. Would you please tell me your fax number?

A: The fax number is 86-38-25456954.

B: I got it ! You will receive the fax in a few seconds.

A: Sure. By the way, do you offer FOB or CIF?

B: Well. We usually offer FOB. And all the details are included in the fax.

A: OK. Thank you.

B: You're welcome. One more thing, Miss Li Hua, your prompt confirmation would be highly appreciated.

A: No problem. Good-bye.

B: Good-bye.

Useful Expressions

1. Have you checked the e-mails and put them into different folders this morning?
   你今天上午检查电子邮件，并把它们放到不同的文件里了吗？
2. Just as you've told me earlier, every morning what I should do firstly is to handle the e-mails.
   就如你先前告诉我的那样，每天早上我应该做的第一件事就是处理电子邮件。
3. It is extremely important for you to organize them in various folders and then forward them to appropriate people since every day our company will receive quite a lot of e-mails.
   我们公司每天要收到大量的邮件，因此，整理电子邮件放入不同的文件夹，并转发给合适的人，这非常重要。
4. E-mail enables us to send or receive a variety of information and documents such as letters, papers, video and audio files to anyone.
   电子邮件使我们能够给任何人发送或接收各种信息和文件，如信函、文件、视频和音频文件。
5. You can export all the e-mails to a mobile disk or to a webmail service.
   你可以导出所有电子邮件到移动硬盘或网络邮件服务。
6. Will you send an e-mail to ABC Toy Company and let them know what our terms of payment are?
   请给 ABC 玩具公司发一封电子邮件，告知他们我们的付款条件。
7. Since we have make an inquiry for your products, please make us an offer within this month.
   我们已对你们的产品进行询价，请在本月内给予报盘。
8. Would you please tell me your fax number?
   您能告诉我你的传真号码吗？
9. Do you offer FOB or CIF?
   你们报离岸价还是到岸价？
10. Your prompt confirmation would be highly appreciated.
    对于您的迅速确认，我们不胜感激。

Situational Dialogues

Using the Sample Dialogue as a model, try to create a new dialogue with your partner.

Situation 1 ▶ Li Yue, an executive secretary of ABC Textile Export Company, is instructing Chen Qin, a junior secretary of the same company, on how to make regular backups of e-mails.

Situation 2 ▶ Suan, a secretary in a foreign trade company, is calling to one of their clients explaining why the fax for offer is late.

Part Two Text A

Business Correspondence

In our day to-day life we exchange our ideas, thoughts and other information with our friends, relatives and other people. Communication through exchange of letters or other media is known as correspondence. We communicate our feelings, thoughts etc. to our friends and relatives through letters that may be called personal letters. A Businessman also writes and receives letters in his day to-day transactions, which may be called business letters.

Actually, business correspondence is a written communication between two parties. Businessmen may write letters to supplier of goods and also receive letters from the suppliers. Customers may write letters to businessmen seeking information about availability of goods, price, quality, sample etc. or place order for purchase of goods. In general, business correspondence may be defined as a media or means through which views are expressed and ideas or information is communicated in writing in the process of business activities.

1. Importance of Business Correspondence

Nowadays business operations are not restricted to any locality, state or nation. Today production takes place in one area but consumption takes place everywhere. Since the businessmen as well as customers live in far off places they don't have sufficient time to contact each other personally. Thus, there arises the need for writing letters. Thus, there arises the need for writing letters. Meanwhile, the importance of letters has increased because of vast expansion of business, increase in demand as well as supply of goods.

1.1 Help in Maintaining Proper Relationship

Nowadays, the businessmen as well as customers are scattered throughout the country. Thus, there is a need to maintain proper relationship among them by using appropriate means of communication. Here business letters play an important role. The customers can write letters to the businessman seeking information about products and businessmen also supply various information to customers. This helps them to carry on business on national and international basis.

1.2 Inexpensive and Convenient Mode

Though there are other modes of communication like telephone, telex, fax, etc., yet business information can be provided and obtained economically and conveniently through letters.

1.3 Create and Maintain Goodwill

Sometimes business letters are written to create and enhance goodwill. Businessmen at times send letters to enquire about complaints and suggestions of their customers. They also send letters to inform the customers about the availability of a new product, clearance sale etc. All this results in cordial relations with the customers, which enhances the goodwill of the business.

1.4 Serves as Evidence

We cannot expect a trader to memorize all facts and figures in a conversation that normally takes place among businessmen. Through letters, he can keep a record of all facts. Thus, letters can serve as evidence in case of dispute between two parties.

1.5 Help in Expansion of Business

Business requires information regarding competing products, prevailing prices, promotion, market activities, etc. If the trader has to run from place to place to get information, he will end up doing nothing. It will simply result in loss of time. But through business letters, he can make all enquiries about the products and the markets. He can also receive orders from different countries and, thus enhance sales.

2. Types of Business Correspondence

Generally, there are three major types of business correspondence in the contemporary office and each has its own function.

2.1 Business Letters

A business letter is usually a letter from one company to another, or between such organizations and their customers, clients and other external parties. Business letters can have many types of contents, for example to request direct information or action from another party, to order supplies from a supplier, to point out a mistake by the letter's recipient, to reply directly to a request, to apologize for a wrong, or to convey goodwill. Thus, we can enumerate the functions of a business letter as follows:

• Promotional Functions

Business organizations have to grow and enlarge, improving the quality of their products, by producing new products and providing better services. The customers have to be kept informed through letters of these developments. Business organizations have to expand their market by tapping new areas. All round expansion is possible only if the organization keeps all the people concerned well informed through letters.

• Informational Functions

Business letters provide valuable data about earlier policies, transactions and all other activities of the organization. Modern business cannot depend on memory as in olden days. Letters are ready references if they are available. New policies can be evolved by studying the earlier ones. It is not only essential to maintain good correspondence but also more essential to make them be available in the files.

• Legal Functions

Business letters can provide evidence in legal disputes, if any, that occur in a transaction. They are useful as legal documents in quotations and offers.

• Goodwill Function

Business letters promote goodwill among parties transacting business. They build a good rapport between parties in a business transaction.

All these functions of a business letter promote sales and improve the image of the firm. So, every business letter is a sales letter if it serves the stated or implied objectives.

2.2 Business E-mail

E-mail is widely used as a form of business communication and overall it is a highly effective communication tool. E-mail is inexpensive, only requiring an Internet connection that is generally already present in the business. Although a printout of e-mails is possible, emails often stay as soft copies because archiving and retrieving e-mail communications is easy to do. From the CEO to the janitorial staff and even temporary employees of the business all can send and receive e-mail.

• Function

Although it cannot and should not replace all face-to-face communication and others forms of communication, internal e-mail usage can cover many areas within the business. Internal e-mails can function as an effective communication for sharing basic information, such as new cafeteria prices, paper use guidelines or security precautions. Sending simple messages to an entire workforce with just the click of a mouse is fast, easy, convenient and can save the company money. If saved, the e-mail can function as proof of a message sent or received, and is easily accessible to remind the recipient of pertinent information. Many businesses use e-mail as part of its marketing efforts to share information with prospects, customers, vendors.

• Format

Business e-mails should be concise and to the point. Use plain text and common fonts with a simple signature line. Fancy graphics, fonts, and backgrounds can take up unnecessary storage space in the recipient's inbox and may load slowly, or not at all. Stick to one topic in a business e-mail and write only the things that are appropriate for anyone to read, as e-mail forwarding makes it possible for originally unintended parties to receive the e-mail. Proper grammar and spelling is very important in business e-mails and attachments should be prepared in a format that any recipient can easily access or download.

• Effects

E-mail has been revolutionary in the world of business communication because information is quickly passed along with instantaneous efficiency and effectiveness. Employees are able to access information from a computer, phone or PDA nearly anywhere, and so are the company's current and potential customers. The use of e-mail within a business can greatly increase productivity for employees and can be a quick way to increase sales as well.

2.3 Business Memos

A memorandum—usually known as a memo—is a document which is most commonly used for internal communication between coworkers or members of a department. You may need to use a memo as an external method of communication if, for example, you need to communicate with clients or other business associates. Business memos should follow strict guidelines in terms of format, with heading, addressee's name, title, address, salutation subject, body, complimentary close and signature. While informal emails may have replaced the interoffice memo in some situations, business memos still have a place in the office for a wide variety of reasons.

• Company Policy Changes

When management changes a company policy that affects all employees in an organization, a business memo is an appropriate method to disseminate the information. The business memo provides the formality and authority that a company-wide policy change requires.

• Announcements

A business memo is an appropriate type of communication to use when making company announcements such as an employee promotion. Companies also use the business memo to welcome new employees who will fill a vital role in the organization. The business memo documents the important announcement. Business memos can also announce a new product line for the company. Management can also send out a business memo to announce that the business hit a target or goal. Other company announcements may include holiday parties, new benefit programs, stock information or the acquisition of a new client.

• Action Request

Business memos are appropriate when management makes a request of all employees. For example, during an open enrollment period for health insurance, the human resource manager can use a business memo to inform and request that workers turn in policy changes by a specific date.

• Reminders

Employers and management can also distribute a business memo to remind workers about a task that workers must complete. A reminder memo can relate to office behavior, such as cleaning up the company break room.

New Words

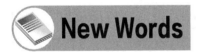

relative ['relətiv] *adj.* 相对的，比较的，相关的 *n.* 亲戚；关系词

communicate [kə'mju:nikeit] *v.* 传达，沟通，交流

transaction [træn'zækʃən] *n.* 交易，办理，处理，事务

supplier [sə'plaiə] *n.* 供应者，供应商

availability [əˌveilə'biliti] *n.* 有效；可得到的人（或物），可用性

sample ['sæmpl] *n.* 样品，样本 *vt.* 采样，取样；品尝，体验

purchase ['pə:tʃəs] *vt.* 购买 *n.* 购买，购买的物品

media ['mi:djə] *n.* 传播媒介，(medium的复数）媒体，新闻媒介

means [mi:nz] *n.* 方法，手段；收入，财产

locality [ləu'kæliti] *n.* 地区，位置，地点，方位

production [prə'dʌkʃən] *n.* 生产，产量，作品，成果

consumption [kən'sʌmpʃən] *n.* 消费，消耗

sufficient [sə'fiʃənt] *adj.* 足够的，充分的

contact ['kɔntækt] *n.* 接触，联系，熟人 *v.*（与）联系，（与）接触

arise [ə'raiz] *vi.* 出现，升起，上升，发生
demand [di'mɑːnd] *n.* 要求，需求 *v.* 要求，查问，需要
scatter ['skætə] *vt.* 散播，撒，驱散 *vi.* 分散，消散
various ['vɛəriəs] *adj.* 各种各样的
convenient [kən'viːnjənt] *adj.* 便利的，方便的
mode [məud] *n.* 方式，模式，样式，风格
goodwill [gud'wil] *n.* 善意，亲切，友好，商誉，信誉
create [kri'eit] *v.* 创造，造成
inform [in'fɔːm] *v.* 通知，告诉，使熟悉，告发
cordial ['kɔːdiəl] *adj.* 热忱的，诚恳的，兴奋的
memorize ['meməraiz] *v.* 记住，记录，记下
dispute [dis'pjuːt] *v.* 争论，辩驳，争议，质疑 *n.* 争论，争端，争吵
competing [kəm'piːt] *adj.* 竞争的，抵触的，相互矛盾的
prevailing [pri'veiliŋ] *adj.* 盛行的，广泛流传的，主流的
promotion [prə'məuʃən] *n.* 提升，促进，晋升，促销
external [eks'təːnl] *adj.* 外来的，外部的，外面的，表面的
content [kən'tent] *n.* 内容，目录，含量 *adj.* 满足的，满意的 *vt.* 使……满足，使……安心
request [ri'kwest] *n.* & *vt.* 请求，要求
enumerate [i'njuːməreit] *vt.* 数，列举，枚举
enlarge [in'lɑːdʒ] *v.* 扩大，增大；详述
expand [iks'pænd] *vt.* 使……膨胀；详述；扩张
tap [tæp] *v.* 开发，利用
concerned [kən'səːnd] *adj.* 担忧的，关心的，关切的，有关的
reference ['refrəns] *n.* 参考，参照；出处，推荐人，推荐函
evolve [i'vɔlv] *v.*（使）逐步形成，（使）逐步演变，进化
quotation [kwəu'teiʃən] *n.* 引语，引用，行情，报价
offer ['ɔfə] *vt.* 提供，提出，（卖方）出价 *n.* 提议，出价
rapport [ræ'pɔːt] *n.* 关系；亲善；一致
implied [im'plaid] *adj.* 含蓄的，暗含的，暗示的
objective [əb'dʒektiv] *adj.* 客观的，真实的 *n.* 目标，目的
overall ['əuvərɔːl] *adj.* 全部的，总体的，全面考虑的 *adv.* 总的来说，总共
printout ['print,aut] *n.* 打印输出
janitorial ['dʒænitə] *n.* 门卫，门警，管理员
temporary ['tempərəri] *adj.* 暂时的，临时的
cafeteria ['kæfi'tiəriə] *n.* 自助餐厅
guideline [gaidlain] *n.* 指导方针，准则
workforce [wəːkfɔːs] *n.* 劳动力；工人总数，职工总数
proof [pruːf] *n.* 证明，证据，校样
pertinent ['pəːtinənt] *adj.* 相关的，切题的，恰当的
prospects ['prɔspekt] *n.* 希望，前景，景色
concise [kən'sais] *adj.* 简明的，简要的

plain [plein] *adj.* 清楚的，简单的，平常的，朴素的
font [fɔnt] *n.* 字体
signature ['signitʃə] *n.* 签署，签名
fancy ['fænsi] *adj.* 引人注目的，时髦的，好的 *n.* 喜爱，幻想，想象力 *vt.* 想象，迷恋
originally [ə'ridʒənəli] *adv.* 原本，起初，独创地
unintended ['ʌnin'tendid] *adj.* 非计划中的，非故意的
download [daunləud] *v.* & *n.* 下载
revolutionary [revə'lu:ʃənəri] *adj.* 革命的
memorandum [ˌmemə'rændəm] *n.* 备忘录；交易备忘录；契约书
associate [ə'səuʃieit] *vt.* 联想，联合 *n.* 伙伴，同事，同伴
header ['hedə] *n.* 页眉
interoffice [ˌintə'rɔ:fis] *adj.* 局间的，各个办公室间的
disseminate [di'semineit] *vt.* 散播，公开，宣传
formality [fɔ:'mæliti] *n.* 礼节，程序，拘谨
acquisition [ˌækwi'ziʃən] *n.* 获得，采集，所获之物
enrollment [in'rəulmənt] *n.* 登记，注册，入伍，入会
reminder [ri'maində] *n.* 提醒物，提示，催单
distribute [dis'tribju(:)t] *v.* 分配，散发，分布

Phrases and Expressions

exchange... with 和……交换
be known as 以……著称
business correspondence 商业通信，商业书信
written communication 书面联络，书面沟通
define as 界定，定义为
be restricted to 局限于
take place 发生
maintain relationship 保持关系
means of communication 通信工具，沟通方式
play an important role 起重要作用
enquire about 询问
at times 有时，偶尔
clearance sale 清仓削价销售
keep a record of 记录
in case of 防备，假如，如果发生
end up doing nothing 在无所事事中告终
order supply 定购供应品
point out 指出，指明，说明
reply to 答复，回答，回复
keep sb. informed of 使某人不断获悉或知晓
legal dispute 法律纠纷
function as 起……的作用
security precaution 安全防范措施
remind sb. of sth. 提醒某人某事
to the point 切题，切中要害

stick to 坚持，遵守；黏附在……上，紧跟，紧随	make a request 请求
e-mail forwarding 邮件发送或转发	health insurance 健康保险
follow strict guideline 遵循严格的方针或准则	human resource 人力资源
hit a target 达到定额	relate to 有关，涉及
	clean up 收拾干净，打扫
	break room 休息室

Notes

1 Customers may write letters to businessmen seeking information about availability of goods, price, quality, sample etc. or place an order for purchase of goods.

本句中，seeking information about... goods 是现在分词短语作目的状语，修饰谓语 write letters。请看下例：

I write, hoping to exorcise some frustration.

我写点东西，希望可以帮助驱散心中的烦闷。

另外，place an order 为固定短语，意为“订购”。请看下例：

If you come down to the old price, we can place an order of a large quantity.

贵方若能降到老价格，我们就向您大量订货。

2 Thus, business correspondence may be defined as a media or means through which views are expressed and ideas or information is communicated in writing in the process of business activities.

本句中，through which... business activities 为“介词 through + 关系代词 which”引导的定语从句，修饰和限定先行词 a media or means。

英语中，常用相应的介词加关系代词来引导定语从句。请看下例：

Do you remember the day on which you joined our club?

你还记得你加入我们俱乐部的那一天吗？

另外，句中 define as 为固定短语，意为“定义为，界定为”。请看下例：

Boxing has been defined as the art of hit without being hit.

拳击已被定义为没有碰撞的碰撞艺术。

3 There arises the need for writing letters.

本句中，地点副词 there 置于句首，句子的主语 the need for writing letters 与谓语 arises 发生倒装。

英语中，在以 here、there、now、then、in、out、up、down、away 等地点方位副词开头的句子里，为表示强调，常将主语和谓语的位置调换。例如：

Here comes the bus.

汽车来了。

There goes the bell.

铃响了。

4 All round expansion is possible only if the organization keeps all the people concerned well informed through letters.

本句中，关系连词 only if 意为“只有当 (只是在 …… 的时候)”，在句中引导条件状语从句。请看下例：

I can buy the house only if a mortgage for 2000 dollars is available.

只有拿到两千美元的抵押贷款，我才买得起那栋房子。

另外，keep sb. informed 为常用短语，意为“随时告知某人某事”。请看下例：

They agreed to keep me informed of fresh developments.

他们同意随时告诉我新的发展。

5 If saved, the e-mail can function as proof of a message sent or received, and is easily accessible to remind the recipient of pertinent information.

本句中，if saved 为 if the e-mail is saved 的省略表达。

英语中，当从句的主语与主句的主语一致时，从句中的主语以及相关系动词可以被省略。请看下例：

If he had worked harder when young, he would be well off now.

如果他年轻时多努力一点，现在就能过得舒服些。

另外，remind of 为固定短语，意为“使 …… 回想起”

Miss lemon reminds her boss of two appointments.

莱蒙小姐提醒她的老板有两个约会。

Exercises

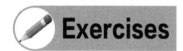

EX. 1 Answer the following questions.

1. According to Text A, what is the definition of business correspondence?
2. Why does the need for writing letters arise in business transactions?
3. What is the advantage of communicating information through letters compared with other modes of communication like telephone, telex, fax, etc.?
4. How do business letters help enhance the goodwill of the business?
5. What situation may call for business letters to serve as evidence?
6. What are the three major types of business correspondence in the contemporary office?
7. What are the legal functions of business letters?
8. What is the advantage of sending simple message to an entire workforce through e-mail?
9. Which type of correspondence is appropriate when management wants to change company policy or make some announcements?
10. Which type of correspondence may be used to remind workers about a task that workers must complete?

EX. 2 **Complete the following sentences with appropriate words or expressions in the box.**

dispute	prevailing	concise	recipient	purchase
in terms of	complaint	in case of	consumption	transaction

1. Had you not helped us, we should have canceled this ________.
2. At the stock market your broker will inquire of other broker if they know of anyone who would like to sell the stock that you want to ________.
3. I always take fuel ________ into consideration when buying a car.
4. Now you can compare the sections of this business letter ________ clarity.
5. There's been a record number of ________ about the standard of service on Britain's railways.
6. Negotiators are looking for a peaceful settlement to the ________.
7. Our guideline would be in conformity to the ________ world market prices.
8. You need to Specify a ________ based on text in either the To: or Cc: line of the e-mail.
9. The executive assistant gave a ________ and firm summary of our company's position.
10. ________ need we can offer you some other brand of the same specification.

EX. 3 **Translate the following sentences into English.**

1. 毫无疑问，电子邮件是重要的信息交流工具。(means of communication)
2. 如果你想咨询有关产品的问题，请与我们的销售部门联系。(enquire about)
3. 初级秘书应该熟悉办公室工作并能独立处理对外商务文书。(business correspondence)
4. 很明显，如今电脑在我们的日常生活中起着很重要的作用。(play an important role)
5. 为了更好地为客户服务，秘书需要具备良好口头及书面沟通技能。(written communication)
6. 一名合格的秘书应该提醒她的主管所有重要的会面。(remind sb. of)
7. 转发功能可让您从其他电子邮件账户查看邮件。(email forwarding)
8. 若该合同涉及任何法律纠纷，地方法院将有最后的决定权。(legal dispute)
9. 我们永远也不会实现目标，除非我们提高生产力。(hit a target)
10. 商誉对一家企业来说是一种无形的资产。(goodwill)

EX. 4 **Translate the following passage into Chinese.**

Generally people say that verbal or non-verbal communication is important as one cannot take back once he says something. It is also similar in the case of writing as one cannot take back what they wrote. Written communication involves any type of interaction that makes use of the written word. It is one of the two main types of communication, along with oral or spoken communication. Written communication is very common in business situations, so it is important for small business owners and managers to develop effective written communication skills. Some of the various forms of written communication that are used internally for business operations include memos, reports, bulletins, job descriptions, employee manuals, and electronic mail. Written communication avenues typically pursued with clients, vendors, and other members of the business community, meanwhile, include electronic mail, Internet Web sites, letters, proposals, telegrams, faxes, postcards, contracts, advertisements, brochures, and news releases.

Part Three Text B

Business Letters

A business letter is a type of correspondence between companies or between companies and individuals, such as customers, clients, contractors or other outside parties. Business letters differ from personal letters in that they are more formal in tone and writing style.

Business letters serve a variety of purposes. They can be used to distribute or seek to obtain information. They can serve as apologies or for other troubleshooting strategies. Other purposes of business letters include being used as a call to action, as an introduction or as a way to seek a position within a company.

1. Essential Qualities of a Good Business Letter

A letter should serve the purpose for which it is written. If a businessman writes a letter to the supplier for purchase of goods, the letter should contain all the relevant information relating to the product, mode of payment, packaging, transportation of goods, etc. clearly and specifically. Thus, to be effective, all business letters need to have some essential qualities and these essential qualities can facilitate quick processing of the request and lead to prompt action.

1.1 Simplicity

Simple and easy language should be used for writing business letters. Difficult words should be strictly avoided, as one cannot expect the reader to refer to the dictionary every time while reading letter.

1.2 Clarity

The language should be clear, so that the receiver will understand the message immediately, easily and correctly. Ambiguous language creates confusion. The letter will serve the purpose if the receiver understands it in the same manner in which it is intended by the sender.

1.3 Accuracy

The statements written in the letter should be accurate to the best of the sender's knowledge. Accuracy demands that there are no errors in the usage of language—in grammar, spellings, punctuation etc. An accurate letter is always appreciated.

1.4 Completeness

A complete letter is one that provides all necessary information to the users. For example, while sending an order we should mention the desirable features of the goods, such as their quality, shape, color, design, quantity, date of delivery, mode of transportation, etc.

1.5 Relevance

The letter should contain only essential information. Irrelevant information should not be mentioned while sending any business correspondence.

1.6 Courtesy

Courtesy wins the heart of the reader. In business letters, courtesy can be shown/expressed by using words like please, thank you, etc.

1.7 Neatness

A neat letter is always impressive. A letter either handwritten or typed, should be neat and attractive in appearance. Overwriting and cuttings should be avoided.

2. Parts of a Business Letter

A business letter represents both you and your employer, so whether the letter comes from you or your administrative staff, it should look and sound professional. When the text is clear and simple and appears balanced on the page, the reader can grasp the message more easily. An effective business letter should cover the following essential parts.

2.1 Heading

The heading of a business letter usually contains the name and postal address of the business, E-mail address, Web-site address, Telephone Number, Fax Number, Trade Mark or logo of the business (if any).

2.2 Date

The date is normally written on the right hand side corner after the heading as the day, month and years. Some examples are 28th Feb., 2016 or Feb. 28, 2016.

2.3 Reference

It indicates letter number and the department from where the letter is being sent and the year. It helps in future reference. This reference number is given on the left hand corner after the heading. For example, we can write reference number as AB/FADept./2016/27.

2.4 Inside Address

This includes the name and full address of the person or the firm to whom the letter is to be sent. This is written on the left hand side of the sheet below the reference number. Letters should be addressed to the responsible head.

2.5 Subject

It is a statement in brief that indicates the matter to which the letter relates. It attracts the attention of the receiver immediately and helps him to know quickly what the letter is about. For example:

Subject: Your order No. C317/8 dated 12th March 2016.

2.6 Salutation

This is placed below the inside address. It is usually followed by a comma (,). Various forms of salutation are:

Sir/Madam: For official and formal correspondence

Dear Sir/Madam: For addressing an individual

Dear Sirs/Dear Madam: For addressing a firm or company.

2.7 Body of the Letter

This comes after salutation. This is the main part of the letter and it contains the actual message of the sender. It is divided into three parts:

(a) Opening part — It is the introductory part of the letter. In this part, attention of the reader should be drawn to the previous correspondence, if any. For example:

With reference to your letter no. 326 dated. 12th March 2016, I would like to draw your attention towards the new brand of television.

(b) Main part — This part usually contains the subject matter of the letter. It should be precise and written in clear words.

(c) Concluding Part — It contains a statement of the sender's intentions, hopes or expectations concerning the next step to be taken. Further, the sender should always look forward to getting a positive response. At the end, terms like *Thanking you, With regards, With warm regards* may be used.

2.8 Complimentary Close

It is merely a polite way of ending a letter. It must be in accordance with the salutation. For example:

Salutation	Complimentary Close
Dear Sir/Dear Madam	Yours faithfully
Dear Mr. Raj	Yours sincerely
My Dear Akbar	Yours very sincerely (express very informal relations)

2.9 Signature

It is written in ink, immediately below the complimentary close. As far as possible, the signature should be legible. The name of the writer should be typed immediately below the signature. The designation is given below the typed name. Where no letterhead is in use, the name of the company too could be included below the designation of the writer. For example:

Yours faithfully

For M/S Acron Electricals

(Signature)

SUNIL KUMAR

Partner

2.10 Enclosures

This is required when some documents like cheque, draft, bills, receipts, lists, invoices etc. are attached with the letter. These enclosures are listed one by one in serial numbers. For example:

Encl : i. The list of goods received

ii. A cheque for Rs. One Thousand dtt. Feb. 27, 2016 (Cheque No....) towards payment for goods supplied.

2.11 Copy Circulation

This is required when copies of the letter are also sent to person apart from the addressee. It is denoted as C.C.. For example:

C.C. :i.The Chairman, Electric Supply Corporation

ii.The Director, Electric Supply Corporation

iii.The Secretary, Electric Supply Corporation

2.12 Post Script

This is required when the writer wants to add something, which is not included in the body of the letter. It is expressed as P.S. For example,

P.S. — In our offer, we provide two years warranty.

3. A Business Letter Sample

To illustrate the format of a business letter, a sample is given in the following table.

Specimen of Quotation Letter

Tel. 508632-35 Fax. 508600	M/s Bharat Fans Bharat Complex Hyderabad Industrial Estate Hyderabad-500032	E-mail: bh@fan.vsnl.net.in Website: http://www.bhfan.com
Ref.-SL/F/2016/12	Dated: August 10, 2016	

M/s Acron Electricals
22/c, Main Road
Darya Ganj, New Delhi-2

Subject: Your letter No. PR/F/2016/27 dated July 27, 2016

Dear Sir,

Thank you for your letter of enquiry. We would be glad to meet your requirements of selling our fan in your retail showroom.

Our quotations are given in the price list enclosed. We offer 10% discount on order above Rs.50,000. Besides, we allow a grace period of 45 days for payment of dues to our regular customers.

We are confident that you will find our prices competitive and our terms and conditions reasonable. We look forward to meeting your requirements.

Thank you,
Yours faithfully,
For M/s Bharat Fans
Sd/-
(Des Gupta)
Sales Manager
Encl: Price List & Terms and Conditions

New Words

contractor [kən'træktə] *n.* 订约人，承包人
troubleshooting ['trʌbl'ʃu:tiŋ] *n.* 发现并修理故障；解决纷争
facilitate [fə'siliteit] *vt.* 促进，帮助，使……容易
simplicity [sim'plisiti] *n.* 简单，单纯，简朴
clarity ['klæriti] *n.* 清楚，明晰
ambiguous [ˌæm'bigjuəs] *adj.* 模棱两可的，含糊不清的
confusion [kən'fju:ʒən] *n.* 混淆，混乱，不确定状态
intended [in'tendid] *adj.* 预期的；故意的
error ['erə] *n.* 错误，过失，误差
punctuation [pʌŋktjʊ'eiʃən] *n.* 标点；强调
desirable [di'zaiərəbl] *adj.* 令人满意的，令人向往的
feature ['fi:tʃə] *n.* 特征，特色；特写；故事片
quantity ['kwɔntiti] *n.* 量，数量；大量
delivery [di'livəri] *n.* 传递，交付，递送
irrelevant [i'relivənt] *adj.* 不恰当的，无关系的，不相干的
neatness [ni:tnis] *n.* 整洁，干净
impressive [im'presiv] *adj.* 给人深刻印象的
overwrite ['əuvə'rait] *v.* 重写；写得过多
represent [ˌrepri'zent] *vt.* 表示，代表，象征
heading ['hediŋ] *n.* 标题，题目，主题；信头，信纸上端所印文字
logo ['lɔgəu] *n.* 商标，标识语；图形
statement ['steitmənt] *n.* 陈述，声明
subject ['sʌbdʒikt] *n.* 话题，主题
salutation [sælju'teiʃən] *n.* 招呼，致敬，问候；(信函开头)称呼语
actual ['æktjuəl] *adj.* 实际的，事实上的
introductory [ˌintrə'dʌktəri] *adj.* 介绍的，引导的，开端的
precise [pri'sais] *adj.* 精确的，准确的；严格的
intention [in'tenʃən] *n.* 意图，目的，意向，打算
concerning [kən'sə:niŋ] *prep.* 关于，涉及，就……而言
merely ['miəli] *adv.* 仅仅，只不过
designation [ˌdezig'neiʃən] *n.* 称呼；指定，任命，命名
letterhead ['letəhed] *n.* 信笺抬头；印有抬头的信纸
faithfully ['feiθfuli] *n.* 忠实地，忠诚地，诚心诚意地
enclosure [in'kləuʒə] *n.* 附件
attach [ə'tætʃ] *v.* 附上，系上，贴上
circulation [ˌsə:kju'leiʃən] *n.* 流通，循环；发行量
addressee [ˌædre'si:] *n.* 收信人
warranty ['wɔrənti] *n.* 保证，担保；保单；保修期
format ['fɔ:mæt] *n.* 格式
specimen ['spesimin] *n.* 样品，样板，范本
retail ['ri:teil] *n.* 零售
enclose [in'kləuz] *vt.* 放入封套，装入
discount ['diskaunt] *n.* 折扣；贴现率 *vt.* 打折扣；贴现
due [dju:] *n.* 税费；会费；应付款

in that 因为，由于，既然
serve the purpose 适合需要，令人满意；管用，能解决问题
mode of payment 付款方式
mode of transportation 运输方式
inside address 信纸左上角的收信人姓名与地址
attract one's attention 吸引某人的注意力
be divided into 被分成
draw one's attention 吸引某人的注意力
with reference to 关于
take steps 采取步骤，设法
look forward to 期待，盼望
complimentary close 结束语，结尾客套语，信尾客套语
as far as possible 尽可能，尽量
in use 在使用中
apart from 除……之外
serial number 序列号
post script（信末签名后的）附言，又及；（正文后的）补充说明
meet one's requirement 合某人的意，符合某人的要求

Abbreviations

C.C. (Carbon Copy) 抄送
p.s. (postscript) 信末签名后的附言
tel. (telephone) 电话
ref. (reference) 参考
encl. (enclosure) 随信附上

Exercises

EX. 5 Answer the following questions.

1. What is the difference between business letters and personal letters according to Text B?
2. What relevant information should be contained in the business letter for purchase of goods?
3. List at least five essential qualities of a good business letter.
4. What does the accuracy of a good business letter demand?
5. What information is usually contained in the heading of a business letter?
6. What information does inside address of a business letter include?
7. What is the definition of subject? And why is it necessary in a business letter?
8. When is enclosure required in a business letter?
9. When is copy circulation required in a business letter?
10. When is P.S. required in a business letter?

Part Four Extended Reading

Text	Notes
E-mail Etiquette[1]	[1] *n.* 礼仪，礼节，规矩
Many people who send business correspondence by e-mail do not realize there is a big difference between using it for that purpose and for communicating with friends and family. When you send a message to a buddy[2] or relative, you can be pretty casual. You can use slang[3] if you want or may even spice it up[4] with inappropriate[5] language if you know the recipient[6] won't have a problem with that. In other words, you can write as if you were speaking to that person.	[2] *n.* 伙伴，好朋友 [3] *n.* 俚语，行话 [4] 增添趣味 [5] 不适当的，不合宜的 [6] *n.* 接受者，收信人
Business correspondence is quite different. Good e-mail etiquette, actually business etiquette in general, dictates[7] that you conduct yourself with professionalism[8]. When you are too casual, use slang or inappropriate language, or send error-filled messages, it leaves a bad impression on[9] the recipients of your message. Here are some basic rules of e-mail etiquette.	[7] *vt.* 规定，决定 [8] *n.* 职业水准，职业化 [9] 留下一个坏的印象
1. Mind Your Manners	
Even in a world where we seem always to be in a rush[10] to get things done as quickly as possible so we can move on to the next task, good manners have not gone out of style.	[10] 匆忙地
You will not sound old fashioned if you always use the words "please" and "thank you." Your recipient will appreciate your politeness.	
Another way to show good manners is to address[11] people you don't know, or only have a formal relationship with, by their title and last name, for example, Mr. White or Ms. Grey. If the recipient of your e-mail prefers being called by his or her first name, he or she will probably correct you. When replying to an e-mail and the sender of the original message has used only his or her first name, then you can safely assume[12] it's okay to use that person's first name as well.	[11] *v.* 称呼；发表演说；提出；处理 [12] *vt.* 假定，设想
2. Watch Your Tone	
Tone is a speaker's, or in the case of e-mail, writer's, way of expressing his or her attitude. It's a difficult thing to convey in writing, but you can usually achieve the correct tone by rereading your message several times before you hit send. Make sure you come across as[13] respectful, friendly and approachable[14]. You don't want to sound curt[15] or demanding.	[13] 被理解为 [14] *adj.* 可接近的，易接近的，亲切的

If you're writing to someone with whom you've communicated before, begin with something friendly like "I hope you are well." E-mail writers often use emoticons[16] to convey a particular feeling: happy, sad, confused or excited. Use good judgment here. If you write to someone frequently and have a less formal relationship with him, then emoticons can be okay. For official e-mail, however, for example, when you're writing to a prospective[17] employer, stick to words only.	[15] *adj.*(言语)简短失礼的，草率的 [16] *n.* 表情符号 [17] 预期的，未来的，可能的
It is always considered poor e-mail etiquette to use all upper case letters[18]. It looks like you are shouting. Do not use all lower case letters[19] either. Some people say it will make it seem like you are mumbling[20].	[18] 大写字母 [19] 小写字母 [20] *v.* 喃喃自语
3. Be Concise[21]	[21] *adj.* 简明的，简要的
Everyone's time is valuable, and you should respect that. Your recipient may have just a moment to read your e-mail and respond to it. When composing[22] your message, be as brief as possible while still making sure to include all pertinent[23] information. Provide as many details as your reader will need to understand what you are trying to convey.	[22] *vt.* 撰写，组成，构成 [23] *adj.* 中肯的，相关的，恰当的
4. Avoid Using Texting Abbreviations[24]	[24] *n.* 缩略语
As a society that spends a lot of time on our phones texting, we have gotten accustomed to[25] using abbreviations for any word. We use U instead of you, UR instead of your, 2 instead of to or too, plz instead of please, and thx instead of thanks. That's fine if your recipient is a friend. Business e-mail should be more formal. Of course, commonly used abbreviations such as Mr. and Mrs., FYI (for your information), inc., and etc. are fine.	[25] 习惯，适应于
5. Use a Professional E-mail Address	
Always use the e-mail address your employer assigned to[26] you for work-related correspondence but avoid using it for anything else. For example, if you are job hunting, use a personal e-mail account[27], but make sure your address looks professional. Consider what it says about you. Are you a sexymom@isp.com or hotdad@isp.com? Maybe. But do you want a prospective employer to think so? Consider getting an address that uses your first initial[28] and last name or your full name. If you are so attached to[29] your address that you do not want to change it, consider adding a second one for professional use only. If your ISP (Internet Service Provider) only provides a single address, look into getting a free account.	[26] 分配给，分派给 [27] 电子邮箱 [28] *n.* 首字母 [29] 喜爱，依恋，附属于

6. Remember That Spelling and Grammar Count[30]	[30] *v.* 重要，有价值
Always proofread[31] your e-mail carefully. You want to be attentive to[32] correct spelling and proper grammar. Use an automatic[33] spell checker if you wish but be careful about relying on it too heavily. If you are using the wrong spelling for a particular use of a word, for example, two vs. to vs. too, it won't pick up[34] your mistake. Don't try to guess the spelling of a word. You should look it up in a free online dictionary.	[31] *vt.* 校对 [32] 注意，关注 [33] *adj.* 自动的，无意识的 [34] 纠正
Good grammar is essential. You can use contractions[35] when you want to convey a more conversational[36] tone. Never use slang or any offensive[37] language.	[35] *n.* 缩写式 [36] *adj.* 会话的，对话的 [37] *adj.* 令人不快的，冒犯的，侮辱的

参考译文

课文A 商务信函

在我们的日常生活中，我们和朋友、亲戚以及其他人交换看法、想法和其他信息。通过书信或其他媒介进行沟通的方式被称为通信。通过信件我们向朋友和亲人传达情感、思想等。这些信件可以被称作个人信函。在日常商业活动中，商人也写信并接收信件，这些信件称为商务信函。

事实上，商务信函是双方书面沟通的一种方式。商人可以写信给供货商，也可以接收供应商的来信。客户可以写信给商家，收集有关商品的供货情况、价格、质量、样品等信息，或者下订单购买商品。总之，商务信函可以被定义为一种媒介或方式，通过这种媒介或方式人们可以在商务活动过程中，以书面方式表达意见或传递信息。

1. 商务信函的重要性

当今商务行动不仅仅局限于某地、某州或某国。如今，生产活动在某地进行时，其产品的消费行为则无处不在。由于居住在相距甚远的地方，商家和顾客没有足够的时间面对面地联系。因此，写信成为一种必要。同时，随着商业行为的大规模扩张以及产品供需的增长，信函的重要性也随之增加。

1.1 有助于维持友好关系

如今，客户、商家均分散在全国各地，因此有必要采用适当的交流手段保持彼此的友好关系。这里商务信件扮演着重要角色。客户可以给商家写信咨询产品信息，商家则把各种信息提供给客户。这有助于他们在全国或全球的范围内开展业务。

1.2 一种成本低廉、方便的方式

虽然存在其他的沟通方式，如电话、电报、传真等，但是通过信件方式，可以经济、方便地收发商务信息。

1.3 创建并维护商誉

有时写商务信函是为了创建和维护商誉，有时商家寄信以便了解投诉情况并听取客户的建议。他们也寄信告知客户有关新产品的推出、清仓降价销售等信息。这使得他们和客户建立了诚挚的关系，并提高了公司的信誉。

1.4 充当证据

我们不能期望经营者记住商人之间的正常谈话中的所有事实和数字，但是通过信件他可以记录下所有这些事实。因此，双方之间万一发生分歧时，信件可以充当证据。

1.5 有助于业务扩展

商务行为需要获取有关其他竞争产品、主流价格、促销、市场活动等方面的信息。如果经营者为获取信息四处奔波，那么他将一事无成。这只能导致时间的浪费。但是通过商务信函，他就可以了解产品和市场情况。他也可以承接来自不同国家的订单，因此促进了销售。

2. 商务信函的种类

在当代办公事务中，通常主要使用三种商务通信方式而且每种通信方式都有自己的功能。

2.1 商务书信

商务书信通常是指一家公司写给另一家公司，或公司与顾客、客户和其他外部人员交流的信件。商务书信可以涉及多种内容，例如，要求对方提供直接信息或采取行动、从供应商那里订货、指出收件人的错误、直接回复请求、为错误道歉或表达善意。因此，商务书信功能列举如下。

• 促销功能

企业必须通过生产新产品、提供更好的服务来发展扩大规模，同时提高产品质量。客户必须通过商务书信来了解这些发展情况。企业也必须通过开发新领域以扩大市场。只有当组织通过信件方式使所有有关人员了解情况时，全方位的扩张才能成为可能。

• 信息功能

商务书信提供该组织的有关早期政策、交易活动以及其他活动的有价值的数据。现代企业不能像过去那样依靠记忆。如果可用的话，信件是现成的参考资料。通过研究早期的政策可以逐步形成新的政策。因此，信件不仅对于保持良好的通信关系来说是必要的，而且更重要的是将它们存档以供查阅使用。

• 法律功能

如果交易中出现法律纠纷的话，商务书信可以充当证据。它们可以用作报价中的法律文件。

• 促进商誉功能

商业书信促进交易各方之间的亲善关系。它们在商业交易各方之间建立良好的关系。

商业书信的所有这些功能促进了销售，提升了公司的形象。因此，如果实现了规定的或隐含的目标，每一封商务书信都是一封销售函。

2.2 商务电子邮件

如今，电子邮件是一种广泛应用的商务交流方式，而且总体上它是一种高效的通信工具。电子邮件成本低，只需要一个互联网连接，而这种连接已经普遍存在于企业中。虽然可以打印邮件，但电子邮件通常以软拷贝的形式存在，这样易于归档和检索。从首席执行官到门卫人员，甚至是企业的临时员工都可以发送并接收电子邮件。

• 功能

虽然电子邮件不能也不会取代所有的面对面的以及其他形式的沟通，但内部电子邮件的使用能涵盖企业内部的许多领域。内部电子邮件可以作为一种有效的沟通方式，共享基本信息，如新的食堂价格、纸张使用指南或安全防范措施等。只需点击鼠标就可以将简单的信息发送给全体员工。这种方式既方便快捷，又可以节省公司的经费。如果将其保存，电子邮件还可以成为收发消息的证据，并且易于用来提醒收件人相关的信息。许多企业使用电子邮件完成部分营销工作，通过电子邮件和潜在的客户、顾客及供应商共享信息。

• 格式

商务电子邮件应该语言简洁、主题明确，应使用纯文本和普通字体，并只留一个签名行。艺术化的图形、字体和背景会占用收件人收件箱中存储空间，并且加载缓慢，甚至完全不加载。在商务电子邮件中，应当紧扣一个主题，只写一些适合任何人阅读的信息，因为转发电子邮件可能会使那些原先并不在计划内的人员接收到邮件。在商务电子邮件中，正确的语法和拼写也是非常重要的，而且附件发送应采用任何收件人都可以轻松地访问或下载的格式。

• 效果

在商务通信领域中，电子邮件是革命性的通信方式，因为通过电子邮件，信息传递迅速、即时、高效。员工以及公司的现有的和潜在的客户在任何地方都能够通过计算机、手机或个人数据助理器获取信息。在企业内部使用电子邮件还可以大幅度提高员工的生产力，快速推动销售。

2.3 商务便函

便函通常被称为备忘录，是常用于同事或部门成员之间进行沟通的文档。你也可以使用便函同外部成员进行沟通，例如，当你需要与客户或其他商务伙伴进行沟通时。商务便函应严格遵循格式准则，应包括标题，收文人的姓名、头衔、地址，称呼，事因，正文，结束语和署名等部分。虽然非正式电子邮件可能在某些情况下已经取代了办公室备忘录，但商务便函由于各种各样的原因在办公领域仍然有一席之地。

• 更改公司政策

当管理层要更改一项对组织所有员工都有影响的政策时，商务便函则是公开传播这一消息的适当方式。商务便函符合公司政策变更的程序和权限要求。

• 发布公告

当要发布如晋升某位职员的公告时，公司则可使用商务便函这种合适的通信方式。公司也可以使用商业便函欢迎将在组织中发挥重要作用的新员工。商务便函记录重要的公告，也用于宣布公司新产品线。管理层还可以发出商务便函，宣布业务达标。公司的其他公告可能包括节日聚会、新的福利计划、股票信息或新增客户信息。

• 要求行动

当管理层需要对所有员工提出要求时，商务便函是可用的适当的方式。例如，在公开购买健康保险期间，人力资源经理可用商业便函来通知并要求所有的员工在某个具体日期之间上缴保费。

• 提示

雇主和管理层还可以通过商务便函提醒员工完成他们必须完成的任务。提示性的便函可以涉及办公行为，如清扫公司的休息室。

课文B 商务书信

商务信函是企业之间或企业与个人之间的一种通信方式，如与顾客、客户、承包商或其他外部人员之间的通信。商务书信与个人书信不同，因为其语气和写作风格都更为正式。

商务信函有各种各样的用途。它们可以用来收发信息，可以用作道歉的方式或解决纷争的策略。商务书信还被用来号召行动，做介绍或者谋求公司里的职位。

1. 优质商务信函必备的属性

信函应该与写信目的相符。如果商家写信给供货商购买货品，信中应明确包含与产品、付款方式、包装、运输等相关的信息。因此，所有的商务信函需要具备一些必要的属性，才能做到有效。这些必备的属性可方便当事人快速处理要求，迅速采取行动。

1.1 简洁性

写商务信函时应使用简单容易的语言。应严格避免使用难词，因为我们不能指望读者每次读信时都去查字典。

1.2 明了性

语言应清楚明了，这样收信人就可以快速、容易、正确地理解书信内容。模棱两可的语言只会引起混乱。如果收信人能以与寄信人所希望的同等方式理解来信的话，这封信就达到了目的。

1.3 精确性

信中陈述的内容在寄信人看来应精确无误。精确性要求语言使用方面无失误——在语法、拼写、标点符号等方面。人们总是欣赏精确无误的信件。

1.4 完整性

一封完整的书信应向使用者提供所有的必要信息。例如，寄出订单时我们应该提及所希望的产品特征，也就是产品的质量、形状、颜色、图案、数量、发货日期、运输方式，等等。

1.5 相关性

信里只应包含必要信息。寄出任何商务信函时均不应提及无关信息。

1.6 礼貌性

礼貌可以赢得读信者的心。在商务书信中，礼貌可以通过使用像“请”“谢谢”等话语来表达。

1.7 整洁性

干净整洁的信件总是使人印象深刻。不管是手写还是打印，信件应该整洁漂亮，避免写得过满和剪切。

2. 商务书信的组成部分

商务书信代表了你和你的雇主，所以不管是谁写的，这封信应该看起来听起来有专业水准。当文本清晰简洁、页面协调时，收信人则可以很容易地领会信息。一封有效的商务信函应该包含以下必要的组成部分。

2.1 信头

商务书信的信头通常包括公司名称、邮政地址、电子邮件地址、网址、电话号码、传真号码以及注册商标或标识（如果有的话）。

2.2 日期

日期一般按年月日写在右上角，位于信头下方。例如 28th Feb., 2016 或 Feb. 28, 2016。

2.3 案号

案号表明信件的编号、来信的部门以及来信的年份。案号便于以后参考。案号写在信纸的左上角，位置低于信头。例如，我们可以将案号写为 AB/FADept./2016/27。

2.4 信内地址

这部分包括收信人或收信公司的名称和完整地址。写于信纸左侧，案号下方。信件的收信人应写成有关负责领导。

2.5 主题

这是一个简短陈述，表明本信的相关话题。它能立刻吸引收信人的注意力，帮助他快速了解这封信关于什么的。例如：

主题：您 2016 年 3 月 12 日编号为 C317/8 的订单

2.6 称呼

称呼写于信内地址下方，后面常用逗号（，）。下面是几种不同的称呼形式：

Sir/Madam: 用于官方及正式信函

Dear Sir/Madam: 用于称呼个人

Dear Sirs/Dear Madam: 用于称呼公司

2.7 正文

这部分位于称呼之后。它是信的主体，含有寄信人的具体信息。它分成三部分：

(a) 开头——这是信的引入部分。在本部分中，应该把读信人的注意力引到以前的信件上（如有的话）。例如，关于您 2016 年 3 月 12 日编号为 326 的来信，请您关注这种这种新型电视机。

(b) 主体——这部分往往包括信件的主题内容。应该准确无误，写作语言应清晰明了。

(c) 结尾——这部分陈述寄信人的意图、希望或对采取下一步行动的期待。而且，寄信人总盼望正面答复。在最后，可能会使用像 Thank you、With regards、With warm regards 等说法。

2.8　信尾客套语

这仅是信件收尾的一种礼貌方法。这部分必须与所用的称呼相符，例如：

称呼	信尾客套语
Dear Sir/Dear Madam	Yours faithfully
Dear Mr. Raj	Yours sincerely
My Dear Akbar	Yours very sincerely（表示非正式的关系）

2.9　签名

签名要用钢笔，签在信末客套语的正下方。签名要尽可能可以辨认出来。写信人的姓名应打印在签名的正下方。写信人的身份在打印姓名下面给出。如未使用信头，公司名称也可以包括在写信人身份一项里。例如:（略）

2.10　附件

当信件附有支票、汇票、账单、收据、清单、发票等时需要使用本部分。这些附件以连续号码逐项列出。例如：

附件: 1. 所收到的货品的清单一张

2. 用于支付所供应货品货款的支票一张：日期为 2016 年 2 月 27 日，金额壹千卢比（支票号码: No...)

2.11　抄送

当信件副本亦寄给收信人之外的其他人时则需要此部分。抄送用 C.C. 表示，例如：

C.C. i.The Chairman,Eletric Supply Corporation

ii.The Director, Eletric Supply Corporation

iii.The Secretary, Eletric Supply Corporation

2.12　附言

当写信人想要补充一些正文没有包括的内容时则需要此部分。附言用 P.S. 表示，例

P.S. ——我们乐于提供两年的质量保证。

3. 商务书信范例

为了说明商务书信的格式，现以下列表格给出一份范例。

报价信范例

电话：508632-35 公司名称：M/s Bharat 电扇公司 E-mail:bh@fan.vsnl.net.in
传真：508600 公司地址：Bharat Complex,Hyderabad Industrial Estate,Hyderabad - 500032 网址：http://www.bhfan.com

案号：-SL/F/2016/12 日期：2016 年 8 月 10 日

M/S Acron Electricals
22/C, Main Road
Darya Ganj, New Delhi-2

主题：您 2016 年 7 月 27 日编号为 PR/F/2016/27 的信件

尊敬的先生：

非常感谢你方的询盘函。我方很高兴能满足贵方的要求，能在贵公司的零售展厅销售我公司的电扇。

我方的报价已在随函的价格表中注明。如订购 5 万卢比货物，我方提供 10% 的订购折扣。此外，我方将允许老客户在 45 天的宽限期内支付应付款。

相信贵公司会发现我方的价格优惠，条款合理。我们期待满足您的要求。

Thank you,
Yours faithfully,
For M/s Bharat Fans
Sd/-
(Des Gupta)
销售经理
附件：价格表 & 条款

Unit 7

Meetings

Part One Dialogues

Sample Dialogue 1

Situation ▶ Lisa is being asked to write up an agenda for her company's Annual General Meeting.

(A—Mr. Black, the general manager of Sunshine Steel Company; B—Lisa, the secretary of Mr. Black)

A: Good morning, Lisa. We'll have our Annual General Meeting this month. I'd like you to write up an agenda for this meeting.

B: OK. No problem. Who will chair the meeting and what will be discussed at the meeting?

A: I will preside over the meeting and we'll discuss the financial report of this year.

B: Is there anything else that you would like to discuss at the meeting?

A: Yes. We'll also talk about the personnel plan and the plan for salary adjustment for the coming year.

B: Are these the three main topics of the meeting?

A: Yes. Please write them into the agenda.The agenda must be prepared before the meeting.

B: OK. I'll do that right away. Is there anything that you expect me to do?

A: Oh, yes. You'd better print and distribute the agenda to the attendees before the meeting.

B: All right. I'll prepare and send all the necessary materials to them before the meeting.

A: Additionally, do well the preparation work for the meeting, including choosing the location, arranging seating, preparing materials and incidentals and so on. Please get all things ready and report back to me as soon as possible.

Sample Dialogue 2

Situation ▶ Lisa is being asked to take minutes at Annual General Meeting.

(A—Mr. Black, the general manager of Sunshine Steel Company; B—Lisa, the secretary of Mr. Black)

A: Lisa, have you got the conference room ready for the meeting?

B: Yes. I've put the minute book and some paper copies of the agenda on the table. And paper and pencils have been laid by their name-card on the conference table for each attendant.

A: Thank you. But do you get the microphone, speakers and projector prepared?

B: Yes. I also have got them ready.

A: Well-done, Lisa! Actually, I've come to tell you that you'll have go to the meeting, make notes and make a record of what has happened.

B: Should I take down whatever everyone says at the meeting?

A: No, it's difficult and unnecessary for you to do that. You just keep proper records of the issues discussed and the resolutions or decisions passed.

B: It sounds a little challenging. And should I type out the minutes from the notes?

A: Yes, of course. You should write up the minutes immediately after the meeting while the information is still fresh your mind. What's more, you must get the minutes confirmed and signed by me before you send any copies of the minutes to the members of the meeting and others who need to be informed.

B: OK. I got it! I believe I can deal with it well.

Useful Expressions

1. I'd like you to write up an agenda for this meeting.
   我想让你给这次会议写份议程表。
2. I will preside over the meeting and we'll discuss the financial report of this year.
   我将主持这次会议，我们将讨论今年的财务报表。
3. We'll also talk about the personnel plan and the plan for salary adjustment for the coming year.
   我们还讨论来年的人事方案和工资调整方案。

4. You'd better print and distribute the agenda to the attendees before the meeting.
你最好在会议前印好并分发出去。
5. Please get all things ready and report back to me as soon as possible.
请把一切准备好，尽快向我汇报。
6. I've put the minute book and some paper copies of the agenda on the table.
我已经把记录簿和会议议程的复印本放在桌子上了。
7. Actually, I've come to tell you that you'll have go to the meeting, make notes and make a record of what has happened.
事实上，我是来告诉你你必须参加这次会议，并且做好笔记，记录会议情况。
8. You just keep proper records of the issues discussed and the resolutions or decisions passed.
你只需要准确记录会议上讨论的问题和通过的决议或问题解决方案。
9. You should write up the minutes immediately after the meeting while the information is still fresh your mind.
会后，你应该趁记忆犹新时马上整理出会议记录。
10. What's more, you must get the minutes confirmed and signed by me before you send any copies of the minutes to the members of the meeting and others who need to be informed.
而且，在把会议记录复印本发给会议成员以及其他需要了解会议情况的人之前，你必须确保会议记录经我确认签字。

Situational Dialogues

Using the Sample Dialogue as a model, try to create a new dialogue with your partner.

Situation 1 ▶ Susan, the secretary of Cloudy Maintenance Co., Ltd., is being required by Mr. Green, the president of Cloudy Maintenance Co., Ltd., to write the agenda for a upcoming Board Meeting.

Situation 2 ▶ Cathy, the secretary of Eastern Printing Equipment Co., is being asked by the general manager of her company to take the minutes for the coming Marketing Regular Meeting.

Part Two Text A

Meetings

A meeting is a gathering of two or more people that has been convened for the purpose of achieving a common goal through verbal interaction, such as sharing information or reaching an agreement. Meetings may occur face-to-face or virtually, as mediated by communications technology, such as a telephone conference call, a Skype conference call or a video conference.

Every organization, large or small, arranges a good number of meetings on certain time interval to discuss and decide on different issues. Companies use business meetings to review company information or establish new operating principles. Most meetings are directed by management, and time is spent helping employees understand the company financial health or operations.

Next to the chairperson, the secretary could be considered the most important member of a meeting and crucial to the smooth running of a meeting as well. It's the secretary's responsibility to schedule meetings, make sure that accurate minutes are kept and follow up with participants afterward, as needed. In order to be effective, a secretary's work will involve three stages: before the meeting; during the meeting; after the meeting.

1. Before the Meeting

The secretary is one of the key role-players before meetings are held. The importance of this role is highlighted in the truism that while a bad chairperson can ruin a meeting, a bad secretary can ruin an organization. To play their role well, secretaries require excellent planning skills and fulfill their responsibilities as follows.

1.1 Set Meeting Objective

Before making any arrangements, the secretary is supposed to consult with the chairperson to reach the final decision on the objective of the meeting, the order of business for the meeting, the way in which the business should be dealt with on the agenda, what business requires discussion and what requires a decision at the meeting.

Under the direction of the chairperson, the secretary can set an objective for the meeting, and make it brief and clearly stated. A concise and to-the-point objective helps determine who should participate in the meeting and whose presence will make it possible to actually meet the specific goals of the meeting.

1.2 Write an Agenda

With a clear meeting objective, the secretary is expected to write the meeting's agenda. An organized meeting needs a well-written agenda, without which the meeting will become over long and inefficient. A detailed, yet flexible agenda can keep your meeting streamlined and focused, ensuring that you meet all of your goals for your meeting in the shortest amount of time. While writing an agenda, the secretary should take the specific goals of the meeting objective into account. If a goal is to communicate the start of a project, set an agenda item that identifies who will present that information and how the information will be shared, such as by PowerPoint presentation. If the goal is to assign actions, set an agenda item that describes how assignments will be made. Every goal should have one or more agenda items aligned directly with it.

To illustrate the format of a meeting agenda, a sample for a business meeting agenda is given in the following table:

Meeting Agenda

***Just Us* Film**
Production Meeting Agenda
Date/Time: January 15, 2016 11:00am-1:30pm
Location: Conference Room B
Attendees:
Joshua Walker — Producer
Shara Jenkins — Writer / Director
Aren Vermont — Creative Director
Dalila Fialho — Director of Circulation
OBJECTIVES
• Review and finalize script
• Develop fundraising strategies for *JUST US* Film
• Finalize Pre-Production Timeline
SCHEDULE

11:00 to 11:15	Check-in, General Updates — Aren Vermont
11:15 to 11:45	Script Review, New Changes — Shara Jenkins
11:45 to 13:00	Fundraising Updates — Dalila Fialho
13:00 to 13:15	Pre-Production timeline — Joshua Walker
13:15 to 13:30	Announcements — All

ROLES/RESPONSIBILITIES
Note-taking: Joshua Walker

1.3 Select the Date and Time

Having consulted with the chairperson, the secretary is required to select a meeting date and time based on the availability of the meeting leader and the most critical invitees. The larger the list of invitees, the harder it is to find a day and time when everyone is available. Accept a time that fits as many schedules as possible. Before setting the time, give thought to time zones. If some invitees will participate by phone or the Internet, consider their working hours as well as your own.

1.4 Choose the Location

As for meeting location, it is a necessity for the secretary to find a conference room that will make it possible to achieve all agenda items. Choose a room large or small enough to comfortably fit the number of people expected to attend. A room that seats 40 is a poor choice for a meeting with 10 people. Likewise, you don't want a crowd squeezing in so tight that it's necessary to bring in extra chairs.

1.5 Arrange for Materials and Incidentals

If presentations are expected, the secretary must make sure that the room is equipped with a projector. If not, make arrangements to bring a projector with you — also make sure you have something to project onto, such as a screen or a white wall. Don't forget to consider the availability of other incidentals, such as white boards with dry erase markers, flip charts and speaker phones for off-site participants. For multi-hour meetings, the secretary had better arrange for food and beverages so that participants stay focused on the topic rather than their stomachs.

1.6 Notify Invitees

Under the direction of the chairperson, the secretary must send out notice of the meeting to all participants well in advance. Along with the meeting notice include an agenda, minutes of the last meeting and any handouts that will be discussed during the meeting. Provide a paper copy of the agenda, minutes from the last meeting and handouts, even if those items were e-mailed to participants ahead of time.

2. During the Meeting

During the course of meeting, the secretary should demonstrate the abilities to listen, comprehend, record accurately, summarize and behave with neutrality, integrity and confidentiality.

The ability to communicate clearly and accurately both in writing and in speech is the most essential attribute of a good secretary, but it is important to remember that the term "secretary" is derived from the word "secrecy", which highlights the upholding of confidentiality regarding the information entrusted to a secretary.

The main responsibilities of the secretary during meetings relate to:

2.1 Arrive in Advance

The secretary is expected to arrive in good time before the meeting with the minutes and with all the relevant correspondence and business matters for that meeting.

2.2 Determine the Attendance

When assisting the chairperson in determining whether all the invitees are present, the secretary needs to circulate the attendance register, record the names of those who are present, convey and record apologies received from those who are absent.

2.3 Announce Apologies

If the meeting is a small group, it is probably unnecessary to take attendance out loud. The person who is taking the minutes will know everyone personally and can indicate who is present and who is absent. In a larger meeting, it may be necessary to send around an attendance sheet or call out names. If an important figure is absent, it may be necessary for the secretary or the chairperson to apologize for his or her absence and offer a brief explanation for it.

2.4 Ratify Previous Minutes

To review the past business transacted, the chairperson of the meeting will usually require the secretary to prepare the minutes of the previous meeting. To this end, the secretary is supposed to obtain approval of the minutes of the previous meeting. If they are approved, he or she should make sure the chairperson signs the approved minutes and note that fact.

2.5 Read Previous Minutes

Minutes are an official of the proceedings of a formal meeting, and are considered in some countries as legal documents, especially for those companies which have many shareholders. The purpose of reading the minutes of last meeting is to provide an accurate and concise record of the business transacted.

2.6 Take Minutes

Unless there is a Minutes Secretary, the company's secretary is usually designated to take notes of the meeting, recording the key points and making sure that all decisions and proposals are recorded, as well as the name of the person or group responsible for carrying them out.

2.7 Provide Information

During the meeting, a secretary is obliged to make sure that the chairperson is supplied with all the necessary information for items on the agenda, and remind the chairperson if an item has been overlooked.

2.8 Act As a Compliance Officer

Acting as a compliance officer implies that the secretary needs to watch out for the instances where the meeting is deemed to be in violation of legislation or institutional regulations or policies. He or she should be sufficiently knowledgeable to ensure that the meeting's resolutions are compliant with the institution's policies, procedures and regulations, as well as with the relevant legislation.

2.9 Create a Relaxing Atmosphere

Secretaries can greet members and make them feel welcome, even late members when appropriate. If possible, serve light refreshments; they are good icebreakers and make your members feel special and comfortable.

Of these, the most important responsibility is that of taking down the minutes. Minutes are a record of proceedings. They are binding on the members present, and can be used as admissible evidence in a court of law. A good set of minutes is not a narrative of who said what during the meeting. Instead, minutes should highlight the decisions and the resolutions made. The record should clearly detail what actions need to be taken in relation to these decisions, by what date, by whom and with what resources. Without such a record it is not possible to hold people accountable for the responsibilities delegated to them. Attempts to record debates, on the other hand, run the risk of detracting from proposals and creating confusion. Nonetheless, the brevity of minutes should not mean that a person who was not present at the meeting would be unable to understand what took place.

3. After the Meeting

The secretary should write up and distribute minutes immediately after the meeting while the information is still fresh in his/her mind. It is advisable for him/ her to prepare a draft of the minutes, consult the chairperson and most senior staff member for approval and then send a copy for duplication and circulation to the members of the meeting and others who need to be informed. The sooner after a meeting the minutes are received, the sooner the members are reminded of things they have undertaken to do.

New Words

gathering ['gæðəriŋ] *n.* 集会，聚集
convene [kən'vi:n] *vt.* 集合，召集
mediate ['mi:dieit] *v.* 调停，斡旋
skype [skaip] *n.* 一种网络即时语音沟通工具
crucial ['kru:ʃəl] *adj.* 决定性的，关键的
smooth [smu:ð] *adj.* 平稳的，流畅的
minute [mai'nju:t] *n.* 备忘，会议记录
participant [pɑ:'tisipənt] *n.* 参与者
involve [in'vɔlv] *vt.* 包含；使忙于；牵涉，使卷入
highlight ['hailait] *vt.* 强调；照亮；使突出
truism ['tru:izm] *n.* 老生常谈，真理
ruin [ruin] *vt.* 毁灭，毁坏 *n.* 毁灭，废墟，崩溃
state [steit] *v.* 陈述，声明，说明，规定
inefficient [ˌini'fiʃənt] *adj.* 无效率的，无能的，不称职的
detailed ['di:teild] *adj.* 详细的
streamlined ['stri:mlaind] *adj.* 流线型的；现代化的
present [pri'zent] *v.* 提出，呈现
illustrate ['iləstreit] *vt.* 说明；(为书)作插图，图解
producer [prə'dju:sə] *n.* 生产者，制造者，制片人
director [di'rektə] *n.* 董事，经理，导演，主管，总监
finalize ['fainəlaiz] *vt.* 完成，确定，最终确定
script [skript] *n.* 剧本，脚本，手稿，手迹
fundraising ['fʌndreiziŋ] *n.* 募捐，资金募集
timeline ['taimlain] *n.* 时间表
invitee [invai'ti:] *n.* 被邀请者
participate [pɑ:'tisipeit] *vt.* 参加，参与
location [ləu'keiʃən] *n.* 位置，定位，地点
achieve [ə'tʃi:v] *v.* 完成，达到，实现
likewise ['laikˌwaiz] *adv.* 同样地，此外
squeeze [skwi:z] *v.* 挤压，塞进
incidental [ˌinsi'dentl] *adj.* 附带的，非主要的，偶然的 *n.* 附带事件；杂项
presentation [ˌprezen'teiʃən] *n.* 介绍，陈述，报告
projector [prə'dʒektə] *n.* 放映机
beverage ['bevəridʒ] *n.* 饮料
handout ['hændaut] *n.* 散发材料，新闻稿，印刷品
demonstrate ['demənstreit] *vt.* 证明，演示，示范
comprehend [ˌkɔmpri'hend] *vt.* 充分理解，领悟
neutrality [nju:'træliti] *n.* 中立
integrity [in'tegriti] *n.* 完整，完善，正直，诚实
attribute [ə'tribjut] *n.* 属性，标志，象征，特征 *vt.* 把……归于
uphold [ʌp'həuld] *v.* 支持，维护，维持
regarding [ri'gɑ:diŋ] *prep.* 关于，至于
entrust [in'trʌst] *vt.* 信赖，信托，交托
circulate ['sə:kjuleit] *vi.* 流通，循环，传播 *vt.* 使流通，使环流
absent ['æbsənt] *adj.* 缺席的，缺乏的
ratify ['rætifai] *vt.* 批准，认可

proceedings [prə'siːdiŋ] *n.* 进程；会议记录
shareholder ['ʃεəhəuldə] *n.* 股东
designate ['dezigneit] *vt.* 指定，选派；标明，把……定名为
proposal [prə'pəuzəl] *n.* 建议，提议
overlook [ˌəuvə'luk] *vt.* 忽视，忽略；远眺；检查
compliance [kəm'plaiəns] *n.* 服从，听从；承诺
imply [im'plai] *vt.* 暗示，意味，隐含，说明，表明
violation [ˌvaiə'leiʃən] *n.* 违反，妨碍，侵犯，违例，犯规
legislation [ˌledʒis'leiʃən] *n.* 立法，制定法律，法律，法规
regulation [regju'leiʃən] *n.* 条例，规则，规章
knowledgeable ['nɔlidʒəbl] *adj.* 博学的，知识渊博的，有见识的
ensure [in'ʃuə] *vt.* 确保，担保获得
resolution [ˌrezə'ljuːʃən] *n.* 解决，决心；决定，决议
atmosphere ['ætməsfiə] *n.* 大气，空气，气氛，气压
refreshments [ri'freʃmənt] *n.* 茶点，点心
binding ['baindiŋ] *adj.* 必须遵守的，有法律约束力的
admissible [əd'misəbl] *adj.* 可容许的，可接受的，有资格加入的
narrative ['nærətiv] *n.* 故事，叙述
delegate ['deligit] *n.* 代表 *v.* 派……为代表，委派，授权，委托
detract [di'trækt] *vi.* 减损 *vt.* 转移
brevity ['breviti] *n.* 短暂，简短，简洁
draft [drɑːft] *n.* 草稿，草图，汇票 *vt.* 起草，征兵，选秀
senior ['siːnjə] *adj.* 地位较高的，年长的，资深的 *n.* 上司；年长者，长辈
duplication [ˌdjuːpli'keiʃən] *n.* 复制，副本
undertake [ˌʌndə'teik] *v.* 承担，从事；保证，答应

Phrases and Expressions

for the purpose of 为了……（的目的）
achieve a common goal 实现一个共同的目标
verbal interaction 言语互动
reach an agreement 达成协议
telephone conference 电话会议
skype conference 网络电话会议
video conference 视频会议系统
on a certain time intervals 按一定的时间间隔
operating principle 工作原理
financial health 财务健康
next to 紧跟在……之后的，仅次于……的
follow up with 跟进，对某一件事采取进一步的行动
fulfill responsibility 履行责任
consult with 与（某人）磋商，相商
reach the final decision 最终决定
on the agenda 在议事日程上，在议事日程中

under the direction of 在……的指导下，在……指导下	obtain approval 获得批准
meet one's goal 达到某人的目标，实现某人的目标	legal document 法律文件，法律文书
take... into account 考虑……的因素	take notes of 把 …… 记下来
give thought to 考虑	be obliged to 必须，不得不，只得
be equipped with 配备，装备	supply with 把……提供给……
erase marker 删除标记	watch out for 警惕，当心，注意
flip chart 活动挂图，配套挂图	be compliant with 符合，与……相容
be derived from 来源于，来自，源自	in relation to 和……有关
to this end 为此，为了这个目的	hold sb. accountable for 要某人对……负责
	run the risk of 冒险
	remind sb. of 提醒某人……

Notes

1 Meetings may occur face-to-face or virtually, as mediated by communications technology, such as a telephone conference call, a Skype conference call or a video conference.

本句中，as mediated by communications technology 是"as + 过去分词"结构，该结构用法很广，可用作定语，相当于非限制性定语从句；也可用作方式状语，相当于方式状语从句。请看下例：

The volcano is still active, as evidenced by the recent eruption.

最近的喷发证明，这座火山仍然活跃。

Owing to the rain the garden party did not take place as advertised.

由于下雨，游园会没有按照广告说的时间举行。

2 Next to the chairperson, the secretary could be considered the most important member of a meeting and he or she is crucial to the smooth running of a meeting.

本句中，next to 是形容词词组作状语的用法，意为"仅次于……的"。

英语中，形容词的主要功能是用作定语和表语，但有时也可用作状语补充说明主语。请看下例：

He arrived home, hungry and tired.

他回到家里，又饿又累。

Unable to afford the time, I had to give up the plan.

由于抽不出时间，我不得不放弃这个计划。

另外，be crucial to 意为"对……至关重要的"。请看下例：

Educational access across the life course will be crucial to family success.

在人生历程各个阶段都能受教育对家庭的成功极为重要。

3 The importance of this role is highlighted in the truism that while a bad chairperson can ruin a meeting, a bad secretary can ruin an organization.

本句中，that while a bad chairperson... an organization 是由 that 引导的同位语从句，

用以说明 truism 的具体内容。

英语中，在复合句中用作同位语的从句叫同位语从句，它一般跟在某些名词后面，用以说明该名词表示的具体内容。可以跟同位语从句的名词通常有 news、idea、fact、promise、question、doubt、thought、hope、message、suggestion、words（消息）、possibility 等。请看下例：

The news that he will be improved is flying about.

他将要提升的消息到处传开。

另外，句中 while 作并列连词用，意思为“而，然而”，表示对比。请看下例：

Some people waste food while others haven't enough.

有些人浪费粮食，然而有些人却吃不饱。

4 The larger the list of invitees, the harder it is to find a day and time when everyone is available.

本句中，the larger the list..., the harder it is to... 是“the + 比较级……, the + 比较级……”，表示“越……越……”。请看下例：

As we all know, the older one gets, the more precious time becomes to him.

众所周知，一个人年龄越大，时间对他就越宝贵。

The longer she waited, the more impatient she became.

她等得越久，就越不耐烦。

5 Likewise, you don't want a crowd squeezing in so tight that it's necessary to bring in extra chairs.

本句中，so tight that it's necessary to bring in extra chairs 是“so + *adj.*+ that”引导的结果状语从句，意为：如此……以至于”。相似的句子结构还有“such + a/an + *adj.* + *n.* + that 从句”请看下例：

The problem is so difficult that none of us can work it out.

这个问题太难了，我们没人能解出来。

He was such an honest man that he was praised by the teacher.

他非常诚实，因而受到了老师的表扬。

6 Without such a record it is not possible to hold people accountable for the responsibilities delegated to them.

本句中，delegated to them 是过去分词短语作后置定语，修饰和限定 the responsibilities。

英语中，过去分词用作定语，带有被动意义和完成意义，其构成的短语通常需后置。请看下例：

The most common procedure for doing this is negotiation, the act of communication intended to reach agreement.

做这件事的最常用的方法是谈判——一种想要达成一致的交流的行为。

另外，句中 hold sb. accountable for... 意为“要某人对……负责”。请看下例：

He is mentally ill and cannot be held accountable for his actions.

他有精神病，不能对自己的行为负责。

Exercises

EX. 1 Answer the following questions.

1. What is the definition of a meeting according to Text A?
2. What is the usage of a concise and to-the-point meeting objective?
3. What should the secretary take into consideration while writing an agenda?
4. How should the secretary choose a conference room?
5. What must the secretary send out to all participants when he or she tries to notify them?
6. What abilities should the secretary demonstrate during the meeting?
7. How can the secretary prepare the minutes of the previous meeting?
8. What does it imply if a secretary acts as a compliance officer?
9. What is a good set of minutes a secretary should take?
10. What should the secretary do immediately after the meeting?

EX. 2 Complete the following sentences with appropriate words or expressions in the box.

be equipped with	entrust	demonstrate	mediate	identify
take into account	ensure	consult with	highlight	crucial

1. United Nations officials have ________ a series of peace meetings between the two sides.
2. Talent, hard work and sheer tenacity are all ________ to career success.
3. You'd better make sure that you ________ the key skills and responsibilities in your present and previous organization in your resume.
4. To evaluate this bid we have to ________ their experience and past performance on similar contracts.
5. A style consultant will ________ how to dress to impress.
6. You should ________ the utilities and methods of maintenance administration.
7. The test should ________ which smokers are most prone to develop lung cancer.
8. We have ________ the matter to our representative, who will have a business discussion with you.
9. I think this issue is troublesome and the customer need to ________ their administration department.
10. We must do everything in our power to ________ the success of the conference.

EX. 3 Translate the following sentences into English.

1. 虽然取得了一些进展，但有关各方尚未能够达成协议。(reach an agreement)
2. 根据需要秘书将安排一次电话会议或视频会议，将有关各方召集在一起。(a telephone conference)

3. 双方都应当表明自己如何履行合同规定的责任。(fulfill one's responsibilities)
4. 这些目标和方向，将配合公司的成长——而不是你自己的个人财务增长。(align with)
5. 开会时间如有变，请提前告诉我们。(in advance)
6. 这家公司的行为不仅不合社会伦理，也违反了法律法规。(in violation of)
7. 区域贸易协定 (RTA) 应符合世贸组织 (WTO) 的规则,并考虑到它们的发展层面。(be compliant with)
8. "会议记录"是指在开会的时候记笔记，这样会后你可以对开会的情况做个记录。(take minutes)
9. 现在我们进入了议事日程上的主要议题。(on the agenda)
10. 此外，可由管理人员指定代表做决定。(designate)

EX. 4 **Translate the following passage into Chinese.**

Face-to-face meetings are the most common way for groups to make decisions, solve problems, educate people, and plan programs and projects. Meetings can be productive and accomplish goals efficiently. However, effective meetings do not happen automatically. Planning the design, the equipment needed and who needs to be involved is critical to a meeting's success. Everyone at the meeting is responsible for its success. Some people have key roles to play, especially the chairperson.

The chairperson is responsible for ensuring that meetings are run effectively and efficiently. The chair must consider both the task functions of the group, i.e., the actions and decisions that are critical to achieve, and the maintenance functions — the relationships, welfare and harmony of the group. Both functions are important and will affect the organization's success. The chair has the lead role in planning, preparing, implementing and evaluating meetings and is responsible for starting and ending on time and involving members in the decisions and discussions.

Part Three Text B

Minutes

Minutes, also known as protocols or, informally, notes, are the instant written record of a meeting or hearing. They typically describe the events of the meeting and may include a list of attendees, a statement of the issues considered by the participants, and related responses or decisions for the issues.

Minutes may be created during the meeting by a typist or court reporter, who may use shorthand notation and then prepare the minutes and issue them to the participants afterwards. Alternatively, the meeting can be audio recorded, video recorded, or a group's appointed or informally assigned secretary may take notes, with minutes prepared later.

1. Purposes of Taking Minutes

Minutes are the official written record of the meetings of an organization or group. They are not transcripts of those proceedings. The minutes should contain mainly a record of what was done at the meeting, not what was said by the members. For most organizations or groups, it is important for the minutes to be taken and they are usually taken for the following purposes.

- Minutes offer the basis of the decisions of the board and the rationale behind them. New boards should be able to piece together what happened in the past from the minutes.
- Minutes are an outline of the issues discussed and serve to justify the board's actions. The minutes should always include all the important facts and should record the action taken by a board.
- Minutes serve as a reminder of future action. The board can evaluate the progress of projects by tracking them in the minutes.
- Minutes should offer pertinent information to third parties not present at the formal meeting. Outsiders, such as potential buyers, can and do examine the minutes to judge the financial condition of the property. The minutes are also reviewed by owners to evaluate the competency of the board.
- Minutes are confidential and, once approved, can be used in court to prove the board acted responsibly or to prove liability.

In general, taking minutes is essential to most meetings, not only for recording purposes but also for follow up action, next steps, and possible disciplinary action that may ensue. The minutes of meetings are a record of discussions and decisions, and over time they might form an important historical record. There might also be a legal requirement for sets of minutes to be produced in an organization–as in the case of a bank or a limited company.

2. How to Take Minutes

Nowadays, lots of organizations, groups, and businesses have meetings where a record needs to be kept of the proceedings and decisions made. The written record of these meeting events are called the "minutes of meetings". The purpose of taking minutes of the meeting is more or less the same in each case — to keep an accurate record of events for future possible reference. However, many people in the position of taking minutes are not clear about how to go about it. Thus, it may be of great help for them to follow the following tips.

- Ensure that all of the essential elements are noted, such as type of meeting, name of the organization, date and time, venue, name of the chair or facilitator, main topics and the time of adjournment. For formal and corporate meetings, minutes include approval of previous minutes, and all resolutions.
- Prepare an outline based on the agenda ahead of time, and leave plenty of white space for notes. By having the topics already written down, you can jump right on to a new topic without pause.
- Prepare a list of expected attendees and check off the names as people enter the room. Or, you can pass around an attendance sheet for everyone to sign as the meeting starts.
- To be sure about who said what, make a map of the seating arrangement, and make sure to ask

for introductions of unfamiliar people.

- Don't make the mistake of recording every single comment. Concentrate on getting the gist of the discussion and taking enough notes to summarize it later. Think in terms of issues discussed, major points raised and decisions taken.
- Use whatever recording method is comfortable for you, a notepad, a laptop computer, a tape recorder, or shorthand. It might be a good idea to make sound recordings of important meetings as a backup to your notes.
- If you are an active participant in the meeting, be prepared! Study the issues to be discussed and have your questions ready ahead of time. If you have to concentrate on grasping the issues while you are making your notes, they won't make any sense to you later.
- Don't wait too long to type up the minutes, especially while your memory is fresh. Be sure to have the minutes approved by the chair or facilitator before distributing them to the attendees.
- Don't be intimidated by the prospect of taking minutes. Concise and coherent minutes are the mark of a professional. The very process of recording minutes can give you a deeper understanding of the issues faced by your organization along with ability to focus on what's important.

3. Format of Minutes

The format of the minutes can vary depending on the standards established by an organization, although there are general guidelines.

• Beginning

Generally, minutes begin with the name of the body holding the meeting (e.g., a board) and may also include the place, date, list of people present, and the time that the chair called the meeting to order.

• Body

Since the primary function of minutes is to record the decisions made, all official decisions must be included. If a formal motion is proposed, seconded, passed, or not, then this is recorded. The voting tally may also be included. The part of the minutes dealing with a routine motion might note merely that a particular motion was "moved by Ann and passed". It is not strictly necessary to include the name of the person who seconds a motion. Where a tally is included, it is sufficient to record the number of people voting for and against a motion, but requests by participants to note their votes by name may be allowed. If a decision is made by a roll-call vote, then all of the individual votes are recorded by name. If it is made by general consent without a formal vote, then this fact may be recorded.

• Closing

The minutes may end with a note of the time that the meeting was adjourned. Minutes are sometimes submitted by the person who is responsible for them (often the secretary) at a subsequent meeting for review. The traditional closing phrase is "Respectfully submitted" (although this is no longer common), followed by the officer's signature, his or her typed (or printed) name, and his or her title.

To illustrate the format of minutes of meetings, here is a sample for meeting minutes available in the following table.

Sample minutes of meetings:

Westleigh Maintenance Company Ltd.

Minutes of Annual General Meeting

Monday, 18 July, 2016

Time and Place

Monday, 18 July, 2016 at 6:00p.m. In Conference Room 2.

Present

Julie Culshaw, Mary Greenhalgh, Vera Sisson, Ingrid Kempster, Edward Kempster, Irene Rodger, Colin Rodger, Gerry Clarke, Edith Pickles, Pat Powell, Heather Pollitt, Roy Johnson.

Apologies

Manoj Hira, Reg Marsden, Lavinia Marsden, John Sillar.

1. Minutes of the last AGM held on 22 July, 2015 were accepted.

2. The accounts for the year ended 31 March, 2016 were accepted.

Although these showed an overall loss, this was due to late maintenance payments, and these had since been paid.

3. Appointment of accountants.

The finance director suggested that we remain with our current accountants, and this was accepted.

4. Appointment of directors.

The current directors were all standing for re-election. There were no nominations for new directors. The current directors were re-elected.

5. Appointment of company secretary.

Julie Culshaw moved a vote of thanks and appreciation to the secretary and other directors in recognition of the amount of work they undertook on behalf of the Company.

Heather Pollitt was elected as secretary.

6. Increase in service charge.

Because of the lack of any surplus to pay for improvements and maintenance, the directors recently looked into the possibility of arranging a bank overdraft. This was not pursued because of the cost and the excessive bureaucracy attached. The possibility of extraordinary payments was also discussed and rejected in favour of an increase in the service charge.

The meeting finally agreed that the directors should prepare a financial projection for the next one to two years, based on an increase in the annual service charge to somewhere between £1100 and £1200.

7. Managing agents.

The directors recently decided to end the relationship with the Guthrie Partnership as managing agents, because it was felt that the directors themselves were able to act more efficiently on behalf of Westleigh and its interests.

However, the advisory services of Alec Guthrie himself would be retained as and when required for legal purposes.

The meeting concluded at 20:15.

Respectfully submitted

Taylor Swift, Secretary to President

New Words

hearing ['hiəriŋ] *n.* 听证会
alternatively [ɔːl'təːnətivli] *adv.* 二者择一地，作为选择，或者
audio ['ɔːdiəu] *n.* 音频；音响设备
appoint [ə'pɔint] *v.* 任命，委派，指定
transcript ['trænskript] *n.* 抄本，副本，笔录
rationale [ˌræʃə'nɑːl] *n.* 依据，理论，原因
justify ['dʒʌstifai] *vt.* 证明……有理，为……辩护
evaluate [i'væljueit] *v.* 评价，估价
examine [ig'zæmin] *vt.* 检查，调查
property ['prɔpəti] *n.* 特性，属性，财产，地产
confidential [kɔnfi'denʃəl] *adj.* 机密的，秘密的
liability [ˌlaiə'biliti] *n.* 责任，债务，倾向
venue ['venjuː] *n.* 会场
facilitator [fə'siliteitə] *n.* 服务商，促进者，帮助者
adjournment [ə'dʒəːnmənt] *n.* 休会，延期，休会期
gist [dʒist] *n.* 要领，要点，主旨
summarize ['sʌməraiz] *vt.* 总结，概述
backup ['bækʌp] *n.* 支持，后援；备份文件
intimidate [in'timideit] *vt.* 恐吓，威胁
prospect ['prɔspekt] *n.* 前景，期望，展望
coherent [kəu'hiərənt] *adj.* 连贯的，一致的
mark [mɑːk] *n.* 记号；标准 *vt.* 做记号；表示
motion ['məuʃən] *n.* 提议；移动；动作，打手势，示意
propose [prə'pəuz] *v.* 提出建议，倡议
second ['sekənd] *v.* 支持，赞成，附和，调派
tally ['tæli] *n.* 记账；记分；一致 *v.* 计算，记录
consent [kən'sent] *n.&v.* 同意，答应
submit [səb'mit] *vt.* 使服从，使屈服；提交，递交
subsequent ['sʌbsikwənt] *adj.* 随后的，后来的
maintenance ['meintinəns] *n.* 维修，维护，保持
nomination [nɔmi'neiʃən] *n.* 提名，任命
surplus ['səːpləs] *n.* 过剩，顺差，盈余 *adj.* 过剩的，多余的
overdraft ['əuvədrɑːft] *n.* 透支
extraordinary [iks'trɔːdnri] *adj.* 非凡的，特别的
reject [ri'dʒekt] *vt.* 拒绝，排斥，驳回，丢弃 *n.* 不合格产品；被拒之人
advisory [əd'vaizəri] *adj.* 顾问的，咨询的，劝告的
retain [ri'tein] *vt.* 保持，保留，记住，聘请
conclude [kən'kluːd] *vi.* 结束，总结

Phrases and Expressions

shorthand notation 速记符号
piece together 拼凑，把……拼合起来
take action 采取行动
go about 从事，着手做，开始做
ahead of time 提前，预先，事先
check off 清点；登记；核对
pass around 分，分发，传送
seating arrangements 安排座位
concentrate on 专心于，把思想集中于，将……集中于……
make sense 有意义，理解，讲得通
second a motion 赞成提议
a roll-call vote 记名投票
remain with 属于，归于
stand for 代表，为……而奋斗，拥护
in recognition of 承认……，为酬答……，按照（功劳等）……
service charge 服务费
in favor of 赞成，支持
financial projection 财务预测

Abbreviations

AGM (Annual General Meeting) 年度例会

Exercises

EX. 5 Answer the following questions.

1. What do meeting minutes typically describe and include according to Text B?
2. Should the minutes contain mainly a record of what was done at the meeting or what was said by the members?
3. Why are the minutes important to outsiders?
4. What role can the confidential minutes play in court once approved?
5. What are the essential elements should be noted in the minutes?
6. How could you get yourself prepared if you are an active participant in the meeting?
7. What does the secretary have to do before distributing the typed minutest to the attendees?
8. What information should be included in the beginning of the minutes?
9. Is it a strict necessity for the secretary to record during the meeting the name of the person who seconds a motion?

10. How may the minutes usually end?

Part Four Extended Reading

Text	Notes
Importance of Business Meeting and Recording a Business Meeting	
1. Importance of Business Meeting	
Meeting is one of the major media of oral communication. It is essentially important for every organization. The basic objective[1] of meeting is to make decisions on some predetermined[2] issues. It has also some other purposes. The importance of meeting is discussed below:	[1] *n.* 目标，目的 [2] *adj.* 预先确定的，预先设定的
• Making Decisions: The foremost[3] objective of any meeting is to take important decisions on some predetermined issue. Decisions are taken here on consensus[4] and it is very crucial to take decisions on routine[5] and non-routine business affairs.	[3] 第一流的，最重要的，最初的，最前面的 [4] *n.* 共识，一致性 [5] *n.* 常规，例行程序
• Exchanging Information: Meeting is arranged also to provide information to the audience about various matters of the organization. Audience also exchange information in meetings.	
• Conveying Organizational Vision, Mission[6] and Operational Plans: Meetings are also called to convey organizational mission, vision and operational plans to the newly appointed[7] employees. Managers or heads of various departments call these types of meetings for the fresher so that they can be better acquainted with[8] organizational culture, mission, vision, plans etc.	[6] *n.* 使命，任务 [7] *adj.* 新任命的 [8] 了解，知道
• Announcing Changes: Another purpose of arranging meeting is to announce the upcoming[9] changes brought in organizational policies, mission, vision, logo[10] etc. before the audience. The causes, benefits and ground of such changes are explained in the meeting so that people understand and accept the probable changes without much resistance[11].	[9] *adj.* 即将来到的 [10] *n.* 标识，商标 [11] *n.* 抵抗，抵抗力
• Negotiation[12]: Meeting is also called for making negotiations between the conflicting[13] parties through fruitful[14] discussion. Sometimes employers and employees or trade union leaders sit in meeting together to reach on some agreement so that organizational activities can be run smoothly.	[12] *n.* 协商，谈判 [13] *adj.* 相矛盾的，冲突的； [14] *adj.* 丰富的，硕果累累，有利的

• Resolving Conflict[15]: In large organizations conflict among people is most common. Healthy conflict helps to increase productivity[16] but unhealthy or undesirable[17] conflict must be resolved immediately after found. Meeting helps the conflicting parties to reach on common understanding and thus resolving or minimizing[18] conflict.	[15] *n.* 冲突，矛盾 [16] *n.* 生产率，生产力 [17] *adj.* 不合需要的 [18] *vt.* 缩小，降低
• Solving Problems: An important purpose of meeting is to provide solution[19] to organizational problems. Problems that are critical and require opinions of most of the members of a board or council[20] must be solved by calling meeting. In meeting diverse [21]thoughts are found that help to face problem suitably.	[19] *n.* 解决办法或方案 [20] *n.* 委员会，（郡、镇等）政务会
• Reviewing and Informing Progress: Meeting is also called for reviewing and informing the progress of any project, plan and activity and so on. Form it the attendants of the meeting are able to know the present status[22] of the projects and can provide their opinions to improve if there is any loophole[23].	[21] *adj.* 各式各样的 [22] *n.* 现状 [23] *n.* 漏洞，观察孔
• Celebrating[24] Success: Meetings are often called to celebrate the success of the organization, completion[25] of any project, achievement of any award etc. It increases the organizational harmony[26] and motivates[27] employees to work united to achieve more.	[24] *vt.* 庆祝 [25] *n.* 完成，完结 [26] *n.* 和谐，协调，融洽，一致 [27] *n.* 利益相关者，股东
• Interaction with External Stakeholders[27]: Every organization is to work with different parties of the society and it must build a long term harmonious[28] relationship with them. Meetings are called to exchange information and to share experience with different stakeholders of an organization so that their interaction with the firm is increased.	[28] *adj.* 协调的，和谐的，融洽的
Evidently[29], meeting has great importance in business. Without it, business activities cannot be performed smoothly. In fact it serves important purposes for an organization.	[29] *adv.* 明显地
2. Importance of Recording a Meeting	
It is standard procedure[30] in most business meetings to record everything of importance that transpires[31] in a meeting. Methods of record-keeping may vary, but the most common method is having a secretary take notes. These notes, or minutes, are usually first circulated[32] in draft form so that all participants have the opportunity to check for accuracy and to make corrections[33] if necessary. This ensures that all participants agree that the record is accurate.The importance of recording a business meeting can be described as follows.	[30] *n.* 程序，手续 [31] *v.* 发生；显露 [32] *vt.*（使）循环，（使）流通，（使）流传 [33] 订正，矫正

• Attendance[34] and Accountability[35]: The names of everyone in attendance at the meeting are usually the first things recorded. This serves two purposes: Absent members can stay in the loop[36] and keep abreast of[37] what they missed at the meeting, and their absence from this meeting becomes part of the public record. If some participants regularly find ways to avoid meetings, they might be more reluctant to skip[38] a future meeting when they realize their repeated absences have been noted.	[34] *n.* 出席率，出席 [35] *n.* 责任制,有责任，有义务 [36] *n.* 回路，圈，环 [37] 了解……的最新情况 [38] *v.* 跳过，略过，漏过
• Reference Purposes: Unfortunately, human memory is fallible[39]. Some participants are likely to have selective memories and forget whatever doesn't substantiate[40] their viewpoint, particularly for controversial[41] issues. A public record is an objective means to remind everyone what was agreed upon and why. It is especially important to have records to refer back to after a significant amount of time has passed and people are no longer sure what transpired. New managers find it helpful to review previous meeting minutes to quickly learn how the organization has been functioning and to detect patterns in behavior of the participants.	[39] *adj.* 容易犯错的 [40] *vt.* 证实，证明 [41] *adj.* 有争议的，引起争议的
• Open Communication: Recording a meeting and making the record available to other interested parties who were not invited to participate in the meeting is a way to be more inclusive[42]. Although the others might not have been able to provide their input during the meeting, they can still see how decisions were made. They will have some knowledge about the decision-making process and will know who the key players were. They will be able to approach[43] meeting participants and offer their point of view if they so choose.	[42] *adj.* 包括的，包罗广泛的，包括……的 [43] *v.* 接近，走近，靠近
• Action Plans: Meetings tend to become more efficient when participants are aware of being recorded; they are more likely to stay on topic. The minutes provide a record of decisions made and who is responsible for taking action[44]. There is an increased chance that these actions will be carried out. Without a record, the participants might not remember who is responsible for the next step of the action plan and disputes[45] might arise[46]. With a public record to refer to, those responsible will be held accountable[47] and expected to proceed as agreed. Unresolved[48] issues won't be forgotten and can be revisited at a subsequent[49] meeting.	[44] 采取行动 [45] *n.* 争议，分歧 [46] *v.* 出现，产生 [47] 追究责任 [48] *adj.* 未解决的，不果断的 [49] *adj.* 随后的，后来的

参考译文

课文A 会 议

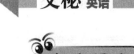

会议是两个或两个以上的人召开的一种集会。在会上，他们借助口头交流，如共享信息或达成协议等形式来实现共同的目标。会议可以是面对面的，也可以是由通信技术作媒介的虚拟会议，如电话会议、Skype 电话会议或视频会议 。

每一个组织，无论其规模大小，在一定的时间间隔内都会安排不少的会议来讨论并决定不同的问题。公司利用商务会议回顾公司的信息或建立新的经营原则。大多数会议由管理层主持，会议有助于员工了解公司的财务状况或经营情况。

秘书被看作是会议中的最重要成员，其重要性仅次于会议主席，并且对于会议的顺利召开至关重要。秘书安排会议，确保准确地记录会议活动，并负责跟进与会者的后续事宜，如有必要的话。为了做到工作有效，秘书的工作将涉及三个阶段：会议召开前、会议期间和会议结束后。

1. 会议召开前

秘书是会议召开前的关键角色之一。这个角色的重要性是不言而喻的，正如老话说的那样，糟糕的会议主席可能毁掉一次会议，而不称职的秘书可能会毁掉一个组织。为了很好地发挥作用，秘书需要具备杰出的策划技能，并履行以下职责。

1.1 设定会议目标

在做任何安排前，秘书应当与主席磋商，就会议目的、议程事项的处理顺序及方式、需要讨论和需要决议的事项等方面达成最终决定。

根据会议主席的指示，秘书可以设定会义目标，并简洁明确地加以说明。一个简明扼要的会议目标有助于确定谁应当参加会议、谁的出席会有可能使会议真正地实现具体的目标。

1.2 写议事日程

明确了会议目标后，秘书将写一份会议的议事日程。有组织的会议需要一份写得极好的议事日程表。如果没有日程表，会议将是冗长而低效的。一份详细的、灵活的日程安排可以使会议流畅地进行，并且目的明确，确保在最短的时间内实现所有的既定目标。在写议事日程的时候，秘书应考虑会议的具体目标。如果目标是传达一个项目启动方面的信息，则可以设置一项议题，确定汇报信息的人选以及共享信息的方式，如使用 PowerPoint 演示文稿。如果这个目标是分配任务，则可以设置一项议题，说明如何进行任务分配。每一个目标都应该有一个或多个与它直接配套的议题项。

为了说明议事日程的格式，下表给出了一个商务会议议程的样本：

会议议程

电影“Just Us”
制作会议议程
日期 / 时间：2016 年 1 月 15 日上午 11:00 —下午 1:30
地点：会议室 B
与会者：
Joshua Walker ——制片人
Shara Jenkins ——作者 / 导演
Aren Vermont ——创意总监
Dalila Fialho ——发行总监
目标
• 审定脚本
• 制定筹资策略
• 确定前期制作时间表
时间安排

11:00 至 11:15	检查，更新材料—— Aren Vermont
11:15 至 11:45	审查剧本，做新的更改—— Shara Jenkins
11:45 至 13:00	更新筹款信息—— Dalila Fialho
13:00 至 13:15	汇报前期制作时间安排—— Joshua Walker
13:15 至 13:30	公告——所有人员

角色 / 职责
会议记录—— Joshua Walker

1.3 选定日期和时间

与会议主席商量后，秘书需要根据会议领导以及最关键的受邀人员的时间空档选定会议的日期和时间。受邀的与会者越多，就越难找出每个人都有空的日期和时间。尽量选定与大多数与会者时间安排相一致的时间。在设定时间之前，还需考虑时区差异。如果与会者通过电话或互联网参加会议，则需要考虑他们以及你自己的工作时间。

1.4 选定会议地点

至于会议地点，秘书需要找一个可能实现所有议程项目的会议室。选择的会议室大小要能充裕地容纳预期与会者的数量。40 座的会议室不适合只有 10 人参加的会议。同样，也不要把大家挤进加座才能坐下的会议室。

1.5 安排材料及杂项

如果要做报告，秘书必须确保会议室配备有投影仪。如果没有，则应该安排带一台投影仪，也要确保配有供投影的设施，如屏幕或白色的墙壁。别忘了提供其他材料，如白板、干的板擦、挂图以及为不在会场的与会者准备扬声器电话。在长达几小时的会议上，秘书最好安排一些食物和饮料，这样参与者就能集中精力关注会议话题，而不是他们的胃。

1.6 通知与会者

经会议主席的指示，秘书必须提前向所有与会者发出会议通知。与会议通知同时发出的还包括会议议程、上次会议记录以及会议讨论所需的任何资料。还需要提供会议议程、上次会议记录和其他资料的纸制复印本，即使这些材料已经通过电子邮件提前发给了与会者。

2. 会议期间

在会议期间，秘书需要具备倾听、理解、准确记录、概括等能力，并能做到中立、正直和保密。

在写作和演讲中具备清晰准确的表达能力是一个优秀秘书的重要特质，但重要的是要记住，"秘书"这个词来源于"保密"，它强调秘书要对组织交托给自己的信息遵守保密原则。

秘书在会议期间的主要职责与下列事项有关：

2.1 提前到场

秘书应当在会议召开之前就到会场，并携带会议记录、所有会议相关信件和会务资料。

2.2 确定出席人数

协助主席确定是否所有的受邀者都出席时，秘书有必要传发考勤登记表，记录到会者的名字，转达并记录的缺席人员的事由。

2.3 宣读缺席人员

如果会议规模小，很可能没有必要公布出勤情况。做会议记录的人认识每一个与会者，能确定到会与缺席的人员。如果会议规模较大，可能发考勤登记表或点名。如果一个重要人物缺席，秘书或主席有必要通报缺席人员，并简要解释。

2.4 获批先前会议记录

为了复阅以前的交易情况，会议主席通常会要求秘书准备以前会议的记录。为此，秘书应该获得批准，才能调出会议记录。如果这些记录获批，他或她应该确保主席在获批的记录上签字，并且秘书还应记录下这个事实。

2.5 宣传先前会议记录

会议记录是正式会议议程的正式记录，在一些国家被认为是法律文件，特别是对于那些有许多股东的公司而言。宣读上次会议记录的目的是提供有关业务往来的一份精确而又简洁的记录文本。

2.6 做会议记录

如果没有专门的会议记录秘书，公司秘书通常被指定为会议做记录。记录关键点，确保记录下所有的决定和提议，以及负责执行决议和提案的个人或小组名字。

2.7 提供信息

会议期间，秘书必须确保主席获得会议议项所需的所有必要资料，并提醒主席是否有议项被忽略了。

2.8 发挥监察作用

担任监察任务意味着，秘书需要密切注意会议违反立法或违反组织规定或政策的情况。他或她应该有足够的见识，以确保会议的决议符合该机构的政策、程序和法规，以及相关立法。

2.9 创造轻松氛围

秘书可以问候与会成员，让他们感到受欢迎，在适当的时候，即使对迟到的成员也应当打招呼。如果可能的话，提供一些点心。因为点心能很好地打破僵局，让你的成员感觉特别和舒服。

当然，在这些职责当中，最重要的是做会议记录。会议记录是会议议程的记录。记录对在场的成员具有约束力，并且可用作法庭上认可的证据。一份好的完整的会议记录并不是记录谁在会议上说过什么话。相反，会议记录应该突出强调会议上做出的决定和采取的决议。记录应该清楚详细地说明针对这些决议需要通过的具体措施是什么，包括采取措施的时间、负责人以及利用的资源。没有这样的记录，不可能让人们对派给他们的职责承担责任。另外，试图记录会议上的争论会有妨碍提案并产生混乱的风险。但是，会议记录的简洁性并不意味着缺席会议的人就无从得知会议内容。

3. 会议结束后

秘书应当在会议结束后趁自己对会议内容还记忆犹新时，立即整理并分发会议记录。明智的做法是准备好一份会议记录的草案，征求会议主席和多数高级职员的同意，然后将副本发给会议成员和其他需要被告知会议信息的成员。会议结束后，会议记录发送得越早，就能越及时地提醒相关人员所承担的工作。

课文B 会议记录

会议记录也被称作记录或非正式的笔记，是对会议或听证会的即时性文字记录。它们通常记载会议的活动，也包括与会者的名单、与会者陈述的问题以及对有关问题做出的答复或决定。

会议记录可在会议期间由打字员或法院记录员创制。他们可用速记符号做记录，然后写成会议记录，再分发给与会者。另外，会议可以采用音频记录、视频记录，或由集团特定的或临时指派的秘书来做笔记，并在会后整理成会议记录。

1. 会议记录的目的

会议记录是一个组织或团体会议的正式书面记录。会议记录不是转录会议事项。该记录应主要记录会议上所做的事情，而不是与会成员讲过的话。会议记录对于大多数组织或团体来说是很重要的。通常，做会议记录有以下几个目的。

- 会议记录为董事会提供决策基础及理论依据。新的董事会可根据会议记录弄清楚过去发生的事情。
- 会议记录概括会议讨论的问题并为董事会的措施提供依据。记录应该包括所有重要的事实，并记录下董事会采取的措施。

- 会议记录可提示未来采取的行为措施。董事会可以通过追查会议记录中的相关记录对项目的进展情况进行评估。
- 会议记录应当为未出席正式会议的第三方人员提供相关信息。外人，如潜在客户，可以并确实会仔细研究会议记录，来判定财产财务状况。老板也可以复查会议记录，以评估董事会的能力。
- 会议记录具有保密性，一经批准，可以在法庭上证明董事会履行的职责或承担的义务。

一般来说，做会议记录对大多数会议来说是极其重要的，不仅是为了记录会议本身，也是为了后续采取的行动和下一步措施，以及随之可能产生的处罚行为。会议记录记载讨论内容和决定，而且随着时间的推移，可能成为一份重要的历史记录。在组织中做成套会议记录也可能是一种法律规定，如银行或有限公司。

2. 如何做会议记录

如今，许多组织、团体和企业都召开会议，会议活动和决策都需要被记录下来。这些会议事件的书面记载被称为“会议记录”。会议记录的目的在每一种情况下基本相同，即准确记录会议事件以供将来参考。然而，许多承担会议记录任务的人，却不清楚该如何记录。因此，采纳以下建议可能是有用的。

- 确保记录下所有重要的内容，如会议类型、组织名称、会议日期、时间、地点、会议主持人的名字、会议主题以及会议结束时间。对于正式会议和公司会议而言，会议记录还需记录先前会议记录的批准事宜，以及所有的决议。
- 根据会议议程提前写好大纲，并留下足够的空白记笔记。如果已经记录下那些话题，可以立即开始记录下一个新的话题。
- 准备好预期与会者的名单并在他们进入会场时进行核对。或者，在会议开始的时候，发签到单让大家签名。
- 确定发言者及其发言内容，制作一张座次表，并务必请求自己不熟悉的人员做介绍。
- 不要犯记录每一句话的错误。应把注意力集中在讨论的要点上，并做足够的笔记，以便以后总结。应考虑会议上讨论的问题，提出的主要观点以及做出的决议。
- 使用任何你觉得顺手的记录方式，如记事本、笔记本电脑、录音机，或速记。对重要会议进行录音，给笔记提供备用素材，这也许是个好主意。
- 如果是会议的积极参与者，你一定要做好准备！提前研究拟讨论的问题，并预备好你拟提出的问题。如果在必须集中精力理解问题的时候，你却在做笔记，那么事后你将理解不了这些问题。
- 不要过很长时间才将会议记录打出来，特别是当你记忆犹新时。一定要先征得会议主席的批准，才能将会议记录分发给与会者。
- 不要一想到做会议记录就被吓倒了。会做简明连贯的会议记录是专业人员的标志。正是做会议记录的整个过程可以让你更深入地了解你的组织所面临的问题，并且使你能够把注意力集中在重要的事情上。

3. 会议记录的格式

会议记录的格式可以根据一个组织建立的标准而有所变化，但也有总的指导准则。

• 开头

一般来说，会议记录都是以举办会议的组织名称开头（例如，董事会），也可能包括会议地点、日期、出席人的名单以及主席宣布会议开始的时间。

• 主体

由于会议记录的主要功能是记录会议做出的决定，所有正式的决定都必须包括在会议记录内。如果一个正式的提议被提出、附议，无论是否通过，都应该记录在内。投票结果也可以案记录在内。涉及常规提议的这部分会议记录可能只会记下某个特定的提案是谁提出的，并在会上通过。谁附议了一项提案，他的名字未必一定要记录在内。当记录投票结果时，记录下投票赞成或反对一项提案的人数即可，但如果与会者请求以实名制记录他们投票，那么可以记录他们的名字。如果一项决议通过记名投票的方式进行表决，则按名字记录下所有的个人投票结果。 如果未经正式投票，而对某项决议达成一致意见，则记录这个事实。

• 结束语

会议记录最后可以写上会议结束的时间。在随后召开的会议上,负责会议记录的人(通常是秘书）有时会呈递会议记录以供复阅。传统的结束语是“谨写”（虽然这种做法不再常见），然后是官员的签名、打印名以及头衔。

为了说明会议记录的格式，下列的表格提供一份会议记录范例。

会议记录范例：

韦斯特利维修有限公司

年度例会会议记录

2016 年 7 月 18 日

时间和地点

2016 年 7 月 18 日（星期一）下午 6:00 在第二会议室举行

与会人员

Julie Culshaw, Mary Greenhalgh, Vera Sisson, Ingrid Kempster, Edward Kempster, Irene Rodger, Colin Rodger, Gerry Clarke, Edith Pickles, Pat Powell, Heather Pollitt, Roy Johnson.

缺席人员

Manoj Hira, Reg Marsden, Lavinia Marsden, John Sillar.

1. 宣读并通过 2015 年 7 月 22 日年度例会的会议记录。
2. 通过截至 2016 年 3 月 31 日的年度财务报告。

   虽然账目显示整体亏损，但这是维修款逾期支付造成的，而现在这些款项已付讫。
3. 任命会计人员。

   财务主任提议我们继续任用现任会计人员，这项提议被采纳。
4. 任命董事。

   目前的董事们都在争取连任。由于没有提名新董事的候选人，现任董事连任。
5. 任命公司秘书。

   Julie Culshaw 提议大家向秘书和其他董事鼓掌致谢，感激并认可他们为了公司的利益所做的大量工作。

   Heather Pollitt 当选公司秘书。

6. 增收服务费。

由于缺少结余资金来支付公司的改建和维修费用，董事们最近研究了从银行透支的可能性。由于附加的花费大和手续烦琐，该提议未得以实施。会议还讨论并否决了公司额外支出一笔钱的可能性，目前还是赞成增收服务费。

会议最后一致同意，董事们应该基于将年服务费提高到1100英镑至1200英镑之间的方案来准备未来一年到两年的财务预测。

7. 管理代理人。

董事们最近决定结束Guthrie公司作为本公司经营代理人的身份，因为他们认为董事们自己能够代表公司为其利益更有效地采取措施。

然而，为法律目的所需，本公司将保留Alec Guthrie本人的法律顾问一职。

这次会议于20:15结束。

谨写

泰勒·斯威夫特（总裁秘书）

Unit 8

Business Trip

Part One Dialogues

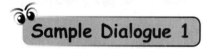

Sample Dialogue 1

Situation ▶ Zhang Ping is confirming a business travel arrangements with her boss.

(A—Zhang Ping, the executive secretary of Shanghai East Asia United International Trade Co.,Ltd.; B—Mr. Peterson, the president of Shanghai of East Asia United International Trade Co.,Ltd.)

A: May I come in?

B: Yes. Come in please.

A: Good morning, Mr. Peterson. Here is a copy of the itinerary I have worked out for you. Will you have a look at it now?

B: Oh, yes. Thank you. Well. Could you tell me some details about the itinerary?

A: OK. I've arranged for you to meet Mr. Brown on Tuesday morning. Does it fit in with your schedule?

B: Good.

A: And the meeting is at 3 o'clock Tuesday afternoon.

B: Ah, it seems to be a busy schedule.

A: Oh, no. According to the time schedule, your negotiations will be completed in three days and you'll be left two days free, if it is all right with you.

B: Oh, that's a good idea. Have you arranged something organized like shopping for me?

A: In fact, shopping is included in the schedule. You can do some shopping in the remaining days. And a city tour is included, too.

B: It sounds great.

A: Please don't hesitate to make any changes. I really wish you can have a pleasant and fruitful business trip.

B: Thank you, Miss Zhang! But there is one more thing, when is the return flight?

A: The return flight is at 10 o'clock Friday morning. Is that OK for you?

Sample Dialogue 2

Situation ▶ Li Fang is booking a hotel room for her executive over the telephone.

(A—a hotel clerk of Palm Tree Hotel; B—Li Fang, the executive secretary of LiChun Industry Co.,Ltd.)

A: Good morning. Palm Tree Hotel. May I help you?

B: Good morning. My executive will be staying in Bing Hai for three days. Have you got any rooms available for the nights of 8th and 9th? I'd like to make a reservation for two nights.

A: All right. What kind of room would you like? Single or double-room?

B: A single room, please.

A: One moment please. I'll just have a look. Yes, we have got a single room available.

B: Is that a single room with an ocean view? You see, my executive usually prefers to stay in a room and enjoy the beautiful ocean view.

A: Yes. It is a room with an ocean view.

B: That sounds fine. Is it a room with shower and toilet?

A: Yes, of course.

B: Then, what is the rate, please?

A: Let me see. A single-room with an ocean view ¥400 per night.

B: What services come with that?

A: It includes morning newspaper, continental breakfast and service.

B: Great.

A: May I have your executive's name and phone number, please?

B: Yes. It's John Hans. It's 88131517.

A: Could spell his name, please?

B: J-o-h-n-h-a-n-s.

A: John Hans. A single room with an ocean view for the nights of 8th and 9th.

B: That's right.

A: Now, your reservation is guaranteed, Miss. Thank you.

B: Thank you. You have been most helpful.

Useful Expressions

1. Here is a copy of itinerary I have worked out for you. Will you have a look at it now?
   这是为您做的行程。您现在能看一下吗?
2. I've arranged for you to meet Mr. Brown on Tuesday morning. Does it fit in with your schedule?
   您和布朗先生的会面安排在星期二上午，和您的时间冲突吗?
3. According to the time schedule, your negotiations will be completed in three days and you'll be left two days free, if it is all right with you.
   根据这个时间安排，您的谈判在三天内能结束。如果您愿意的话，将有两天自由支配的时间。
4. Please don't hesitate to make any changes.
   如果您想改动的话，请一定告诉我。
5. I really wish you can have a pleasant and fruitful business trip.
   希望您能旅行愉快并有所收获。
6. Have you got any rooms available for the nights of 8th and 9th?
   请问 8 号和 9 号晚上还有空房间吗?
7. What kind of room would you like? Single or double-room?
   请问您要预定什么样的空间? 单人房还是双人房?
8. A single-room with an ocean view ¥400 per night.
   一间海景单人房每晚 400 元。
9. It includes morning newspaper, continental breakfast and service.
   它包括晨报、欧式早餐和我们的服务。
10. Now, your reservation is guaranteed, Miss.
    现在，您已成功预订了酒店，女士。

Situational Dialogues

Using the Sample Dialogue as a model, try to create a new dialogue with your partner.

Situation 1 ▶ Xu Ying, a secretary of Fuyang Cocoon Silk Company Ltd., is confirm the business travel itinerary with John Smith, her boss.

Situation 2 ▶ Zhang Ping, a secretary in Ningbo Qihua Supply Chain Service Co., Ltd., is reserving a hotel room for Jane Gates, her executive.

Part Two Text A

Business Travel Arrangements

A business travel is a trip undertaken for work or business purposes, as opposed to other types of travels, such as for leisure purposes or regularly commuting between one's home and workplace. The necessity to conduct business travels may involve many reasons, such as visiting customers or suppliers, attending meetings at other company locations, marketing or promoting a new or an existing product , etc.

In some large companies, there is a department which is in charge of the travel arrangements for its staff. However, in many small companies, it is left to the secretary to make travel arrangements for her boss or other employees.

Making travel arrangements can be very stressful which takes a good deal of planning and foresight. However, despite the stress, planning a trip can be a great opportunity to show your company your capabilities and skills, earning the confidence of your superiors. Therefore, it is a necessity for a secretary to know how to arrange a business trip and she can start by dividing her actions into three stages: making preparations, planning an itinerary and contacting travel agency.

1. Making Preparations

One of the most important things to keep in mind when planning a trip for your boss is to never make assumptions. When you're assigned the task of taking care of business travel details, write down all of the information that you're given and make full preparations for arranging a business travel.

1.1 Know the Budget

Determine what sort of budget exists for the trip. This will serve as a useful reference point throughout the planning process. It is also helpful to break the global budget down into ingredients such as airfare, transportation, accommodations, etc. Some assistants will have to determine the budget themselves; others will need to ask the executive or the accounting department.

1.2 Go to the Archives

If possible, contact any assistants or staff members who were responsible or involved in the executive's travel arrangements on prior trips to see what sort of insights can be collected from their experiences. They may have already done much of the fact-finding labor for you, and they may have made blunders you will want to avoid.

1.3 Traveler's Details

Gather the details necessary for making reservations and booking flights. These should include the traveler's:

Full name (as it appears on drivers license or ID)

Email address

ID/drivers license number

Phone number (necessary in cases of cancellation or delay)

Credit card number and expiration date

Address

Have these legible and organized details on hand when it comes time to make the actual reservations and bookings.

1.4 Permission Granted

Make sure the executive's passport is valid and will not be expiring in the near future. Certain countries require vaccination forms and Visas, so these matters should also be taken into account and dealt with if necessary, as should travel insurance.

1.5 To and From the Airport

Don't forget to take this important detail into consideration. Will the executive be driving his own vehicle to the airport (and leaving it in long term airport parking), or will somebody else be driving him? Will he use a car service, taxi, public transportation? How much luggage will the executive be taking, and must any of it be checked?

1.6 The Schedule

This may be the most important part of the preparations. Make a list of exact dates and time the traveler needs or desires to be at each destination, from the beginning of the trip to the end, including when she needs or desires to reach home. Accuracy is critical here, so make sure to double check every detail.

Know the exact location, time, and nature of each meeting, engagement, or event the traveler will be attending. This information will become crucial when it comes time to deal with transportation and hotel reservations. The more information you can gather, the more effective you can be.

1.7 Flight Preferences

Make a list of the traveler's airline, airport, and travel class preferences. Standard travel classes are: first, business, and economy. Be sure to inquire about the traveler's seating preferences within the preferred class: aisle, window, front or back of plane, exit row, bulkhead seat, etc. Also, does the traveler have meal preferences or restrictions? Will he need Wi-Fi or a power connection in order to work while in the air?

1.8 Transportation Preferences

Determine what sort of transportation the executive will want use during the trip: car/limousine service, Uber, rental, taxi, or public. Some companies get car rental discounts, so find out if your company has such an arrangement. In the case of car rental, you will of course need to inquire about the type of car.

1.9 Hotel Preferences

When it comes to choosing a hotel, find out where her priorities lie: proximity to business engagements, proximity to airport, comfort and quality, a particular hotel or hotel chain, etc. In the case of a conference, check the option of booking a room in the hotel hosting the conference.

Of course you'll want to inquire about preferences such as room (single, double, twin, or suite), bed size, meals, gym, spa, Wi-Fi, etc.

1.10 Travel Agent

And of course, find out if the traveler prefers to work with a particular travel agent or agency, or if your company has an internal travel department that handles travel arrangements.

1.11 Research and Return

After gathering all of the above information, do not run to the phone or computer to start booking flights and making reservations. You'd better do some added research (unless you've got a reliable agent doing the research for you), and go back over all the above information. And then you need to record your findings and sit down with the executive for a second time to present him with any thoughts or suggestions.

2. Planning an Itinerary

As a secretary, it's your responsibility to make travel arrangements for your executive and keep him or her as productive and stress-free as possible. There are a lot of details to figure out, reservations to make, and schedules to coordinate. And even if you plot out every last detail of the trip, there's still no guarantee your executive won't experience a travel snag. So the best thing you can do is to create the perfect travel itinerary for him.To draft an itinerary, you need to keep in mind the following tips.

2.1 Format Your Itinerary

Be sure to set up the document in a way that makes it look clear and concise. This includes arranging everything on the page in a good way, putting each event's title on a new line, drafting a paragraph about the itinerary entry below and having time attached to each event.

2.2 Focus on Goals and Priorities

No matter what kind of trip it is, there will be a fundamental goal or priorities that your boss has probably communicated to you. If not, get these kinds of details in order to plan only the stops that truly fit into the overall plan.

2.3 Offer Maps of Hard to Reach Places

Some experienced planners recommend putting maps of each event location into the itinerary. This can end up saving everyone time in case the traveling executive or other party gets lost between itinerary trip points.

2.4 Fill in Itinerary Entries with Details

Give your boss more than just the time and place. Adding nice details about anything related to the trip points can really add value to an itinerary.

Address the five Ws. Many who are writing various kinds of documents use these five markers to generate relevant detail: who, what, why, when and how. Even though the fifth one does not start with W, calling these inquisitive words the "five Ws" helps for the purpose of recall.

2.5 Be Flexible

Always be receptive to input from the boss. Travel plans may change, and rolling with up-to-date changes can really make the difference between a great itinerary and one that doesn't get much use.

3. Contacting Travel Agency

Having the itinerary ready, you need to call the travel agency and make the arrangements. Confirm that the travel is for business. Corporate executives are permitted to book business class (seating between first class and coach) on flights lasting three hours or longer.

Ask the travel agent to e-mail you and the traveler a copy of the itinerary before issuing tickets. Read the itinerary carefully. Make sure that flights, hotels and car rentals show confirmation numbers. Give special attention to the spelling of the traveler's name. Any misspellings will show up on the airline ticket. If the name on the ticket and the name on the passport do not match, the executive won't be allowed aboard the flight.

When you are satisfied and the itinerary is correct, call the travel agency again telling them when to issue the ticket. Most ticketing is done through e-ticket. Both you and the traveler will receive an e-mail containing the e-ticket. Print the executive a copy for use at the airport to secure boarding passes.

New Words

undertake [ˌʌndə'teik] *vt.* 承担，从事

leisure ['leʒə] *n.* 闲暇，安逸

commute [kə'mjuːt] *v.* 往返，上下班交通

foresight ['fɔːsait] *n.* 预见，先见，深谋远虑

despite [dis'pait] prep. 虽有，尽管

capability [ˌkeipə'biliti] *n.* 性能，才能，能力

superior [sjuː'piəriə] *adj.* 较高的；较好的 *n.* 上级；较好的人或事物

necessity [ni'sesiti] *n.* 需要，必需品

itinerary [ai'tinərəri] *n.* 旅行计划，行程表

assign [ə'sain] *vt.* 分配，指定，指派

budget ['bʌdʒit] *n.* 预算

determine [di'təːmin] *v.* 决定，决心，确定

ingredient [in'griːdiənt] *n.* 成分，原料，配料

accommodation [əˌkɔmə'deiʃən] *n.* 膳宿，住处

archive ['ɑːkaiv] *n.* 档案，档案馆 *vt.* 存档

prior ['praiə] *adj.* 优先的，在前的

insight ['insait] *n.* 洞察力，见识，深刻的理解

fact-finding ['fæktˌfaindiŋ] *adj.* 实情调查的 *n.* 寻求事实

blunder ['blʌndə] *n.* 大错 *v.* 失策，绊倒

cancellation [kænsə'leiʃən] *n.* 取消，撤销，废除

expiration [ˌekspaiə'reiʃən] *n.* 终止，期满

legible ['ledʒəbl] *adj.* 清晰的，易读的，可辨认的

passport ['pɑːspɔːt] *n.* 护照
valid ['vælid] *adj.* 有效的，有根据的，合法的
expire [iks'paiə] *vi.* 终止，期满，失效
vaccination [ˌvæksi'neiʃən] *n.* 接种疫苗
visa ['viːzə] *n.* 签证 *vt.* 办理签证
luggage ['lʌgidʒ] *n.* 行李
accuracy ['ækjurəsi] *n.* 准确性，精确度
critical ['kritikəl] *adj.* 关键的，批评的，爱挑剔的
preference ['prefərəns] *n.* 偏爱，优先
preferred [pri'fəːd] *adj.* 首选的，有优先权的
aisle [ail] *n.* 侧廊，（席位间的）通道
bulkhead ['bʌlkhed] *n.* 隔板，隔舱
limousine ['liməziːn] *n.* 豪华轿车，接送旅客的交通车
priority [prai'ɔriti] *n.* 优先，优先权，优先考虑的事
proximity [prɔk'simiti] *n.* 接近，邻近
suite [swiːt] *n.* 套房
spa [spɑː] *n.* 温泉浴场，水疗
reliable [ri'laiəbl] *adj.* 可靠的
coordinate [kəu'ɔːdinit] *v.*（使）协调，（使）一致
guarantee [ˌgærən'tiː] *n.* 保证，担保 *vt.* 保证，担保
snag [snæg] *n.* 障碍，困难
fundamental [ˌfʌndə'mentl] *adj.* 基础的，根本的
generate ['dʒenəˌreit] *vt.* 形成，造成，产生，引起
inquisitive [in'kwizitiv] *adj.* 好奇的，爱打听的，求知欲强的
receptive [ri'septiv] *adj.* 易接受的，愿意接受的
confirm [kən'fəːm] *v.* 证实，确定
coach [kəutʃ] *n.* 经济舱；（火车）客车车厢；长途客运大巴
rental ['rentl] *n.* 租费，租借
misspelling [ˌmis'speliŋ] *n.* 拼错
e-ticket [iː-'tikit] *n.* 电子机票
print [print] *v.* 印刷，打印 *n.* 印刷字体，印刷物
secure [si'kjuə] *adj.* 安全的，牢靠的，稳妥的 *vt.* 使安全，获得

Phrases and Expressions

as opposed to 与……对比，而不是
travel agency 旅行社
keep in mind 记住，牢记
make assumptions 做出假设
break... down into 把……分解成或拆成
accounting department 财务部，会计部门
make reservations 预约，预定，订房间
book flights 预订航班
drivers license 驾照
credit card 信用卡
on hand 在手边，现有
take into account 考虑，重视
travel insurance 旅游保险，旅行保险
to and from 往返，来往于
take into consideration 考虑到，顾及
make a list of 列出……的清单

when it comes time to do sth. 每当……的时候
inquire about 询问，打听
plot out 提出……纲要
attach to（使）贴（系，粘，依附）在……上
fit into 适应，融入，符合
end up（以……）结束，最终成为，变得
in case 万一，以免
add to 增加，添加
make the difference 有影响，产生差别
confirmation number 确认号
boarding pass 登机牌，登记证

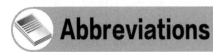

Abbreviations

ID (identification) 身份证

Notes

1 However, despite the stress, planning a trip can be a great opportunity to show your company your capabilities and skills, earning the confidence of your superiors.

本句中，earning the confidence of your superiors 是一个现在分词短语，在句中作状语，表示伴随状态。despite the stress 是介词短语，在句中作让步状语，其中 despite 意为“尽管；虽然有”。请看下例：

Despite numerous failures, they continued to conduct the experiment without flagging.

尽管实验几次都失败了，他们仍毫不气馁地继续进行。

另外，动词不定式词组 to show your company your capabilities and skills 在句中作后置定语，修饰和限定 opportunity。

英语中，动词不定式 to do sth. 作定语时，常后置修饰限定前面的先行词。请看下例：

The desire to succeed is deeply rooted in human nature.

成功欲在人性中根深蒂固。

2 One of the most important things to keep in mind when planning a trip for your boss is to never make assumptions.

本句中，when planning a trip for your boss 是连词 when 引导的时间状语从句，其中 when 和 planning 之间省略了 you are。动词不定式 to never make assumptions 在句中作表语。请看下例：

The purpose of education is to develop a fine personality in children.

教育的目的是发展儿童完美的品格。

另外，one of the most important things 是“one of + 形容词最高级 + 名词复数”结构，意为“最…… 之一”。请看下例：

We are in one of the most severe recessions in modern times.

我们正在经历现代最严重的一段经济衰退。

3 Certain countries require vaccination forms and Visas, so these matters should also be taken into account and dealt with if necessary, as should travel insurance.

本句中，if necessary 是“if + 形容词”结构，这类结构通常可视为在 if 与形容词之间省略了“主语 + 动词 be 的适当形式”。这类省略结构中有的已构成相对固定的搭配，如：if necessary（如果需要），if possible（如果可能）等。请看下例：

If possible, let me know beforehand.

如果可能，可在事前通知我。

另外，句中 as should travel insurance 是“as + 助动词 + 主语”的倒装句结构，表示“与前面的情况一样；也应该这样”，相当于 travel insurance should be taken... necessary, too。请看下例：

Women cadres should have the world in view, as should women in the rural areas.

妇女干部应该看世界，农村妇女也应该看世界。

4 No matter what kind of trip it is, there will be a fundamental goal or priorities that your boss has probably communicated to you.

本句中，no matter what kind of trip it is 是“no matter + 疑问词（what, who, when, which, where 等）+ 主语 + 谓语”结构，在句中常引导让步状语从句，意为“无论，不管”。请看下例：

Jenkins would reward all investors, no matter when they made their investment.

无论投资人何时投资，詹金斯都会让他们得到回报。

另外，that your boss has probably communicated to you 是一个定语从句，修饰和限定 a fundamental goal or priorities。

5 This can end up saving everyone time in case the traveling executive or other party gets lost between itinerary trip points.

本句中，in case the traveling... between itinerary trip points 是由连词 in case 引导的条件状语从句。

英语中，in case 作连词用时，常用于引导条件状语从句和目的状语从句，引导条件状语从句时，意为“假使，如果”；引导目的状语从句时，意为“以防，免得”。请看下例：

In case they're late, we can always sit in the bar.

要是他们来晚了，我们总可以在酒吧里坐一坐。

Be quiet in case you wake the baby.

轻点儿，别吵醒婴儿。

另外，end up 为固定词组，意为“结束；告终”，其后常接介词短语、形容词、动名词等。请看下例：

I don't want you to end up out of pocked.

我不希望你最后亏本。

You could end up running this company if you play your cards right.

你要是处理得当，到头来这个公司能归你掌管。

If you don't work hard, you'll end up nowhere.
如不努力工作，你将一事无成。

Exercises

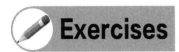

EX. 1 **Answer the following questions.**

1. What is a business travel according to Text A?
2. Why is planning a trip a great opportunity for a secretary?
3. What is one of the most important things to keep in mind when you are planning a trip for your boss?
4. What details of the traveler are necessary for making reservations and booking flights?
5. What may be the most important part of the preparations for arranging a business trip?
6. What should a secretary know about his or her executive's hotel preferences?
7. List at least three tips on how to plan an itinerary.
8. Why does the itinerary need to be flexible?
9. What should the secretary ask the travel agent to do before ticket are issued?
10. Why should the secretary give special attention to the spelling of the executive's name on the ticket?

EX. 2 **Complete the following sentences with appropriate words or expressions in the box.**

coordinate	expire	undertake	make the difference	proximity
blunder	in case	legible	take into consideration	preference

1. If you ________ the project, you are bound to encounter difficulties.
2. These priorities may ________ the most pressing needs and the opportunities available.
3. He had lived illegally in the United States for five years after his visitor's visa ________ .
4. Please ensure application is complete and ________ to avoid errors or delays in processing.
5. Her superior used to say he had a strong ________ for deluxe suite.
6. We wanted to be here early ________ the maintenance supervisor had forgotten to deal with it.
7. The manager's job is to plan, organize and ________.
8. Marriages in ________ of blood are forbidden by the law.
9. An embarrassing ________ nearly ruined the secretary's career before it got off the ground.
10. But preparation can ________ between being productive and just being tired.

EX. 3 **Translate the following sentences into English.**

1. 结果令人非常不满意，和主管们所期望的恰恰相反。(as opposed to)

2. 作为一名行政助理，他负责公司的一些行政工作。(in charge of)
3. 那位秘书通过旅行社拿到了她老板的签证和机票。(travel agency)
4. 秘书很容易做出这样一种设想，即她的老板偏爱住豪华套房。(make the assumption)
5. 需不需要我在那里为您预订一个房间？（make reservation)
6. 我要订一张 25 号星期四去北京的飞机票。(book a flight to)
7. 必须以信用卡或银行汇票支付。(credit card)
8. 对于个人旅游者来说，则需要如酒店预订房间的证明、机票、旅游保险等。(travel insurance)
9. 先生，给您造成不便真是抱歉。但是如果您没有确认好，那我们可一点儿办法也没有了。(confirmation number)
10. 在登机手续办理处，你可以拿到登机证和行李标签。(boarding pass)

EX. 4 **Translate the following passage into Chinese.**

Once a secretary discovers that her boss has to travel for business, she must learn the exact dates of the anticipated trip. If you are responsible for making travel arrangements for everyone in your department or office, you must determine if other staff members are traveling at the same time as well. Depending on the company you work for, you may have to determine the budget for the travel expenses or contact the accounting department to see if the money is in the budget for the trips. You must find out what hotels are in the area where your boss will be traveling, if she has any preferences, and get the costs and availability of rooms.

Another part of making travel arrangements includes taking care of the travel needs for your boss while she is away. You must know if your boss needs transportation to the airport or if she will be reimbursed for the cost of parking her car at the airport. You should provide a printed copy of the itinerary for your boss to use when she arrives at her destination, so she will know her daily schedule and the addresses of the hotel and the location of the meeting or conference. You can reserve a rental car in advance that will be available upon her arrival or arrange for the hotel shuttle to take her to the hotel. A secretary's duties when making travel arrangements includes ensuring that every aspect of the trip is covered.

Part Three Text B

Business Travel Booking

1. Overview

With a multitude of options offered for trains, planes and hotels, business travel booking becomes a minefield when selecting what's best for your boss. As a secretary or personal assistant, you need to make sure your boss' business trips always go smoothly.

The first thing is to consider whether your company have a travel policy or not. Most companies will have one in place to control what and where their employees book, and can heavily influence your choices. After company regulations come the needs and desires of the person you're booking for.

Typically, there are 3 main ways to book business travel:

- Manage the bookings yourself and book each item individually.
- Use an online service to handle all bookings.
- Employ a Travel Management Company (TMC).

Assuming you don't use a Travel Management Company to do the work, there are 3 stages to handle business travel bookings perfectly.

1.1 Pre-booking

- Research

A little work early on can save a lot of time later. Take into account what the business trip entails and how you can deliver the best response to each aspect. For example, certain countries require visas or immunizations. Make sure you get advice on the steps needed to be taken and be wary of schedule. Think about the itinerary. It's easy to make the experience more efficient if you can save the traveler's time.

- Create traveler profiles

Some online booking tools allow you to quickly create profiles, enabling you to seamlessly pass essential personal preferences to travel suppliers, including your boss' loyalty scheme numbers, seating or room preferences. Even if you handle all the bookings yourself, it is worth ensuring you have all this information on hand.

1.2 Booking

Before you start, make sure you are clear on what is required. The cheapest train tickets and hotel rooms are usually those which have the least flexibility. They may save money initially but if plans change and you are unable to transfer, this will have to be written off.

Booking everything separately can be very time consuming due to the number of options. Create a database of all the numbers or web addresses you require, and remember you may need to become a member of many individual organizations such as airlines, train companies and hotel chains.

A simple way to simplify this is to utilize search aggregators, such as lastminute. com, booking. com or cheap flights. com. These search multiple brands, rank the results and remove the need for multiple logins.

If cost is the main consideration, consider the following:

- The further in advance the more you can save, and this doesn't just go for flights, the trend is the same for hotels and for rail bookings too.
- Consider avoiding flexible tickets to save money. (e.g. It's often cheaper to book three advance rail tickets giving no flexibility than it is to buy a fully-flex rail ticket.) Sometimes the best solution is to book a fixed outbound ticket and a flexible ticket on the return.

- Consider the full cost of a trip, not just the component parts, e.g. It's worth paying £100 per night for a hotel that is on site, rather than £80 per night for one a few miles out but incurs a £15 taxi each way.
- Consider starting internal meetings later to allow non-peak train travel for all attendees — this may save 60% per attendee.
- Pay attention to what you are being charged, it's easy to go through a whole booking process and not notice all the extras.

If business travel booking is a more regular part of your job duties, you may want to look at an online travel booking tool. Advantages of using a business travel booking tool include:

- No merchant fees — Booking directly on BA.com will include these, but by using a Travel Management Company you avoid these and can save over £50/seat.
- Payment terms — Web bookings require card payment up front, but by using a Travel Management Company you are able to hold seats and prices until the ticketing deadline.
- 24 hour support — Airlines don't all operate 24 hours a day, if your boss is on the other side of the world and needs to call at 3am in the morning to change their return flight, this becomes an issue.
- Impartial, expert advice — e.g. South African Airways is not going to tell you that the leg room in their first class cabin on Heathrow to Cape Town is smaller, yet more expensive, than BA's business class.

(Note: Having all bookings in one place makes it easier to manage your business travel, track business travelers and analyze data.)

1.3 Post Booking

Once the travel bookings are completed, it's time to ensure the traveler is up to speed with what they need to provide and do. Important considerations include:

- Travel Documentation.

Make sure you prepare and organize any necessary documentation that your boss may need. These can include train and plane tickets/reference numbers, accommodation loyalty cards, passport, visas and immunization certificates.

- Travel Insurance.

Make sure they have sufficient travel insurance, there are countless options these days and by shopping around you may be able to select a better package.

2. Bookings for Different Purposes

Owing to the different purposes of bookings, there may be different bookings as follows: hotel booking; restaurant booking; ticket booking; conference room booking; vehicle booking and banquet booking etc. In this part, we will mainly focus on hotel booking, restaurant reservation and ticket booking.

2.1 Hotel Booking

If you are a personal assistant, you must know how to book a hotel for someone else. In fact, part of your job responsibilities and duties will be to book hotels for your boss. As you learn many aspects of your job, you must learn preferences of your employer and thus anticipate the needs of your employer.

• Gather information on the trip.

You should know the destination of the trip and its purpose. If your boss will be attending an event such as a seminar you should book their hotel room within the hotel at which the event is planned. If the event will be at a different venue, you need to research hotels near that venue. You will need to know how many days your boss will be in that area. It is your job to look for credit card. Knowing how many occupants will be in the room will also be helpful.

• Book the hotel room.

Call the hotel and book the reservation. Provide the clerk with name, credit card information, and a contact number. You will then state specifications for the hotel room and any extras that are needed.

• Make transportation arrangements.

Make transportation arrangements for your boss to and from the hotel. Some upscale hotels will provide concierge services. The concierge will make any arrangements needed for guests of a certain status. This includes dinner reservations, tee times for golf, and even special accommodations as needed. If your boss is of celebrity status, you may want to call the concierge of the hotel directly.

Here is an example for hotel booking.

Gentlemen,

Would you have a single room available from Monday afternoon, July 6, through the night of Friday, July 10. Please send me rates for a single room with bath. I'd appreciate an immediate reply so I can make reservations right away. Thank you.

Yours Sincerely

Jane Gates

2.2 Restaurant Reservation

Learning to make restaurant reservations will help you make the most of your dining experience. It can also help you get into fine restaurants that are heavily booked. Here are some tips on how to make restaurant reservations.

- Call as far ahead of time as possible. Most restaurants will accept reservations a few days in advance, and exclusive fine dining venues will often accept (or even require) reservations weeks or months in advance. If you make your reservations more than a few days in advance, it is best to call the day of the dinning to quickly confirm your reservation.
- Be as courteous as possible when booking a reservation. If you are attempting to book a tough reservation, remember that your attitude on the phone will go a long way. Be confident but polite; avoid giving the impression that you feel entitled to a reservation.
- Visit the restaurant in person. A further strategy for booking a tough reservation is asking for

availability in person rather than over the phone. This shows that you are willing to put a bit of effort into securing a table. A host is also much less likely to be dismissive or unhelpful when dealing with you face-to-face.

- Call ahead or cancel if you are running late. Once you've secured your reservation, call ahead and apologize if it looks like you'll be up to 20 minutes late. If you are running much later than that, consider canceling and rescheduling your dinner. Remember that reservations are made for a reason — to make sure as many guests as possible are served on each night. If you are late, it affects other guests' reservations.

Here is an example for ordering a table.

Dear Sir,

We wish to entertain at dinner at Beijing Restaurant on March 29 at 6 in the afternoon.

This will be a party of seven people, and a private dining room would be preferable. We will need the service of a wine steward and we will prefer mainly seafood.

Please let us have information as to the approximate cost by return mail if possible.

Sincerely,

Zhang Ping

2.3 Tickets Booking

Tickets booking mainly include booking the tickets of transportation and the tickets of entertainment. The former refers to the tickets of various ways of transportation like train, airplane, bus, etc, which a business travel booking mainly involves. Here, we just focus on how to book flight tickets over the Internet.

- Determine your final destination, the day you need to leave, and the day you will return. Just as if you were going to book a flight over the phone, you need to outline the basics of your trip before booking a flight over the Internet.
- Choose whether you need plane tickets only or some other package such as plane tickets and a rental car or plane tickets and a hotel room, and select the appropriate option. Many online sites offer package deals along with the plane tickets. If you need a hotel or rental car, selecting a package may save some money.
- Enter the locations and dates in the appropriate fields. In the "from" field, enter where you are flying from. In the "to" field, enter where you are flying to. In the "departure" field, enter the date you wish to leave; in the "return" field, enter the date you wish to return.
- Select the number of tickets you need. Many sites have a drop-down menu allowing you to select how many adults, children, or seniors will be flying. Enter the appropriate number for your trip. If you're an adult traveling alone, simply leave the default at "1" for one adult.
- Press the "search" or "find tickets" button on the screen. After all the information has been entered, the online site will search for plane tickets matching your needs. You will then select which flight you need based on airline or price. After making a selection, simply follow the instructions on the website to purchase your ticket electronically.

3. Confirm, Change, or Cancel a Reservation

After a reservation is made, you need to confirm the reservation if there is no change of your schedule or plan. However, if there are any changes, you need to change your reservation and sometimes cancel your reservation. Here are some examples.

3.1 Confirm a Reservation (Confirm a telephone order for rooms)

Gentleman,

This will confirm reservation made by phone on March 12 for a suite to accommodate one of our executives from March 18 through March 22, at a daily rate of $ 80.

The cost will be paid by check.

Yours Sincerely,

Susan Smith

3.2 Change a Reservation (Change the reservation for the flight tickets)

Gentleman,

On May 10, I reserved a round ticket on your flight 262 from New York to Shanghai, leaving at 9 a.m. on Wednesday, May 15 with return to New York scheduled for May 20.

I will not be able to make the trip to Shanghai at that time, but instead will go there on May 18, and return on May 23. Please send me confirmation of this change.

Yours Sincerely,

Li Hua

3.3 Cancel a Reservation (Cancel the reservation for a car)

Dear Sir,

On June 20 I reserved a car for two weeks for Mr. Peterson, the efficiency consultant who came from the headquarters. He planned to stay with us for about half a month. However, as Mr. Peterson will not be able to travel that time as planned, please cancel the reservation immediately. Thank you.

Yours Sincerely,

Linda

New Words

booking ['bukiŋ] *n.* 预约，预订

minefield ['mainfi:ld] *n.* 充满隐伏危险的事物，雷区

policy ['pɔlisi] *n.* 政策，策略，保险单

assuming [ə'su:miŋ] *conj.* 如果，假设

deliver [di'livə] *vt.* 交付，发表，递送

immunization [ˌimju:nai'zeiʃən] *n.* 免疫接种

seamlessly ['si:mlis] *adv.* 无缝地，天衣无缝地

require [ri'kwaiə] *v.* 要求，规定

initially [i'niʃəli] *adv.* 首先，最初，开头

time-consuming ['taim-kənˌsju:miŋ] *adj.* 耗费时间的
separately ['sepərətli] *adv.* 分别地，个别地
simplify ['simplifai] *vt.* 简化，使简单
aggregator ['ægrigeitə] *n.* 聚集，集合
multiple ['mʌltipl] *adj.* 多种多样的，许多的 *n.* 倍数
rank [ræŋk] *n.* 等级，列 *v.* 列为，排名，排位
login ['lɔgin] *n.* 登录，注册
solution [sə'lu:ʃən] *n.* 解决办法，方案
incur [in'kə:] *vt.* 招致，遭受，惹起
charge [tʃɑ:dʒ] *v.* 要价，索价
extra ['ekstrə] *adj.* 额外的 *n.* 额外之物
deadline ['dedlain] *n.* 最后期限，截止时间
impartial [im'pɑ:ʃəl] *adj.* 公正的，不偏不倚的
analyze ['ænəlaiz] *vt.* 分析，解析
documentation [ˌdɔkjumen'teiʃən] *n.* 文件，证明文件
countless ['kauntlis] *adj.* 无数的
banquet ['bæŋkwit] *n.* 宴会 *vt.* 宴请，设宴
anticipate [æn'tisipeit] *vt.* 预期，预料，预计；预先考虑并满足
seminar ['seminɑ:] *n.* 研讨会，(大学的)研究班
occupant ['ɔkju:pənt] *n.* 占有者，居住者
upscale ['ʌpskeil] *adj.* 高消费的，高端的 *vt.* 提高，提升
concierge [ˌkɔ:nsi'εəʒ] *n.* 门房，看门人
status ['steitəs] *n.* 地位，状况，状态，身份
rate [reit] *n.* 价格，费用
exclusive [iks'klu:siv] *adj.* 排外的；唯一的
tough [tʌf] *adj.* 强硬的；棘手的，难办的
dismissive [dis'misiv] *adj.* 拒绝的，放弃的，轻视的
apologize [ə'pɔlədʒaiz] *vi.* 道歉，赔罪
entertain [ˌentə'tein] *v.* 娱乐，使有兴趣；招待
preferable ['prefərəbl] *adj.* 更好的，更合意的
steward ['stjuəd] *n.* 乘务员；管家；干事；管理员
approximately [əprɔksi'mətli] *adv.* 大约，近似地
departure [di'pɑ:tʃə] *n.* 出发，离开
drop-down [drɔp-daun] *adj.* 下拉的
instruction [in'strʌkʃən] *n.* 指令；教学
accommodate [ə'kɔmədeit] *vt.* 供给住宿；使适应；容纳
confirmation [ˌkɔnfə'meiʃən] *n.* 确认，证实
headquarter [ˌhed'kwɔ:tə] *n.* 总部 *vt.* 设总部于
specification [ˌspesifi'keiʃən] *n.* 规格，详述

Phrases and Expressions

in place 在适当的位置
loyalty scheme number 忠实顾客奖励计划号
be written off 被冲销，被注销
hotel chain 连锁酒店
outbound ticket 出境机票
go through 通过；经历；完成
merchant fee 商户手续费
payment terms 付款条件，付款方式
up front 预先付款
first class cabin 头等舱
business class 二等舱，商务舱
speed with 加速
loyalty card 优惠卡
immunization certificate 预防接种证
owing to 由于，多亏
tee times for golf 高尔夫球的发球时间
be of celebrity status 名人身份
entitle to 有资格，有权
put effort into 对某事付出或投入精力
package deals 套餐，一揽子交易
confirm a reservation 确认预订
cancel a reservation 取消预订
round ticket 往返机票

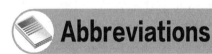

Abbreviations

TMC (Travel Management Company) 旅行管理公司，差旅管理公司，商旅管理公司
BA (British Airways) 英国航空

Exercises

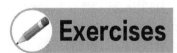

EX. 5 Answer the following questions.

1. What is the first thing the secretary should consider when making business travel bookings?
2. What should the secretary do before making business travel bookings?
3. What does the author think of the cheapest train tickets and hotel rooms?
4. List at least three ways in which the secretary can save money while making business travel bookings.
5. What are the advantages of using a business travel booking tool while making bookings?
6. What do any necessary travel documentation usually include?
7. What information should the secretary provide for the hotel clerk while booking a hotel room?

8. What can you consider doing if you are up to over 20 minutes late for your dinner reservation?
9. What may you do to save some money if you need the plane tickets along with a hotel or a rental car?
10. What do you need to do if there are some changes of your schedule or plan after a reservation is made?

Part Four Extended Reading

Text	Notes
The Art and Science of Traveling Light[1]	[1] 轻装旅行
Reasons for Traveling Light Of all the travel skills you might acquire, traveling light is the one most likely to result in enjoyable, productive[2], stress-free travel experiences. For two thousand years, seasoned[3] travelers have written of its many important benefits, including:	[2] *adj.* 多产的，富有成效的 [3] *adj.* 老练的，经验丰富的
• Security—With a much-reduced need to hand your belongings[4] over to the care of others, you are less likely to lose them to theft, damage, or misrouting[5]. Similarly, you foil[6] those who would enlist[7] your unsuspecting aid as a conveyor of contraband[8] goods. Attaining peace of mind is rarely this easy.	[4] *n.* 物品，行李，财产 [5] *n.* 错误指向，误转 [6] *vt.* 挫败，击退，阻挠 [7] *vt.* 征募，获得……支持 [8] *n.* 违禁品，走私品
• Economy[9]—You can laugh at checked baggage fees. You don't have to pay porters and others to carry and store stuff for you. You are more able to take public transportation, rather than limos[10], shuttles[11], and taxis. You can even walk. All of which also bring you into more intimate[12] contact with the people and places that you have come to visit.	[9] *n.* 经济，节约 [10] *n.* 豪华轿车 [11] *n.* 短程穿梭运行的飞机（或火车，汽车） [12] *adj.* 亲密的，亲近的
• Mobility[13]—Less stuff means greater mobility, thus more options. With no checked or awkward-to-manage luggage to limit your travel alternatives[14], you can better cope with delayed transportation & missed connections, and exploit[15] unexpected opportunities. You can switch to other flights when space is available, and use alternate transport (trains, rental cars, etc.) when it isn't. You needn't arrive at airports as early (no waiting for luggage check-in[16]), and will be among the first to leave. You can board trains, trams, and coaches with alacrity[17]. You won't feel compelled to take the first hotel room offered, but can comfortably walk down the street should the ambience[18] be unsuitable or the price unreasonable. You can sell your airplane seat on full flights. You can travel as an air courier[19]. You can be more spontaneous[20].	[13] *n.* 流动性，机动性 [14] *n.* 供替代的选择 [15] *vt.* 利用，开发 [16] 行李托运 [17] *n.* 轻快，敏捷 [18] *n.* 周围环境，气氛 [19] *n.* 航空快递员或导游 [20] *adj.* 自发的，不由自主的

- Serenity[21]—Traveling lightly reduces stress: it is simply a more hassle-free[22] way to get about. You have more time, because packing takes little. You waste less energy hauling[23] stuff. You know what you have, where everything is, and that it's sufficient. We've all seen those anxious folks at the airport, struggling with too much baggage, concerned that they have lost track of something, or left it behind. Foreign travel can be particularly challenging[24], because it is unfamiliar and less predictable[25]. But the one-bag traveler copes by operating from a solid, familiar, and—most important— well-considered foundation, with fewer unnecessary things to worry about.
- Ecology[26]— All of the above are concerned with short-term benefits to you. But traveling light also yields[27] long-term benefits to the planet. Less stuff to manufacture[28]. Less use of vehicles and other equipment to move you and your belongings about. Less fuel for those vehicles that do move you. Less greenhouse gas production. Greater likelihood of upcoming generations[29] being around and able to do some traveling of their own. (It's not often that the most convenient option is also the most environmentally responsible.

A Trick[30] to Traveling Light

If there's a "trick" to traveling light, it's the understanding and proper use of a packing list. Apart from that, however, there's no single specific secret. Traveling light is a skill comprised of[31] a very large number of very small considerations. Taken individually, many of these might seem relatively unimportant; collectively[32], however, this selection of small sanities[33] makes it possible to journey for extended periods of time, carrying no more than will fit in a surprisingly small bag.

Typical travelers shouldn't expect the transition[34] to happen overnight (unless they're extraordinarily[35] diligent). The proficient one-bag traveler will have mastered the three core elements of light travel, illustrated here in order of importance.

- Packing Moderation[36]— abandoning the foolishness of lugging[37] around too much stuff.
- Weight Reduction — find travel-friendly versions of items that you do carry
- Bag Optimization[38]— understanding what to look for in efficient and effective luggage.

Packing List for a Stress-Free Business Trip

When packing for your business trip, the biggest thing you can do is to decide what needs to go with you, and what can stay at home. Consider a small handful of categories your travel gear[39] will fall into when preparing for the trip.

[21] *n.* 平静，从容
[22] *adj.* 省事的，无忧的
[23] *vt.* 拖拉，拽
[24] *adj.* 挑战性的
[25] *adj.* 可预知的
[26] *n.* 生态，环境
[27] *vt.* 出产，生产
[28] *v.* 制造
[29] 接下来的几代人
[30] *n.* 诡计，花招，把戏，诀窍
[31] 由……组成
[32] *adv.* 共同地，集体地，总体地
[33] *n.* 神智健全
[34] *n.* 转变，过渡
[35] *adv.* 非常，格外
[36] *n.* 适度，节制
[37] *vt.* 拖，拉，用力拖动
[38] *n.* 优化，最佳化
[39] *n.* 工具，装备

• First order of business — your attire[40] — What is the dress code for your trip? — Is it the same for all functions, or will you need a versatile[41] wardrobe? — How long are you going for? — What is the weather going to be like at your destination? These are questions you should have sorted out[42] beforehand. Bring what you need, and only that. If you will be attending a board meeting, followed by a night of bar hopping[43] with clients, you're going to need some options. Bring clothes that pack well (wool suits get the wrinkles out like it's their job). Have an extra outfit[44] for each function at the ready.	[40] *n.* 服装，穿衣 [41] *adj.* 多才多艺的，通用的，多功能的 [42] *vt.* 整理，选出，分类 [43] 逛酒吧 [44] *n.* 套装，服装，装束
• Up next–work related items Once you have the wardrobe for your entire trip planned out, make sure you have all work related items ready. This does not mean simply have your laptop and charger[45] packed up and thrown in the suitcase. Do you need to bring hard copies of sales reports with you? Are you visiting a vendor[46] who will want drawings of your most recent construction project? If you assume the hotel or your meeting locations will have printing capabilities for you to easily access, you're setting yourself up for a potentially disastrous[47] situation. Make copies of what you need on your last day at the office before the trip. Your work items checklist: Printed handouts[48] Business cards Pens and a notebook Laptop, mouse and charger	[45] *n.* 充电器 [46] *n.* 厂商，供应商 [47] *adj.* 灾难性的，损失惨重的 [48] *n.* 宣传品，小册子，讲义材料
• Batting third[49]–electronics and entertainment We have these two lumped[50] together because in this day and age, they are often times one and the same. This doesn't mean forget the book at home for your in-flight entertainment. It's always a good idea to take a break from the screen, and reading books (fiction or nonfiction) is a great way to keep your mind sharp.	[49] 第三棒 [50] *vt.* 把……归并到一起
• Bring your chargers with you These little guys are items we take for granted[51] when we're in the middle of our office and home lives. They are always where we need them to be. It is easy and more common than you might think to leave essential phone accessories[52] at home when rushing out to catch a flight.	[51] 想当然，认为理当如此 [52] *n.* 附件，配件

Check your list the night you're done packing, but make some time in the morning to double check your work. Did your toothbrush and deodorant[53] make it into your toiletries[54] bag? You might have charged your phone at night; make sure that charger makes it into the suitcase. Take the few minutes to ensure you're ready to roll. Once you've packed and prepared in an orderly way, you're a step ahead of everyone else. Get to the airport on time, relax with a good book while you wait in the terminal[55] knowing you're ready to roll.	[53] *n.* 除臭剂，防臭剂 [54] *n.* 化妆品，洗漱品 [55]*n.* 航站楼

参考译文

课文 A　商务旅行安排

与其他类型的旅行，如以休闲或以定期上下班为目的的旅行相反，商务旅行是以工作或商务为目的而进行的旅行。有必要进行商务旅行的原因可能有很多，如拜访客户或供应商、参加在其他公司场所举行的会议、营销或促销新的或现有产品等。

在一些大公司，有专门为员工负责安排旅行的部门。然而，在许多小公司，为老板或其他员工安排旅行的工作则由秘书来完成。

安排旅行可能很有压力，需要大量的策划和远见。然而，尽管有压力，策划旅行也是你向公司展示能力和技能的机会，从而获得上司的信任。因此，秘书有必要知道如何安排商务旅行，她可以将其行动过程分为三个阶段：做好准备工作、规划行程表和联系旅行社。

1. 准备工作

在为老板安排旅行时，需要牢记的最重要的事情之一是永远不要假设。当接到负责安排商务旅行具体细节的任务时，你需要记下提供给你的所有信息，并为安排商务旅行做好充分准备。

1.1　了解预算

确定此次旅行的预算是多少，这将成为整个旅行策划的有用参考数据。而且将总额预算细分成如机票、交通、住宿等具体预算，这样做也很有用。一些助理必须自己确定预算；而其他人则需要问行政主管或会计部门。

1.2　去档案室

如果可能的话，联系所有在主管以往的旅行中曾负责过或参与过安排事宜的助理或员工，看看从他们的经验中可以获得哪些见解。他们或许已经做了很多实情调查的工作，并且他们犯过的错，你不会重蹈覆辙。

1.3　旅行者的详细资料

收集预订机票和做其他预订时所需的详细信息。这些信息应该包括旅行者的：

全名（注：与驾驶证或身份证上的全名一致）

电子邮件地址

身份证 / 驾驶证号码

电话号码（注：在取消或延误的情况下，非常必要）

信用卡号码和有效日期

地址

当实际预订时，随身携带这些易读的、有条理的详细资料。

1.4　许可

确保主管的护照有效，并且在近期不会过期。某些国家要求接种疫苗表和签证，因此，必要的话，秘书还应考虑这些问题，而且也要考虑旅游保险问题。

1.5　往返机场

别忘了考虑这个重要的细节。主管是自己开车去机场并将车长期停在机场呢？还是有人开车送他去机场呢？他会乘坐汽车、出租车、公共交通工具吗？主管要带多少行李？所有的行李都要托运吗？

1.6　日程安排表

这可能是准备工作中最重要的一部分。列出旅行者需要或想去每个目的地的确切日期和时间，从旅程开始到结束，包括她需要或想要回到家的日期和时间。在这个环节，精确度至关重要，所以确保反复检查每一个细节。

了解旅行者拟参加或参与的每次会议、会面以及活动的确切地点、时间和性质。这些信息对于安排交通和酒店预订非常重要。你收集的信息越多，你的工作就越有效。

1.7　搭机喜好

列出旅行者对航空公司，机场和舱位的喜好。标准的客舱分为头等舱、商务舱和经济舱。务必询问旅行者在首选舱内的座位喜好：通道、窗口、飞机前面或后面、紧急出口座位以及隔座等。而且，旅行者是否有膳食喜好或禁忌？他是否需要 Wi-Fi 或电源连接以便在飞行途中工作？

1.8　交通喜好

确定主管在旅行中想用何种交通工具：豪华轿车、租的高级车、租车、出租车或公共交通工具。有些公司可享有汽车租赁折扣，所以你要清楚你的公司是否有这样的安排。租车时，您当然要询问汽车类型。

1.9　住店喜好

在选择酒店时，应该先弄清楚主管优先考虑的因素：靠近商务活动、邻近机场、酒店的舒适度和质量、一个特定的酒店或酒店连锁等。如果要参加一个会议，应查看是否可以选择在举办该会议的酒店预订房间。当然，你还需要询问主管有关房间各方面的喜好，如房间类型（单人房、双人房、带两张单人床的双人房，或套房）、床的大小、膳食、健身房、水疗中心、无线网络连接等。

1.10 旅行代理人

当然，你还应当弄清楚旅行者是否更喜欢与某个特定的旅行社或代理人合作，或者你的公司是否有一个内部旅行部门，专门负责旅行安排事宜。

1.11 调查与返回

收集上述所有信息后，不要急于在电话或电脑上开始预订航班和做其他预订。你最好再做一些额外的调查（除非你已经有一个可靠的代理人为你做调查），再看一遍上面所有的信息。然后你要记录下你的结论，接着再和主管一起坐下来，向他提出你对此次旅行的想法或建议。

2. 规划行程

作为一个秘书，你的责任是为你的主管安排旅行，并确保他或她的商务旅行尽可能地富有成效、轻松愉快。你需要解决许多细节问题，做各种预定，并协调日程安排。然而，即使你计划好旅行的每一个细节，也无法保证你的主管在旅途中不会遇到困难。所以你能做的最好的事就是为他制定完美的行程表。要拟定一张行程表，你需要记住以下几点建议。

2.1 格式化旅程表

务必使文档的设置清晰、简洁。这包括在页面上美观地编排所有旅行事项，另起一行写上每一事项的标题、在每个日程项下加上一段说明，并对每一事项附上具体的时间。

2.2 关注目标和重点

不管是什么样的旅行，老板都可能给你传达基本目标和优先事项。如果没有，你应当设法获取这些信息资料，这样就只需安排真正符合总体旅行计划的行程。

2.3 对于难找之处，提供地图

一些经验丰富的策划人建议把每项活动地点的地图列入行程表。万一旅行中的主管或其他人员在行程中迷路，这样做最终可以节约大家的时间。

2.4 填写旅程项细节

给老板的旅程表不应只包括时间和地点。在旅程表中添加任何与旅行点相关的细节都可真正地使旅程表更有价值。

可用五个W来解决这些细节。许多正在写各种文档的人都使用这五个标记生成有关细节：谁，什么，为什么，何时以及如何。尽管第五个标记不是以字母 W 开头，但将这些疑问词称作“五 W”有助于记忆。

2.5 灵活性

随时接受老板的信息补充。旅行计划可能改变，而且能随着最新的变化而变化才能真正地使优秀的旅程表与其他无用之物区别开来。

3. 联系旅行社

准备好旅程表后，你需要给旅行社打电话，做旅行安排。向他们证实此次旅行为商务旅行。可以为公司主管人员预订持续飞行三小时或更长时间的航班的商务舱（即介于头等舱和经济舱之间的座位)。

要求旅行社在出票以前，给你和旅行者用电子邮件发送一份旅程表副本。仔细阅读旅程表，确保航班、酒店和租车都有确认号。需特别注意旅行者的名字拼写是否有误。任何拼写错误都将在机票上显示出来。如果机票上的名字和护照上的不一致，主管将不允许搭乘航班。

当你感到满意而且旅程表正确无误，再次给旅行社打电话，告知他们何时可以出票。大多数票务是通过电子票的方式完成。你和旅行者都会收到一封含有电子票的电子邮件。为主管打印一张电子机票，以便获取登机牌时使用。

课文B　商务旅行预订

1. 概述

由于有大量的火车、飞机、和酒店可供选择，所以在做出最适合你老板口味的选择时，商务旅行预订已成为你需要小心应付的工作。作为秘书或私人助理，你要确保老板的商务旅行始终顺利进行。

首先要考虑的是你所在的公司是否有旅行政策。大多数公司已有适当的政策来管制员工预订什么、在哪儿预订。这可能在很大程度上影响你的选择。在考虑公司规章制度后，接下来要考虑你要为之做预订的人的需求和愿望。

通常，预订商务旅行主要有三种方式：

- 亲自预订并单独预订每一项。
- 使用在线服务来处理所有的预订。
- 雇用差旅管理公司(TMC)。

假设你不雇用旅行管理公司，那么可以分三个阶段来圆满地完成商务旅游预订工作。

1.1　预定前

- 调查

先前的一点点工作就可以为后来节省大量时间。你要考虑商务旅行涉及的各个方面，以及应对各方面采取的最佳措施。例如，某些国家需要签证或免疫接种。确保你在采取必要性措施方面听取了相关建议，并留意时间安排表和旅程表。如果能节省旅行者的时间，你就能轻松地使他的旅行更高效。

- 创建旅行者档案

一些在线预订工具允许你快速创建档案，使你能够持续地向旅行代理人传递必要的有关个人喜好的资料，包括你老板的忠诚奖励计划号，以及对座位或房间的喜好。即使自己处理所有的预订，确保你手上有这些信息也是必要的。

1.2　预订

在开始预订前，你必须明确预定所需。最便宜的火车票和酒店房间通常可变通性最小。起先，它们或许省钱，但如果计划有变，而你又无法改签，起初省下的钱也会被抵销。

由于可供选择的数量较多，分开预定所有的东西非常耗时。创建一个你所需要的信息和网址的数据库，并记住可能还需要成为许多组织中的会员，如航空公司、铁路公司和酒店连锁集团。

简化这一工作的简单方法就是使用搜索聚合，如 lastminute. com、booking. com 或 cheap flights. com 等网址。这些网址可搜索多个品牌，对搜索结果排名，并且无须多次登录。

如果成本是主要的考虑因素，可考虑以下建议：

- 预订的时间越早，省下的钱就越多。不仅预定航班是这种情况，预订酒店和火车票也是如此。
- 为了省钱，可考虑不买可改签票（如：提前买三张不可改签的火车票通常要比购买一张完全可改签火车票便宜）。有时最好的解决办法是预订一张固定的去程票和一张可改签的返程票。
- 考虑旅行的整体花费，而不仅仅是单项费用。如：每晚支付 100 英镑入住现场的酒店是值得的，而不是住在几英里以外的酒店，虽然那里每晚只需支付 80 英镑，却要产生单程 15 英镑的出租车费。
- 考虑延后召开内部会议，以便所有的与会者能避开火车旅行的高峰期。这样做可使每位与会者节约 60% 的花费。
- 注意你所交付的费用。在执行整个预订过程中，很容易忽视所有的附加费用。

如果商务旅行预订是你的常规工作，或许你想看看在线旅游预订工具。使用商务旅行预订工具的优点包括：

- 无商家费用——直接在英国航空网站上预定将包括这些费用，但是通过旅行管理公司则可避免这些商户费，并可每座节省 50 英镑。
- 付款条件——网站预订需要信用卡预先支付，但是通过旅行管理公司，你可以保留座位和价格直到售票截止日期。
- 24 小时支持——航空公司并不都是一天 24 小时运行。如果你的老板在世界的另一边，需要在凌晨 3 点打电话更改回程航班，这就将成为一个重大的问题。
- 公正、专业的建议——例如，南非航空公司是不会告诉你从希思罗飞往开普敦航班，其头等舱的腿部活动空间更小，但其价格却高于英国航空的商务舱。

（注：在同一个地方的进行所有预订工作，你会更容易处理好商务旅行安排工作，记录商务旅客的行踪并分析数据。）

1.3 预订后

一旦旅游预订完成，就该确保旅行者抓紧时间准备他们所需要提供的资料。要考虑的重要事项包括：

- 旅行文件。

确保准备并安排好老板可能需要的全部必要材料。这些材料可能包括火车票、飞机票或其票号、住宿优惠卡、护照、签证以及免疫证。

- 旅行保险。

确保他们有足够的旅行保险。如今，有许多旅行保险种类可供选择，通过货比三家，你或许能选择更好的套餐。

2. 不同用途的预订

由于目的不同，可能有如下不同的预订：酒店预订、餐厅预订、票务预订、会议室预订、车辆预订和宴会预订等。在这部分，我们将主要关注酒店预订、餐厅预订和订票。

2.1　预订酒店

如果你是私人助理，你必须知道如何为别人预订酒店。事实上，为老板预订酒店是你工作职责的一部分。在了解自己工作的方方面面时，你必须也了解你老板的喜好，从而预测他的需求。

• 收集旅行信息。

你应该了解旅行的目的地和目的。如果你的老板将去参加一个活动，如研讨会，你应该在策划这次活动的酒店为其预订酒店房间。如果活动将在不同的地点进行，你需要搜索附近的酒店。你需要知道老板在那个地方会待多少天。此外，办信用卡是你的工作，知道房间里住多少人也是有帮助的。

• 预订酒店房间。

打电话预订。向酒店职员提供姓名、信用卡信息和联系号码。然后，说明拟预订的酒店房间规格以及任何必要的附加要求。

• 安排交通。

安排好老板往返于酒店的交通工具。一些高端酒店将提供礼宾服务。礼宾接待员会为有一定地位的客人做任何必要的安排。这包括预订晚餐、预订高尔夫开球时间甚至根据需要提供特殊条件。如果你的老板是知名人士，你或许可以直接给礼宾接待员打电话。

下面是一个有关预订酒店的例子。

先生：

请问 7 月 6 日周一下午至 7 月 10 日周五晚上有没有空余的单人房？请告知带浴室的单人房房价。如贵方能立即回复以便我能马上预定，我将不胜感激。谢谢！

真诚的，

简 · 盖茨

2.2　预订餐厅

学会预订餐厅将有助于使你的用餐体验更加美好，还有助于你进入到预订很多的高级餐厅。在这里，有一些关于如何预订餐厅的建议。

- 尽早地打电话预订。大多数餐厅将提前几天接受预订，而高档的用餐场所往往会提前几周或几个月就接受（甚至要求）预订。如果你提前好几天预订，最好在用餐当天打电话快速确认你的预订信息。
- 预订时尽可能有礼貌。 如果预订很棘手，记住你在电话中的态度将起重要作用。要自信，但也要有礼貌；不要让人觉得你认为享受预订服务是理所应当的。
- 亲自去餐厅。 对于棘手的预订，还需要的一项策略就是亲自去预订，而不是通过电话。这样做表明为了就餐，你愿意付出努力。当和你面对面打交道时，餐厅主人也不太可能拒绝你，或不给予帮助。
- 如果你迟到，提前打电话说明或取消预订。 一旦预订，如果你可能会晚到 20 分钟，提前打电话道歉。如果你晚到的时间超过 20 分钟，则需考虑取消和重新安排你就餐。请记住，所有的预订都是出于一个原因，即确保每晚有尽可能多的客人用餐。如果你迟到了，会影响到其他客人的预订。

下面是一个有关餐厅预订的例子。

亲爱的先生：

我们打算3月29日下午6点在北京饭店用晚餐。就餐者共七人，希望能预订一个包间。我们还需要酒侍一名，菜肴以海鲜为主。

如有可能，请回信告知大致价格。

诚挚的，
张平

2.3 订票

订票主要包括预订各种交通工具和娱乐活动的票。前者指的是乘坐如火车、飞机、公共汽车等各种交通运输工具的票，这也是商务旅行预订工作主要涉及的内容。这里，我们只重点谈谈如何在互联网上预订机票。

- 确定你最终的目的地、出发日和返程日。正如你用电话预订机票一样，在网上预订机票前，你需要列出你此次旅行的基本信息。
- 选择是否只需要机票还是需要一些其他套餐，如机票加租车，或者机票加酒店房间，并做出适当的选择。许多在线网站都提供连同机票一起的套餐服务。如果你需要酒店或租车，那么选择套餐可节省一些钱。
- 在相应域输入地点和日期。在“从”域，输入出发地；在“到”域，输入目的地。在“离开”域，输入你想离开的日期；在“返回”域，输入你想返回的日期。
- 选择你需要的机票数量。许多网站都有一个下拉菜单，让你选择有多少成人、儿童、或老年人坐飞机。输入准确的票数。如果你是一个成年人单独旅行，只需保留成人票“1”张的默认值。
- 在屏幕上单击“搜索”或“找票”按钮。输入全部信息后，在线网站将搜索与你需求匹配的飞机票。然后，根据航空公司或价格，选择你需要的航班。选择后，只需按照网站上的说明，以电子方式购买机票即可。

3. 确认、更改或取消预订

预订后，如果日程安排或计划没有变化，则需要确认预订信息。但是，如果有任何变化，则需要更改预订，而且有时会取消预订。下面是一些例子。

3.1 确认预订（确认电话预订的房间）

先生：

此信是为了确认3月12日通过电话为我公司一位主管预订的套房。入住时间是3月18日至3月22日，每日房价为80美元，并以支票支付。

真诚的，
苏珊·史密斯

3.2 更改预订（更改机票预订）

先生：

我在5月10日预订了纽约飞上海262号航班的往返机票。5月15日周三上午9点出发，计划5月20日返回。

但我将不能按计划出发去上海，而要推迟到5月18日出发，5月23日返程。请确认此更改并告知我。

诚挚的，
李华

3.3　取消预订（取消车辆预订）

亲爱的先生：

6月20日我为我公司总部的效率顾问彼得森先生预订了一辆汽车，租赁期是两周。彼得森先生原计划在这里停留半个月，但现在却不能按原计划出行。请立即取消此预订。谢谢！

诚挚的，
琳达

Business Contracts and Negotiation

Unit 9

Part One Dialogues

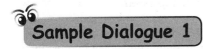

Sample Dialogue 1

Situation ▶ Li Mei is consulting a business and commercial law attorney about a business contract.

(A—Li Mei, the executive secretary of East Building Materials Trade Company; B—John Norman, a business and commercial law attorney)

A: Good morning, Mr. Norman.

B: Good morning, Miss Li. What can I do for you?

A: I am just wondering if you can help me make sense of this contract? I don't quite understand this phrase...

B: OK. Let me see, "The two undersigned are in agreement to the following terms. Party A shall be responsible for furnishing Party B with materials as follows." Well, that's kind of complicated way to say you both agree to something and sign your names to certify.

A: So if I sign here, that makes me Party A, am I right?

B: Yes. Then you have to abide by all the requirements listed in this contract for Party A.

A: Oh, I see. What about this phrase, "Terms and conditions of this agreement are void in the case of natural disaster or acts of God."

B: That means unless something very serious arise, like an earthquake, a tsunami, a flood and so on, you will be bound to the contract and can't get out of it.

A: That is so serious, huh?

B: Sounds like it. Before you sign this contract, be sure to read it carefully so that you are sure it's what you exactly want.

A: Good idea! What's more, I think I'll probably have to get a dictionary to help me understand the contract better. Thank you a lot, Mr. Norman!

B: You're welcome, Miss Li. Good-bye!

Sample Dialogue 2

Situation ▶ Wang Lin is negotiating business with a client.

(A—Wang Lin, the senior secretary of Chunhui Plastics Industry Company; B—Mr. Anderson, the client from Australia)

A: Welcome to China, Mr. Anderson.

B: Nice to meet you, Miss Wang.

A: Nice to meet you, too, Mr. Anderson. Shall we get down to business?

B: All right.

A: Our representative in your country faxed a letter saying that you showed an interest in some of our products on display at the Oct. Exhibition there. Now we'd like to know if you have any specific requirements in mind.

B: Yes, we have. I've brought with me a list of the quantity of your products we'd like to import for the second half of this year. And the articles we require should be durable and the colors should be bright and attractive. Here is a copy of it.

A: Good. Well, Mr. Anderson, most of the items listed are available this year. And I am sure that the quality of our products will meet your requirements. I hope we can come to an agreement and sign the contracts soon to enable timely delivery.

B: I hope so, too. Furthermore, there are one or two points I'd like to go over with you.

A: Go ahead, please!

B: Could you give us a higher discount if we allow you a later delivery?

A: Usually we'll give our clients 2% discount in that case.

B: Thank you, Miss Wang. What are your normal export terms?

A: We normally export CFR.

B: All right. When can we meet again for more specific details, Miss Wang?

A: What about tomorrow morning at 10 o'clock? I'll come over to your hotel.

B: I'll be expecting you, then.

Useful Expressions

1. The two undersigned are in agreement to the following terms.
   下面签名的双方同意以下条款。
2. So if I sign here, that makes me Party A, right?
   那么如果我在这里签字的话，那我就算是甲方了，对吗？
3. You have to abide by all the requirements listed in this contract for Party A.
   你必须遵从本合同中列出的对甲方的所有要求。
4. Terms and conditions of this agreement are void in the case of natural disaster or acts of God.
   出现自然灾害或不可抗力时，本协议中的各条款和条件无效。
5. That means unless something very big happens, like an earthquake or a tsunami, you will be bound to the contract and can't get out of it.
   这意思是说除非有某些大事发生，如地震和海啸，否则你必须履行合同内容而且不能逃避责任。
6. Our representative in your country faxed a letter saying that you showed an interest in some of our products on display at the Oct. Exhibition there.
   我们公司在贵国的代理人发来一封传真说您对我们公司十月份在贵国展会上展示的产品有兴趣。
7. I've brought with me a list of the quantity of your products we'd like to import for the second half of this year.
   我带来了我们公司今年下半年要从你们这里进口的产品的数量清单。
8. I hope we can come to an agreement and sign the contracts soon to enable timely delivery.
   我希望我们能达成协议，尽快签订合同以保证准时发货。
9. Furthermore, there are one or two points I'd like to go over with you.
   另外，我还有一两点想和您商量一下。
10. Could you give us a higher discount if we allow you a later delivery?
    如果我方允许贵方迟些时间交货，贵方能给我方高一些的折扣吗？

Situational Dialogues

Using the Sample Dialogue as a model, try to create a new dialogue with your partner.

Situation 1 ▶ Wang Shan, a secretary in Mechanical and Electrical Equipment Company, is consulting with Jack Chen over a business contract, who is a business law attorney.

Situation 2 ▶ Zhang Yue, a senior secretary in Machine Tools Industry Company, is negotiating business with Tom Jackson, a client from the United States.

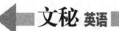

Part Two Text A

Business Contracts

A contract is a voluntary, deliberate, and legally binding agreement between two or more competent parties. A contractual relationship is evidenced by an offer, acceptance of the offer, and a valid (legal and valuable) consideration. Each party to a contract acquires rights and duties relative to the rights and duties of the other parties. However, while all parties may expect a fair benefit from the contract, it does not follow that each party will benefit to an equal extent. Existence of contractual-relationship does not necessarily mean the contract is enforceable, or that it is not void or voidable.

A contract and an agreement are similar in nature as they both describe two or more people that seem to agree on the same thing. However, a contract must be an agreement, but an agreement is not necessarily a contract. Whenever two or more persons' minds meet on any subjects, no matter how trivial, there is an agreement. But it is only when all the participating members intend to be legally obliged by the terms of the agreement that a contract comes into existence. If it composes only a social or moral obligation, however, it is not a contract and is not legally enforceable. Typically, the subject matter of the contract must involve a business transaction, as distinguished from a purely social transaction.

There are many reasons to have a written contract. A written contract ensures that all of the terms of your agreement are documented. If a disagreement or a negative situation arises, there will be a document that the parties can refer back to in order to get the relationship back on track. In short, a solid written contract can save money and strengthen a business relationship by helping to avoid litigation altogether.

1. Essential Elements of a Contract

A contract is much more than an agreement between two people. There must be an offer and acceptance, intention to create a legally binding agreement, a price paid (not necessarily money), a legal capacity to enter a contract of your own free will, and proper understanding and consent of what is involved. Any duress, false statements, undue influence or unconscionable dealings could make a contract illegal and void.

1.1 Offer and Acceptance

A contract is formed when an offer by one party is accepted by the other party.

An offer is a definite promise to be bound, provided the terms of the offer are accepted. This means that there must be acceptance of precisely what has been offered. For example, a used car dealer offers to sell B a Holden panel van for $1,000, without a roadworthy certificate. If B decides to buy the Holden panel van, but insists on a roadworthy certificate being provided, then B is not accepting the used car dealer's offer. Rather, B is making a counter offer. It is then up to the used car dealer to accept or reject the counter offer.

An offer must be distinguished from mere willingness to deal or negotiate. For example, X offers to make and sell to Y calendars featuring Australian paintings. Before any agreement is reached on size, quality, style or price, Y decides not to continue. At this stage, there is no legally binding contract between X and Y because there is no definite offer for Y to accept until the essential terms of the bargain have been decided.

Acceptance occurs when the party answering the offer agrees to the offer by way of a statement or an act. Acceptance must be unequivocal and communicated to the offer, otherwise, the law will not deem a person to have accepted an offer merely because they have not expressly rejected it.

1.2 Intention to Create Legal Relations

A contract does not exist simply because there is an agreement between people. The parties to the agreement must intend to enter into a legally binding agreement. This will rarely be stated explicitly but will usually be able to be inferred from the circumstances in which the agreement was made. For example, offering a friend a ride in your car is not usually intended to create a legally binding relation. You may, however, have agreed with your friend to share the costs of traveling to work on a regular basis and agree that each Friday your friend will pay you $20 for the running costs of the car. Here, the law is more likely to recognize that a contract was entered into.

Commercially based agreements are seen as including a rebuttable intention to create a legally binding agreement. However, the law presumes that domestic or social agreements are not intended to create legal relations. For example, an arrangement between siblings will not be presumed to be a legally binding contract. A person who wants to enforce a domestic or social agreement needs to prove that the parties did intend to create a legally binding agreement.

1.3 Consideration

Consideration is the price paid for the promise of the other party. The price must be something of value, although it need not be money. Consideration may be some right, interest or benefit going to one party or some forbearance, detriment, loss or responsibility given, suffered or undertaken by the other party.

So long as consideration exists, the court will not question its adequacy, provided that it is of some value. For example, the promise to pay a peppercorn rent in return for the lease of a house would be good consideration. Of course, the consideration must not be illegal or impossible to perform.

1.4 Legal Capacity

Not all people are completely free to enter into a valid contract. The contracts of the groups of people listed below involve problematic consent, and are dealt with separately, as follows:

• People who have a mental impairment

Capacity to give consent involves a general understanding of the nature of the contract (not necessarily its fine details). A person with a mental impairment, for example, may have the capacity to understand some contracts (e.g. buying a loaf of bread), but not to understand other, more complicated contracts (e.g. buying a car on credit). Thus, people with mental impairments are sometime vulnerable to being bound by contracts they do not fully understand.

When a person with a disability did not understand the general nature of the contract, a court can intervene to set aside the contract.

• Young people (minors)

The term young person is used here to refer to anyone under the age of 18 years. Sometimes legal writing refers to minors or infants.

Contracts binding on young people generally include contracts for the supply of "necessaries", such as food, clothing, a place to live, medicine, and so on, and those related to the young person's education, apprenticeship or something very similar.

There are two classes of contracts which are not binding on a young person, namely, contracts that are not for necessaries; and contracts for the repayment of money lent or to be lent (that is, any form of credit contract).

• Corporations

A corporation is an artificial body created by law. The corporation has a legal existence separate from the individual people who comprise it. However, a company has the legal capacity of a natural person and therefore has the capacity to enter contractual relations. This is so even if there is an express prohibition contained in the company's constitution. Such transactions are not deemed void and beyond the company's powers simply because the exercise of such powers is in breach of the restrictions placed in the company.

• Prisoners

During their imprisonment, prisoners may enter contracts, including contracts to buy and sell property. The usual restrictions about supervision and censorship of anything coming into the prison still apply.

1.5 Consent

Entering into a contract must involve the elements of free will and proper understanding of what each of the parties is doing. In other words, the consent of each of the parties to a contract must be genuine. Only where the essential element of proper consent has been given is there a contract that is binding upon the parties.

Proper consent may be affected by duress. Duress is held to have occurred where there has been actual or threatened violence either to the other contracting party directly or to their immediate family, near relatives or close associates. The duress may be made by someone acting under the instructions of the party to the contract. The net effect, though, will have been that a party has been forced into the contract by being deprived of their free will to act.

Proper consent may be affected by undue influence. Undue influence is exercised by taking unfair and improper advantage of the weakness of the other party, to the extent that it cannot be said that that party intended voluntarily to enter into the contract.

1.6 Legality

For a contract to be enforceable, the terms and conditions of the agreement between the parties must be legal. They must also be capable of being performed and not offend public policy goals. A commonly encountered situation of this sort arises in the context of non-competition clauses in employment agreements. Where the terms of the non-competition agreement extend too far into the future, or are too wide in their geographic scope, the courts have struck them down on the basis that it is against public policy to unfairly restrict commercial competition or an employee's right to earn a living.

Contracts are important to facilitate commercial relationships. The absence of any essential element may leave the parties with just an unenforceable set of terms. Such a situation can be avoided by proper planning and engaging legal counsel early on in the negotiation process.

2. *How to Write an Effective Business Contract*

Contracts may follow a structure that can include the following items:

- details of the parties to the contract, including any sub-contracting arrangements.
- duration or period of the contract.
- definitions of key terms used within the contract.
- a description of the goods and/or services that your business will receive or provide.
- payment details and dates, including whether interest will be applied to late payments.
- key dates and milestones.
- required insurance and indemnity provisions.
- guarantee provisions, including director's guarantees.
- damages or penalty provisions.
- renegotiation or renewal options.
- complaints and dispute resolution process.
- termination conditions.
- special conditions.

Entering into a contractual business relationship with another party is a serious task and should only be entered into after giving real thought about the relationship you want. Don't fall into the trap of entering into agreements haphazardly or with complete trust of the other party. so you'll need to familiarize yourself with some guidelines on how to create a clear, concise and complete business contract.

2.1 Use Language You Can Understand

There's no need to be intimidated by a false sense that a business contract has to be written in "legalese." The best contracts, particularly in the small business context, are written in plain English where both parties know exactly what they're signing and what the provisions mean. Just be sure that the terms you write are specific as to each party's obligations and the specific remedies that you have in the event that the other party violates the agreement. Also, keep in mind that certain terms have specific meaning in the law.

The easiest way to write a contract is to number and label each paragraph and only include that topic in the paragraph. By segmenting the contract into individual units, it will be more easily understood by the parties (and by a court should it come to that).

2.2 Be Detailed

The rights and obligations of each party should be laid out in specific language that leaves little room for interpretation. If you want delivery on the 15th of each month, use the specific number instead of writing, "mid-month". If you and the other party agree to a new term or decide to change an existing term in the agreement, be sure to add a written amendment to the contract rather than relying on an oral agreement. A court may or may not accept the oral agreement as part of the contract.

2.3 Include Payment Details

It's important to specify how payments are to be made. If you want to pay half up front and the other half in equal installments during the life of the contract, state that, as well as the terms under which you will release payment. For example if you contract with someone to paint your business offices, you might want a provision stating that your regular payments are contingent upon a certain number of rooms being painted to your satisfaction. Whenever possible, list dates, requirements and methods of payment (cash, check, credit). Contract disputes often center on money, so you'll want to be as specific as possible.

2.4 Consider Confidentiality

Often when entering a business contract, the other party will gain access and insight into your business practices and possible trade secrets. If you do not want the other party sharing this information, you should include a clause that binds the other party from disclosing your business information or information included in the contract to other parties.

2.5 Include Details on How to Terminate the Contract

Contracts aren't meant to last forever. If one party continually misses payments or fails to perform their duties, you want to have a mechanism in place so that you can (relatively) easily terminate the contract. It could be a mutual termination agreement (when the objectives of each side have been met through the contract) or more likely an agreement that either side can terminate if the other side violates a major term of the contract, after giving proper notice of its intent to terminate.

2.6 Consider State Laws Governing the Contract

Contracts can stipulate which state's laws will govern in the event there's a dispute. If the other party is located in another state, you should include a clause that states which state laws will govern. If you don't, and there's a dispute, there may be a whole other legal argument (which costs more money) about which state's laws should be applied to the contract. Avoid this headache and agree to it at the inception of the contract, when both parties are agreeable.

2.7 Include Remedies and Attorneys' Fees

Especially if you believe that it's more likely that you'll sue over the contract (as opposed to the other party suing you), you might want to include a clause that awards attorneys' fees to the winning party. Without this clause, each party will have to pay for their own attorneys.

2.8 Consider a Mediation and Arbitration Clause

In the event of a dispute, it may be advantageous to include a provision that requires the parties enter either mediation or arbitration, or both. Mediation is a voluntary process where both parties try to work out their issues directly, with the help of a neutral third party mediator. Any settlement must be approved by both parties. Arbitration is a more adversarial process where the arbitrator hears both sides' arguments and makes a decision that both parties must abide by. It's akin to a trial setting, but the arbitration process is much quicker and cheaper than litigating in court.

2.9 Consider the Help of a Legal Professional

Writing a business contract that protects your interests while balancing your business objectives is critical to your business' success. Learning how to write a business contract is the first step on the road to success. But while you should get acquainted with the legal terms and processes for writing a contract, sometimes it's best to have an attorney review your contract before it takes on the force of law. Find a business and commercial law attorney near you for assistance.

New Words

deliberate [di'libərit] *adj.* 深思熟虑的
binding ['baindiŋ] *adj.* 有约束力的
contractual [kən'træktjuəl] *adj.* 合同的，契约的
evidence ['evidəns] *n.* 证据；迹象 *vt.* 表明；使明显；显示；证实
offer ['ɔfə] *n.* 发价，发盘，报价，开价
acceptance [ək'septəns] *n.* 受盘；承兑，认付
enforceable [in'fɔ: səbl] *adj.* 可强行的，可强迫的；可实施的
void [vɔid] *adj.* 无效的
voidable ['vɔidəbl] *adj.* 可撤销的
trivial ['triviəl] *adj.* 琐碎的，无价值的
oblige [ə'blaidʒ] *vt.* 强制，强迫；使负债务
litigation [ˌliti'geiʃən] *n.* 诉讼；打官司
consent [kən'sent] *n.&vi.* 同意；准许，赞同
duress [djuə'res] *n.* 胁迫；强制
undue ['ʌn'dju:] *adj.* 不适当的；过度的，过分的
unconscionable [ʌn'kɔnʃənəbl] *adj.* 昧着良心的；不合理的
dealing ['di:liŋ] *n.* 行为，交易
bound [baund] *adj.* 有义务的；受约束的
provided [prə:'vaidid] *conj.* 如果；假如；在……的条件下
roadworthy ['rəudwə:ði] *adj.* 适于公路行驶的
reject [ri'dʒekt] *vt.* 拒绝；排斥
willingness ['wiliŋnis] *n.* 自愿，乐意
negotiate [ni'gəuʃieit] *v.* 谈判，协商；交涉
feature ['fi:tʃə] *vt.* 以……为特色
bargain ['bɑ:gin] *n.* 交易；契约，协定 *vi.* 讨价还价；达成协议

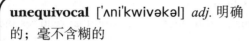

unequivocal ['ʌni'kwivəkəl] *adj.* 明确的；毫不含糊的
expressly [iks'presli] *adv.* 明确地；清楚地
rarely ['rɛəli] *adv.* 很少；难得
explicitly [iks'plisitli] *adv.* 明白地，明确地
commercially [kə'məːʃəli] *adv.* 商业地
rebuttable [ri'bʌtəbl] *adj.* 可辩解的，可反驳的
presume [pri'zjuːm] *v.* 假设，假定；推定
sibling ['sibliŋ] *n.* 兄弟，姐妹
enforce [in'fɔːs] *vt.* 强制；实施；强迫
consideration [kənsidə'reiʃən] *n.* 对价
forbearance [fɔː'bɛərəns] *n.* 债务偿还期的延展
detriment ['detrimənt] *n.* 损害，伤害；造成损害的事物
question ['kwestʃən] *v.* 对……表示异议
peppercorn ['pepəkɔːn] *n.* 花椒；胡椒
lease [liːs] *n.* 租约；租契；租期 *vt.* 出租；租得
problematic [prɔblə'mætik] *adj.* 问题的；有疑问的
impairment [im'pɛəmənt] *n.* 损伤，残损；损害
vulnerable ['vʌlnərəbl] *adj.* 易受攻击的；易受伤的
disability [ˌdisə'biliti] *n.* 无能；残疾
intervene [ˌintə'viːn] *vi.* 干涉，干预；介入；调停
minor ['mainə] *n.* 未成年人
infant ['infənt] *n.* 未成年人，法定未成年者
apprenticeship [ə'prentisˌʃip] *n.* 学徒期；学徒身份
repayment [riː'peimənt] *n.* 偿还；付还的钱
corporation [ˌkɔːpə'reiʃən] *n.* 公司；法人
artificial [ˌɑːti'fiʃəl] *adj.* 人造的；虚伪的
comprise [kəm'praiz] *vt.* 构成；包含
prohibition [prəuhi'biʃən] *n.* 禁止，禁令
constitution [ˌkɔnsti'tjuːʃən] *n.* 章程，法规
imprisonment [im'prizənmənt] *n.* 关押，监禁
censorship ['sensəʃip] *n.* 审查制度；审查机构
genuine ['dʒenjuin] *adj.* 真正的；坦率的，真诚的
instruction [in'strʌkʃən] *n.* 命令；指示
improper [im'prɔpə] *adj.* 不合适的
legality [li'gæliti] *n.* 合法，正当；合法性
offend [ə'fend] *vt.* 违反；触犯
encounter [in'kauntə] *vt.* 遭遇；不期而遇；对抗
facilitate [fə'siliteit] *vt.* 促进；帮助
sub-contracting [sʌb-'kɔntræktkiŋ] *n.* 合同转包；分包制；承包制
duration [djuə'reiʃən] *n.* 合同有效期；持续
milestone ['mailstəun] *n.* 重要阶段；里程碑；划时代事件
indemnity [in'demniti] *n.* 保证；赔偿；免除债务
provision [prə'viʒən] *n.* 规定；条款
penalty ['penəlti] *n.* 违约罚金；处罚
renewal [ri'njuəl] *n.* 延期；补充；更新；继续
termination [ˌtəːmi'neiʃən] *n.* 终止；结束
haphazardly [hæp'hæzədli] *adv.* 不规则地；随意地

legalese [ˌliːgəˈliːz] *n.* 法律措辞，法律术语
segment [ˈsegmənt] *vt.* 分割；划分
interpretation [inˌtəːpriˈteiʃən] *n.* 解释，阐释
delivery [diˈlivəri] *n.* 交货
amendment [əˈmendmənt] *n.* 修正草案；改动，修正
installment [inˈstɔːlmənt] *n.* 分期付款
terminate [ˈtəːmineit] *v.* 结束；终止；解除
mechanism [ˈmekənizəm] *n.* 机制；原理；途径
intent [inˈtent] *adj.* 热切的；专心的 *n.* 意图；目的
stipulate [ˈstipjuleit] *v.* 规定；要求
inception [inˈsepʃən] *n.* 开端；初期；成立
agreeable [əˈgriəbl] *adj.* 准备同意的；可接受的
attorney [əˈtəːni] *n.* 律师
mediation [ˌmiːdiˈeiʃən] *n.* 调停；调解；仲裁
arbitration [ˌɑːbiˈtreiʃən] *n.* 仲裁；公断
advantageous [ˌædvənˈteidʒəs] *adj.* 有利的；有益的
neutral [ˈnjuːtrəl] *adj.* 中立的
mediator [ˈmiːdieitə] *n.* 调解人
adversarial [ˌædvəˈsɛəriəl] *adj.* 对立的；对抗的；对手的

Phrases and Expressions

be relative to 和……有关系，随……而转移；与……相对
it follows that ... 由此得出结论……
to an equal extent 在同等程度上
come into existence 存在；形成；成立
moral obligation 道义上的责任；道德上的义务
business transaction 商务交易；业务往来
be distinguished from 不同于，与……加以区别
refer back to 重新提及，查阅
get... back on track 使……回到正轨或步入正轨
in short 简而言之，总之
panel van 厢式货物运输车
insist on 坚持，强调
a counter offer 还盘，反要约
by way of 经由；用……方法
infer from 从……中推导出
at a peppercorn rent 空有其名的租金；极低的租金；名义租金
in return for 作为……的报酬；替换
mental impairment 精神损害
be binding on 对……有约束力的
credit contract 信贷合同，信用合约
express prohibition 明示禁止
be in breach of 违反
be deprived of 丧失；被剥夺
to the extent that... 达到这种程度以致……
non-competition clause 非竞争性条款
strike down 驳回；取消
earn a living 谋生，维持生活
in the event that... 假如，在……的情况下
be contingent upon 视……而定

to one's satisfaction 使某人满意 center on 以……为中心；重点在于…… gain insight into 了解，熟悉；看透，识破 sue sb. over sth. 以某事为由起诉或控告某人	in the event of 倘若；如果发生 abide by 遵守，服从 be akin to 类似，近于 the force of law 法律效力，法律约束力 get acquainted 认识，熟悉

Notes

1 However, while all parties may expect a fair benefit from the contract, it does not follow that each party will benefit to an equal extent.

本句中，it 作主句的形式主语，代替主语从句 that each party will benefit to an equal extent。其中，it follows that 是一固定结构，意为“由此断定”。请看下例：

It follows that specialization will lead to increased production.

由此看来专业化会导致产量增加。

另外，本句中 to an equal extent 为固定短语，意为“在相同的程度上”。请看下例：

If one experiment was helped by the wind, the other was hindered to an equal extent.

如果一个实验受到顺风的帮助，另一个实验则受到同等程度的逆风的阻碍。

2 But it is only when all the participating members intend to be legally obliged by the terms of the agreement that a contract comes into existence.

本句中，主干为“it is + 被强调成分 + that...”结构的强调句型，被强调部分是 only when all the participating... the agreement 这个时间状语从句。

在强调句型中，被强调的部分放在前面，其他部分置于 that 之后，被强调部分可以是主语、宾语、表语或状语。请看下例：

It is only when money wages move that instability declares itself.

只有当货币工资移动时，不稳定才会出现。

另外，come into existence 为固定短语，意为“形成；产生；成立”。请看下例：

Contracts arise when a duty does or may come into existence, because of a promise made by one of the parties.

一方做出一个诺言，即产生了一个义务，合同就有可能产生。

3 So long as consideration exists, the court will not question its adequacy, provided that it is of some value.

本句中，so long as 是固定短语，相当于 as long as，意为“只要”，通常引导一个状语从句。请看下例：

The president need not step down so long as the elections are held under international supervision.

只要选举在国际监督下进行，总统就不用下台。

另外，本句中连词 provided 意为“如果；假如；在……的条件下”，在句中引导条件状语 that it is of some value。

英语中，引导此类条件句的连词还有 assuming; providing; supposing。请看下例：

Provided that there is no opposition, we shall hold the meeting here.

假如无人反对，我们就在这里开会。

4 Only where the essential element of proper consent has been given is there a contract that is binding upon the parties.

本句中，Only + 地点状语从句（where the essential element of proper consent has been given）置于句首，引起主句发生部分倒装。

英语中，当副词 only 置于句首，强调方式状语、条件状语、地点状语、时间状语等状语时，主句要进行部分倒装。请看下例：

Only when we had studied the data again did we realize that there was a mistake.

只有当我们再次研究了这些数据的时候，我们才意识到出了一个错。

另外，本句中 be binding upon 为常用表达，意为“对……有约束力”。请看下例：

This agreement and its terms shall be binding upon the Clients' heirs, executors, administrators and assigns.

本协议及其条款对客户的（财产）继承人、遗嘱执行人、财产管理人和财产受让人都具有约束力。

5 Undue influence is exercised by taking unfair and improper advantage of the weakness of the other party, to the extent that it cannot be said that that party intended voluntarily to enter into the contract.

本句中，to the extent that 意为“达到这种程度以致……”，在句中引导结果状语从句。请看下例：

Society progresses to the extent that reason can suppress the passions.

社会已经进步到理性可以抑制激情的阶段了。

另外，本句中 take advantage of 为固定短语，意为“利用；占……的便宜”。请看下例：

People concentrate in cities not only to get jobs but to take advantage of cultural facilities.

人们聚集在城市不仅是为就业，而且是为享用文化设施。

Exercises

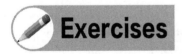

EX. 1 Answer the following questions.

1. What is the definition of a contract according to Text A?
2. What is the link between a contract and an agreement?
3. What are the essential elements of a contract according to Text A?
4. Is any offer a definite promise to be bound?
5. Does the consideration of a contract have to be money?
6. According to Text A, what kind of people may have no legal capacity to give consent to a contract?

7. What factors may affect the parties' proper consent to a contract in accordance with Text A?
8. What does the legality of a contract mean?
9. What clause should you include in a contract if you don't want the other party to share with other parties the information related to your business practices?
10. Based on Text A, what is meditation and arbitration?

EX. 2 **Complete the following sentences with appropriate words or expressions in the box.**

penalty	deprive of	mediate	legality	in the event of
voidable	terminate	intimidate	consent	in breach of

1. We have also found that a regional presence can be an effective way to ________ disputes.
2. A ________ contract is one in which one or more parties have the power to end the contract.
3. The buyer then may elect to ________ the transaction by giving timely and appropriate notice to the seller.
4. The contract was ended by mutual ________.
5. The principle of ________ should govern all their actions and decisions.
6. Attempts to ________ people into voting for the governing party did not work.
7. The maximum ________ is up to 7 years imprisonment or an unlimited fine.
8. ________ difficulties, please do not hesitate to contact our Customer Service Department.
9. The commission of inquiry ruled that the company was ________ contract.
10. Years of secretarial work has ________ the executive assistant ________ her energy or vigor.

EX. 3 **Translate the following sentences into English.**

1. 你必须遵从本合同中列出的对甲方的所有要求。(abide by)
2. 这份声明指出，这家公司将对恶意诽谤保留控告权。(sue over)
3. 我们要合理控制贷款风险，包括审查申请人资质以及完善信贷合同。(credit contract)
4. 采取欺诈或者胁迫手段订立的合同无效。(duress; void)
5. 如果雇员在非竞争性条款通过时没有达到成年年龄，则该条款无效。(non-competition clause; invalid)
6. 本条款并无意改变或增加组织的法律义务。(provision; legal obligations)
7. 如能最优惠地考虑我方还盘，我们将不胜感激。(counter-offer)
8. 对这份协议任何条款的增加或者修改，对当事人都不产生约束力。(be binding upon)
9. 接受报价中的条款就会产生一份合同。(acceptance)
10. 诉讼过程将视这些国家的现有法律而定。(litigation process; be contingent on)

EX. 4 **Translate the following passage into Chinese.**

The terms and conditions of a business contract specify the rights and obligations of each party. These can vary widely depending on the nature of the business arrangement. Common examples can include the amount of payment, when payment is due, the specific nature of the work involved and how long the agreement will remain in effect. Terms can also include possible remedies if one party is found to be in breach of the contract.

A contract may be deemed invalid if it can be shown that one of the parties was mentally incompetent at the time of entering into the agreement. A contract may also be voided if one party was under the influence of drugs or alcohol and the other party was aware of the first party's condition.

A business contract must be for a legal purpose to be considered valid. If, for example, one party knowingly contracted to deliver stolen merchandise for a second party, the second party would have no legal recourse if the first party failed to deliver the goods to their intended destination.

Part Three Text B

Business Negotiation

Negotiation is a process where two or more parties with different needs and goals discuss an issue to find a mutually acceptable solution. In business, to negotiate is to deal or bargain with another or others, as in the preparation of a treaty or contract or in preliminaries to a business deal.

Negotiation skills are important in both informal day-to-day interactions and formal transactions such as negotiating conditions of sale, lease, service delivery, and other legal contracts.

1. Importance of Negotiation in Business

Good negotiations contribute significantly to business success, as they:

• help you build better relationships.

• deliver lasting, quality solutions — rather than poor short-term solutions that do not satisfy the needs of either party.

• help you avoid future problems and conflicts.

Negotiating requires give and take. You should aim to create a courteous and constructive interaction that is a win-win for both parties. Ideally a successful negotiation is where you can make concessions that mean little to you, while giving something to the other party that means a lot to them. Your approach should foster goodwill, regardless of the differences in party interests.

2. Negotiation Process

Every time you negotiate, you have to make choices that affect whether you achieve a successful outcome for your business. To get the best outcomes, you need to understand the steps involved in the negotiation process.

2.1 Planning Your Negotiation

No amount of preparation is too much in approaching complex or high-stakes negotiations. Plan both your approach to the subject under negotiation, and your tone and communication style.

In approaching the subject of your negotiations:

- set your objectives clearly in your own mind (including your minimum acceptable outcome, your anticipated outcome and your ideal outcome).
- determine what you'll do if the negotiation, or a particular outcome, fails.
- determine your needs, the needs of the other party and the reasons behind them.
- list, rank and value your issues (and then consider concessions you might make).
- analyze the other party (including their objectives and the information they need).
- research the market and consult with colleagues and partners.
- rehearse the negotiation.
- write an agenda — discussion topics, participants, location and schedule.

In deciding your communication style, familiarize yourself with successful negotiating strategies. Arm yourself with a calm, confident tone and a set of considered responses and the tactics you anticipate.

2.2 Engaging with the Other Party During the Negotiation

- Introduce yourself and articulate the agenda. Demonstrate calm confidence.
- Propose — make your first offer. The other party will also make proposals. You should rarely accept their first offer. Evidence suggests that people who take the first proposal are less satisfied and regret their haste.
- Check your understanding of the other party's proposal.
- Remember your objectives.
- Discuss concepts and ideas.
- Consider concessions, then make and seek concessions.
- Suggest alternative proposals and listen to offered suggestions.
- Paraphrase others' suggestions to clarify and acknowledge proposals.
- Give and take.

2.3 Closing the Negotiation

Take a moment to revisit your objectives for the negotiation. Once you feel you are approaching an outcome that is acceptable to you:

- look for closing signals; for example:
  - — fading counter-arguments.
  - — tired body language from the other party.
  - — negotiating positions converging.
- articulate agreements and concessions already made.
- make "closing" statements; for example:
  - — "That suggestion might work."

— "Right. Where do I sign?"

- get agreements in writing as soon as you can.
- follow up promptly on any commitments you have made.

3. Negotiation Skills

Effective negotiation skills are those tactics and techniques that the adept negotiator employs during the course of negotiations in order to both create and claim value for herself and her counterparts. Effective negotiation skills include BATNA identification, effective use of emotions at the bargaining table, caucusing, delineating your zone of possible agreement, and other skills geared toward an integrative bargaining outcome rather than a distributive, or haggling, bargaining outcome. What follow are some effective negotiation skills.

3.1 Preparation Is Key

Know about the party you're negotiating with so you can capitalize on your strengths and the party's weaknesses. If the other party is very experienced, that means he also has a history that could contain useful information. If possible, talk to business associates who have dealt with this person before. Many negotiators develop patterns and certain styles that you may be able to use to your advantage.

If you are a buyer, make sure you are thoroughly familiar with the product or service that will be the subject of the negotiation. If the other party senses you are weak on such details, you may be a prime target for a bluff or another technique designed to create anxiety and uncertainty. Psychology plays a crucial role in your ability to make the most of the other party's lack of preparation and anticipate their next move.

Most negotiators have a price target or goal in mind before they start. It should be based on realistic expectations considering all the constraints that will undoubtedly surface. These may include budget limits, direction from management, pressure to make sales goals, and a myriad of other external forces. During the course of the negotiation, the goal may change based on changes in scope and other unforeseen actions by either party. While your ultimate goal should be realistic, this should not constrain your first offer or counteroffer.

Before you start the negotiation, ensure that the other party is fully empowered to make binding commitments. You don't want to find yourself in a position where you believe you've struck a deal, only to discover that your agreement must be approved by someone higher in the chain of command.

3.2 Have a Strategy

There are basic principles that apply to every negotiation. The first offer is usually the most important and the benchmark by which all subsequent offers will be judged and compared. You'll never get what you don't ask for, so make your first offer bold and aggressive. The asking price is just that, and will typically include a margin to give away during negotiations. Don't worry about insulting the other party. As long as your offer is not ridiculous, the other side will continue the negotiations in hopes of settling at a better number.

As a buyer, do not disclose your budget or other limitations in your negotiating position. A favorite trick of salesmen is to reorganize the product specifications, schedule and other limitations in order to sell you an inferior product to fit your budget. You want the best product you can get for the money you have to spend, so employ an approach that maintains the possibility of spending less than you had originally planned.

Always have something to give away without hurting your negotiating position. If you're submitting a price proposal to a buyer, consider inserting decoys and red herrings for the other party to find. For example, if you are bidding a project, consider including some nice-to-have items that aren't critical to the success of the project. You could also include spare parts that may or may not be needed in the end. If the buyer takes those items out to reduce the overall cost, you haven't lost anything but it may help the buyer reach his price target. Such distractions will help to divert the other party from attacking the meat of your proposal. Employing this strategy must be viewed in the context and in consideration of what other bidders may be doing. If you know that the only way to win the bid is to provide a bare bones cost, then this strategy may not be appropriate.

Watch for clues such as body movement, speech patterns and reactions to what you say. Be prepared to suspend or cancel negotiations if you feel things are getting nowhere or the other party seems stuck in their position. Indicate your reluctance to continue under those conditions and make the other side wonder if you are ever coming back. If they are on the hook to cut a deal, they will feel the pressure to move. Be patient even if the other party isn't. This can be difficult for those with a passion for instant gratification, but the last thing you want is for the other party to think you're under the gun to finish quickly.

From a contractual standpoint, a counter-offer automatically rejects all previous offers. Once an offer is made, you should expect an acceptance or rejection of your offer, or a counter-offer that keeps the negotiation open. If your offer is rejected and you are asked to submit a new and better offer, do not fall into that trap. That would be tantamount to negotiating with yourself, and you should never do this.

3.3 Find the Leverage

In addition to exploiting the other party's weaknesses, concentrate on taking maximum advantage of your strengths. If you're the only source available for a particular product, you have tremendous leverage across the board. If economic conditions have created a market in which the product you're selling is in great demand and low supply, that gives you more bargaining power to name your price. If you are the buyer in a depressed economy, you normally have the advantage of too much supply and lower demand. The current housing situation is a classic example of what happens when supply vastly outweighs the demand and market prices fall dramatically.

Establish a strong foundation early in the process by demonstrating your knowledge and expertise of the negotiation subject matter. This may intimidate those on the other side and put them on their heels before they've a chance to establish their own credibility. Playing catch-up in a tough negotiation can be challenging, so it's much better to take the initiative and steer the process in the direction you want.

3.4 The Offer

An offer is more than just a dollar amount. It must encompass all of the elements of the bargain and will normally comprise the basis for a contract that formalizes the agreement. If you make an offer without nailing down all of the specifics, you may find out later that there was no meeting of the minds with the other party. The basis of the bargain should include: offer price (in proper denomination), statement of work (scope), identification and quantities of goods or services, delivery schedule, performance incentives (if any), express warranties (if any), terms and conditions, and any documents incorporated by reference.

Trading one element for another—such as a lower price for a more relaxed schedule—is a common tactic. These bargaining chips should be kept in your hip pocket until you need them to close the deal and get the price you want. While your primary focus is normally on price, you should always keep all the other components of the deal in the forefront of your mind. Don't be pressured into accepting boilerplate contracts represented as the "standard of the industry" or something that "we always use". Everything, including the fine print, is open to change. If the other party refuses to alter onerous terms, consider taking your business elsewhere.

3.5 Go for a Win-Win Solution

Throughout the negotiation, try to determine what you believe to be an acceptable outcome for the other party. It may be a combination of different things that aren't necessarily tied solely to price. For example, the delivery date may be the most important thing to the other party, while product quality may be your primary driver.

Understanding the other side's priorities is just as important as understanding your own, so figure out what you would do if you were in his shoes. When constructing your offers, attempt to satisfy some of his priorities if doing so doesn't weaken your overall position. Be prepared to give up the little things in exchange for the big things you don't want to concede. Know your limits and how far you're willing to go on all aspects of the deal.

While you have the power to influence the negotiation process in your favor, your goal should be to secure a good deal without extracting the last pound of flesh from the other party. This is especially true if you will be negotiating with the same party on a recurring basis. The most effective negotiators are professionals who know their business and don't let personalities and irrational behavior interfere with their mission. They are capable of making the other party believe they got the best deal they could under the circumstances.

3.6 Closing the Deal

Successful negotiation is like horse-trading in that it requires a sense of timing, creativity, keen awareness and the ability to anticipate the other party's next move. Negotiation is also like chess in that each move should be designed to set up not only your next move, but several moves down the line. Generally, your moves should get progressively smaller, and you can expect the same from the other party.

New Words

negotiation [ni,gəuʃi'eiʃən] *n.* 协商，谈判
mutually ['mju:tʃuəli] *adv.* 相互地；彼此
treaty ['tri:ti] *n.* 条约，协议
preliminary [pri'liminəri] *adj.* 初步的，初级的；预备的 *n.* 准备工作；初步措施
lasting ['lɑ:stiŋ] *adj.* 持久的，恒久的
win-win [win-win] *adj.* 双赢的，对各方都有益的
foster ['fɔstə] *v.* 培养；促进
high-stakes [hai-steiks] *adj.* 高风险的，高利害性的
minimum ['miniməm] *n.* 最低限度；最小量 *adj.* 最小的，最低的
anticipated [æn'tisipeitid] *adj.* 预期的，预先的
rehearse [ri'hə:s] *v.* 排练，排演；详述，复述
tactic ['tæktik] *n.* 战术；策略
articulate [ɑ:'tikjulit] *adj.* 发音清晰的；善于表达的 *v.* 清楚地和清晰地讲；善于表达
haste [heist] *n.* 匆忙；急速，紧迫；轻率
paraphrase ['pærəfreiz] *vt.* 复述；意释；释意
clarify ['klærifai] *v.* 澄清；阐明；解释
fade [feid] *vi.* 褪去，逐渐消逝；凋谢，衰老
counterargument ['kauntə'ɑ:gjumənt *n.* 反驳，抗辩
converge [kən'və:dʒ] *vi.* 聚集，汇集；融合
adept ['ədept] *adj.* 精于……的，擅长……的
caucus ['kɔ:kəs] *vi.* 召开（参加）核心会议；磋商
delineate [di'linieit] *vt.* 描绘，描述
gear [giə] *vt.* 使适应；调和 *n.* 用具，装备
integrative ['intigreitiv] *adj.* 综合的，一体化的
haggle ['hægl] *n.* 讨价还价；争论 *v.* 讨价还价；争论不休；使疲惫
thoroughly ['θʌrəli] *adv.* 彻底地；认真仔细地
bluff [blʌf] *n.* 欺骗；恐吓；虚张声势 *v.* 虚张声势；吓唬；愚弄
constraint [kən'streint] *n.* 约束，限制，强制
surface ['sə:fis] *vi.* 浮出水面；显露 *n.* 表面；外观，外表
scope [skəup] *n.* 范围；眼界，见识；余地
unforeseen ['ʌnfɔ:'si:n] *adj.* 未预见到的，无法预料的
ultimate ['ʌltimit] *adj.* 极限的；最后的
constrain [kən'strein] *vt.* 约束，限制；强迫
empower [im'pauə] *vt.* 授权，准许
benchmark [bentʃmɑ:k] *n.* 基准，参照
bold [bəuld] *adj.* 明显的；大胆的，无畏的
aggressive [ə'gresiv] *adj.* 侵略的，侵犯的，攻势的
insult ['insʌlt] *vt.* 辱骂；侮辱，凌辱；损害 *n.* 侮辱，凌辱；损害

inferior [in'fiəriə] *adj.* 低劣的；下级的，下等的
decoy [di'kɔi] *n.* 圈套，诱饵
bid [bid] *n.* 出价，投标 *vt.* 出价，投标；恳求；命令
divert [dai'vəːt] *vt.* 使转移，转移注意力；分散
suspend [səs'pend] *v.* 暂停，推迟，暂缓
reluctance [ri'lʌktəns] *n.* 不情愿，勉强
passion ['pæʃən] *n.* 激情，热情，热心
gratification [ˌgrætifi'keiʃən] *n.* 满足，满意，满足感
rejection [ri'dʒekʃən] *n.* 拒绝；摒弃
tantamount ['tæntəmaunt] *adj.* 相等的，相当的
leverage ['liːvəridʒ] *n.* 杠杆作用；影响力；优势，力量
exploit [iks'plɔit] *vt.* 利用；剥削；开采
tremendous [tri'mendəs] *adj.* 极大的，巨大的，惊人的
depressed [di'prest] *adj.* 情绪低落的，沮丧的；萧条的
outweigh [aut'wei] *vt.* 在重量上超过；比……重要
dramatically [drə'mætikəli] *adv.* 戏剧性地，引人注目地
challenging ['tʃælindʒiŋ] *adj.* 有挑战的；富有挑战性的
steer [stiə] *v.* 引导；驾驶；操纵，控制
encompass [in'kʌmpəs] *vt.* 围绕，包围；包含或包括某事物
formalize ['fɔːməlaiz] *vt.* 使正式，形式化
denomination [diˌnɔmi'neiʃən] *n.* 面额
incentive [in'sentiv] *n.* 动机，诱因；刺激，鼓励
onerous ['ɔnərəs] *adj.* 繁重的；麻烦的；负有义务的
combination [ˌkɔmbi'neiʃən] *n.* 结合，联合体
concede [kən'siːd] *v.* 承认；让步，容许；承让
extract [iks'trækt] *vt.* 提取，选取；获得
irrational [i'ræʃənəl] *adj.* 无理性的，不合理的，荒谬的
horse-trading [hɔːs-'treidiŋ] *n.* 讨价还价；精明的谈判

Phrases and Expressions

bargain with 与（某人）讨价还价
make a concession 做出让步，妥协
regardless of 不管，不顾，不论
achieve an outcome 实现成果，取得某种结果
arm oneself with 武装自己
engage with 与……接洽；与……开战；忙于
make a commitment 做出承诺
at the bargaining table 在谈判桌上
capitalize on 充分利用某事物，从某事物中获利
to one's advantage 对某人有利
a prime target 首要目标
give away 放弃；泄露
in hope of 怀着……的希望，希望
red herring 转移注意力的话
in consideration of 考虑到，由于
be stuck in 困于；停止不前

be on the hook 陷入困境
be under the gun 处于紧张状态
from a contractual standpoint 从合约的角度看
fall into a trap 陷入圈套，坠入陷阱
in addition to 除……之外
take maximum advantage of 最大程度地利用
across the board 全面性的，全面
be in great demand 畅销，有很大需求
put sb. on one's heels 使某人紧跟在后面
play catch-up 弥补；追赶
take the initiative 采取主动
nail down 明确；确定
close the deal 结束交易；达成交易
be pressure into doing sth. 被迫做某事
boilerplate contract 定型合同，样板合同
be in sb.'s shoes 处于某人的位置或立场
in exchange for 交换，调换
in sb.'s favor 得某人欢心，对某人有利
on a recurring basis 重复地，反复地
interfere with 干预，妨碍，干扰

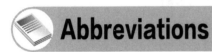

Abbreviations

BATNA (Best Alternative To a Negotiated Agreement) 谈判协议最佳替代方案

Exercises

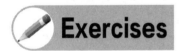

EX. 5 Answer the following questions.

1. What is the definition of negotiation according to Text B?
2. Why are good negotiations important to business success?
3. How many steps are typically involved in the negotiation process? And what are they?
4. List at least three things that need to be done in approaching the subject of your negotiations.
5. List at least three things that need to be done while engaging with the other party during the negotiation?
6. Why do you need to know about the party you're negotiating with before you start a negotiation?
7. How should you make the first offer since the first offer is the benchmark by which all subsequent offers will be judged and compared?
8. What should the basis of the bargain include according to Text B?
9. What kind of negotiators can be regarded as the most effective ones in accordance with Text B?
10. Why does the author compare negotiation to chess?

Part Four Extended Reading

Text	Notes
Employment Contracts	
Employment contracts are binding[1] agreements between an employer and employee. They spell out every detail, including how long the contract period will last, what the compensation[2] will be, and other employment issues. They can benefit both the large companies and the smallest businesses, especially if you have valuable trade secrets you need to protect.	[1] *adj.* 有约束力的；应履行的 [2] *n.* 补偿，赔偿
There are times and places for employee contracts. As an employer, you should be aware of the various factors to consider when thinking about employee contracts. Certainly, there is no requirement that you have to enter into a written employee contract with every employee that you have. However, there are some situations in which it makes sense[3] to enter into an employment contract with your employees.	[3] 有意义；理解；讲得通
Why Should You Use an Employment Contract?	
• They protect trade secrets: Many small businesses have trade secrets. Whether it's a recipe[4] for your signature[5] bagels or a production method, it must be protected. An employment contract can have a non-disclosure agreement[6], which prohibits employees from sharing trade secret information during and after their contract period is over.	[4] *n.* 食谱；处方；秘诀 [5] *n.* 签名 [6] 保密协议
• Non-compete: Don't want your employee to work for a competitor or start his own business just down the street? You can include non-compete agreements[7] within your contracts to prevent current and past employees from doing just that. (In California, where non-competes are unenforceable[8] for the most part, employers can use non-solicitation agreements[9] and nondisclosure agreements to protect their trade secrets, client lists, and employees when an employee leaves.)	[7] 非竞争协议 [8] *adj.* 不能强制的，不能执行的 [9] 不劝诱协议
• Ensures steady employment: With an employment contract, you have a promise from an employee that you will have access to their skills as long as you provide work for a specified period. While the at-will employee[10] can quit whenever he or she wishes, employees with contracts are less likely to resign[11] because of the benefits and guaranteed work and risk of breaching[12] the contract.	[10] 任意制雇员，临时工 [11] *v.* 辞职；放弃 [12] *vt.* 违背；破坏

• Better talent acquisition[13]: An employment contract may attract better talent to your company. A good employee will value the benefits of a contract, and if you can offer them a worthwhile opportunity, you may lock in the best talent long-term.	[13] *n.* 获取；取得
When Should You Use an Employment Contract?	
If you are not sure when to use an employment contract, these are a few situations that call for them:	
• You have extensively[14] trained an employee and you want him or her to work for you for a specified amount of time before being allowed to resign. That way you don't waste resources and time training them.	[14] *adv.* 广大地，广泛地
• You will be exposing that employee to trade secrets that could easily help a competitor[15] if they were shared.	[15] *n.* 竞争者；对手
• You can commit[16] to a time frame and supply enough work to that employee so that you don't breach the contract.	[16] *v.* 把……托付给；承诺，使……承担义务
What Is Included in an Employment Contract?	
First and foremost[17], a good employment contract will spell out what exactly you expect the employee to do (the parameters[18] of their job). In addition, the contract will spell out what your employee can expect from you (normally a salary). However, there are other terms that you can include in an employment contract, such as:	[17] 首先，首要 [18] *n.* 参量；限制因素；决定因素
• The term of employment (A period of months or years, until the completion of a project, or indefinitely[19]).	[19] *adv.* 无限期地；不定期地
• Terms relating to the responsibilities of the employee.	
• Benefits such as health, life or disability insurance[20] or retirement accounts[21].	[20] 丧失工作能力保险 [21] 退休账户
• Vacation and sick day policies.	
• Reasons and grounds for termination[22].	[22] *n.* 终止，结束
• Covenants[23] not to compete that will limit the employee's employment opportunities if he or she is terminated or otherwise leaves the company.	[23] *n.* 盟约；契约
• Nondisclosure agreements relating to your company's trade secrets or client lists.	
• An ownership agreement stating that all materials produced by the employee during his employment are owned by the company.	
• Assignment clauses[24] stating that any patents[25] procured[26] by the employee during his employment must be assigned to the company.	[24] 转让条款 [25] *n.* 专利；专利权 [26] *vt.* 取得，获得
• A method for resolving disputes relating to employment (such as mediation[27] or arbitration[28]).	[27] *n.* 调停，调解 [28] *n.* 仲裁，公断

At Will Employment Concerns	
Generally speaking, employees that are under contract are not "at will" employees because the contract will spell out the specific grounds[29] on which the employer can terminate the employee.	[29] *n.* 根据，理由
However, there are other employees that are required to sign written agreements that state that their employment is at will, meaning that the employer can fire them at any time for any reason ,so long as the reason is not illegal[30].	[30] *adj.* 非法的；不合法的
In addition, the employee is free to quit at any time. Employers that work with at will employees often get their employees to sign employee handbook acknowledgment[31] or other documents that state that the employee knows his or her employment is at will. These documents, unlike "regular" employment contracts do not limit an employer's ability to terminate an employee.	[31] 员工手册签阅
Disadvantages of Using Employee Contracts	
However, with all the advantages that can come to you with an employment contract, you should never lose sight of[32] the potential[33] disadvantages. Remember that an employment contract is a two way street[34] — you have obligations[35] that you must fulfill[36] as well. If an employee does not turn out how you want, or if the needs of your business change, you will have to renegotiate[37] the employment contract.	[32] 忽略 [33] *adj.* 潜在的，有可能的 [34] 必须有所妥协的情感场面或人际关系 [35] *n.* 债务；义务，责任 [36] *vt.* 履行；执行 [37] *v.* 重新谈判或协商
As an example, if you have hired an employee under a two year contract only to find out six months into the project that you no longer need the employee, you cannot simply fire him. Instead, you will probably have to renegotiate the contract or settle with[38] your employee as to how much money you owe.	[38] 与……达成协议，与……成交
Another disadvantage of employment contracts is that, once under the terms of the contract, you are required to act with according to the "covenant of good faith and fair dealing." This means that you have to act in good faith and in accordance with[39] the terms of the contract. Therefore, if you breach a term of the contract in bad faith, you will not only be in breach of[40] the contract, but you may also have breached your duty to act in good faith, which could lead to further legal ramifications[41].	[39] *n.* 与……一致，依照 [40] 违反 [41] *n.* 分叉；衍生物，后果
While carefully considered and well-written employment contracts offer certain benefits and protections for employers, they also carry some risk. If you have any questions about the validity[42] of your contracts, or whether you should even use them, you may want to contact an employment law attorney licensed[43] to practice in your state.	[42] *n.* 效力；正确性 [43] *vt.* 许可，颁发执照

参考译文

课文A 商务合同

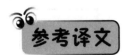

合同是两个或两个以上的有行为能力的当事人经过深思熟虑自愿订立的具有法律约束力的协议。证明契约关系存在的要素有要约、接受以及有效的（即合法并有价值）对价。合同每一方获得的权利和义务与合同其他各方的权利和义务相对。然而，尽管各方当事人都期望在合同中公平受益，但这并不意味着每方当事人都能平等受益。契约关系的存在并不一定意味着合同是可执行的，有可能是无效的或可撤销的。

契约和协议在本质上是相似的，因为它们都描述了两人或者多人似乎在同一件事上达成一致。然而，合同必须是协议，但协议未必是合同。两人或多人在任何时候、任何事情上意见一致，都可形成协议，无论事情多么微不足道。但是，只有当所有当事人愿意履行协议条款规定的有法律效力的义务时，一份合同才得以产生。然而，如果协议只构成社会或道德义务，它便不是合同，也不具备法律上强制执行的效力。通常，合同的标的必须包括业务交易，其不同于纯粹的社会交易。

签订书面合同的原因很多。书面合同确保协议的所有条款都记录在案。如果出现分歧或负面情况，则会有一份文件供当事人参阅，从而使关系恢复正常。总之，一份可靠的书面合同有助于完全避免诉讼，从而省钱并加强业务关系。

1. 合同的基本要素

合同不只是两人之间的协议。合同必须具备要约和接受、建立合同关系的意愿、对价（不一定是钱），自愿缔结合同并正确理解合同的行为能力以及对合同内容的同意等要素。任何胁迫、虚假资料、不正当压力或不合理的交易都可能使合同非法并且无效。

1.1 要约和接受

当一方当事人提供的要约由另一方当事人接受时，一份合同即产生。

如果要约的条款被接受，要约则是明确的有约束力的承诺。这意味着必须要对要约条件完全接受。例如，一位二手车经销商提供要约，以1000美元销售给B方一辆没有道路通行证的霍顿厢式货车。如果B方决定购买霍顿厢式货车，但坚持要经销商提供道路通行证，那么B方并没有接受二手车经销商的要约。相反，B方正在提出反要约。这时，将由二手车经销商决定接受或拒绝B方的反要约。

要约必须区别于纯粹的交易或谈判意愿。比如，X方主动提出给Y方制作和向Y方出售以澳大利亚绘画作品为特色的日历。在就日历尺寸、质量、款式或价格方面达成任何协议之前，Y方决定不跟进。那么，在这个阶段，X方和Y方之间没有产生具有法律约束力的合同，因为直到协议基本条款被决定时，Y方才有明确的要约可接受。

当受要方通过一项声明或决议书同意提供的报价时，接受即产生。接受必须是明确的，并传达给要约方。否则，仅仅根据受要方没有明确拒绝要约这一行为，法律是不会承认他已经接受了报价这一事实。

1.2 建立合同关系的意愿

合同不会仅仅因为人与人之间有一份协议而存在。协议各方必须具备达成具有法律约束力的协议的意愿。这一点很少有明确的规定，但通常可以从达成协议的详细事项中推断出来。例如，主动请朋友搭你的车，这通常不是建立具有法律约束力关系的意愿。然而，你可能已和朋友协商好定期分摊上班的路费，并同意每周五你的朋友向你支付 20 美元的车费。这时，法律则很有可能承认合同被签订。

商业性协议被视为包括建立一个具有法律约束力协议的可驳回的意愿。然而，法律假定家庭或社会协议本意并非是创造法律关系。例如，兄弟姐妹之间的一种安排将不被推定为具有法律约束力的契约。要想强制执行一份家庭或社会协议，当事人需要证明协议各方确实有创建一个具有法律约束力协议的意愿。

1.3 对价

对价即对另一方的承诺所支付的报酬。报酬必须是有价值的东西，虽然未必是钱。对价可能是合同一方具有的权利，享有的利益或好处，也可能是合同另一方经受的债务延缓条例，遭受的损害、损失或承担的责任。

只要对价存在并有一定价值，法院就不会质疑其是否充分。例如，允诺支付极少的租金租赁一所房屋将是好的对价。当然，对价物必须是合法的、可执行的。

1.4 法律行为能力

不是所有的人都能随意地缔结有效合同。下列人群缔结的合同在“同意”真实性问题上存在疑问，要区别对待：

• 精神障碍者

给予同意的能力指的是能大致理解合同性质的能力(不一定是合同的详细细节)。例如，一个有精神障碍的人，可能有能力理解一些合同（如：买面包），但不能理解其他更复杂的合同(例如：购买汽车)。因此,有精神障碍的人易于受到其无法充分理解的合同的制约。

当丧失行为能力的人不能理解合同的一般性质时，法院可以介入，将合同作废。

• 年轻人（未成年人）

在这里，术语“年轻人”是指年龄在 18 周岁以下的人。有时法律文件上称作未成年人或法定未成年者。

对未成年人有约束力的合同一般包括提供“必需品”的合同，如食品、服装、居所、医药，等等，以及与年轻人的教育、学习或类似东西有关的合同。

有两类合同对未成年人不具有约束力，即非供应“必需品”的合同以及还款合同（也就是任何形式的信贷合同)。

• 公司

公司是依法产生的非自然法人。公司的合法地位与组成它的员工是分开的。然而，公司具有一个自然人的法律行为能力，因此它能够缔结合同关系，即使公司章程明文禁止这一做法。仅仅是因为行使这种权力违反了该公司的有关限制性规定，这些交易不会被视为无效，也不会被认为越权。

• 囚犯

服刑期间，服刑人员可以签订合同，包括买卖财产合同。有关对进入监狱的任何东西进行监督和审查的这些常规限制性规定仍然适用。

1.5 同意

签订合同必须包括自由意志以及对当事人行为的正确理解等要素。也就是说，合同各方当事人的同意必须是真实的。只有满足真实性同意的必备条件时，签订的合同才对当事人有约束力。

胁迫可能会影响到同意的真实性。当直接对合同另一方当事人或对其直系亲属、近亲亲属或关系密切的人施加实际的暴力行为或进行暴力威胁时，胁迫这种行为则被认为已经发生。胁迫可能是合同一方当事人指示他人进行的行为。然而，胁迫带来的净效应是：合同一方被剥夺了行为的自由意志而被迫签订合同。

不正当影响也可能会影响到同意的真实性。即通过不公平和不正当地利用对方当事人的弱点给对方施加不正当影响，以致该方当事人不能自愿签订合同。

1.6 合法性

一份合同要具有可执行性，双方协议的条款和条件必须是合法的。他们还必须具备的可执行性，而且不违反公共政策目标。这种情形常见于就业协议的非竞争条款情况中。当非竞争协议条款规定的未来期限过长，或规定的地理范围太宽泛，法院可宣布这些协议条款无效，理由是该协议违反了公共政策、不合理地限制了商业竞争或员工谋生的权利。

合同在促进商业关系方面起着重要作用。缺失任何必要性的要素都可能使当事人签订的合同成为不可执行的空文。在谈判过程中，适当的规划并咨询法律顾问可以避免这种情况。

2. 如何草拟一份有效的商业合同

合同的结构可包括下列内容：

- 合同各方当事人的详细情况，包括任何分包安排。
- 合同有效期。
- 定义合同中使用的关键术语。
- 描述你公司将得到或提供的货物和 / 或服务。
- 付款细节及日期，包括是否对逾期付款加收利息。
- 关键日期和阶段。
- 要求保险和赔偿条款。
- 担保条款，包括董事的担保书。
- 赔偿损失的条款。
- 重新谈判或续订合同权。
- 投诉和纠纷解决程序。
- 终止条款。
- 特殊条款。

与另一方缔结商业合同关系是一件严肃的事情，只有真正考虑过你想要的这种关系后才可签订。不要随意或因为完全信任对方而陷入签约陷阱。因此，你需要熟知有关如何草拟一份清晰、简明、完整的商务合同的准则。

2.1 用你能理解的语言

你没有必要因为一种错误的认识——即必须以“法律术语”来草拟商业合同，而对合同望而生畏。最好的合同，尤其是在小企业中，都是用浅显的英语写的，双方都确切地知道他们签订的内容和条款。但要确保你写的条款具体规定了合同双方各自的义务，以及补救措施，如果对方违约的话。另外，请记住某些条款在法律上有特定的含义。

草拟一份合同的最简单的方法是给每个段落编号命名，并且一个段落只包含一个主题。将合同分成单个的段落，以便合同各方（以及法院，如果涉及的话）更容易理解。

2.2 详细

合同各方的权利和义务都应该以具体的语言拟定，不留任何阐释空间。如果你要每月15日交货，应在合同中写明具体的数字而不是“每月中旬”字样。如果你和另一方都同意一条新的条款或决定更改协议中现有条款，务必要在合同中增加一份书面修正案，而不是依赖口头协议。法院将口头协议视为合同的一部分的可能性未定。

2.3 包括付款细节

明确付款方式，这一点很重要。如果你想在合同有效期内先付一半，再等额分期支付另一半的话，那么必须在合同中明确说明，并确定你放款的条件。例如，如果你与某人签订合同，让他来粉刷你的办公楼，你可能需要订立一项条款，说明你的定期付款条件是取决于被粉刷得令你满意的房间数量。只要有可能，你应该列出日期，要求和付款方式（现金、支票、信用卡）。合同纠纷往往以金钱为中心，所以你要尽可能详细具体。

2.4 考虑保密性

通常，在签订一份商业合同的时候，对方将有机会接触并了解你公司的商业行为，也可能是商业秘密。如果你不希望对方散发这些信息，你应该订立保密条款来约束对方，防止对方将你公司的商业信息或合同包含的信息透露给任何第三方。

2.5 包括有关如何终止合同的细节

合同不会永远持续下去。如果合同一方一直不付款或不履行其职责的话，你需要设立某种机制，以便你能（相对）容易地终止合同。这可能是一份相互终止协议（当双方通过合同已实现各自的目标时）或更有可能是一份单方终止协议，即如果乙方违反了合同的主要条款，甲方在适当告知乙方终止合同的意愿后，即可终止合同。

2.6 审议适用本合同的州法律

合同可以规定 一旦产生纠纷时，适用哪个州的法律。如果合同另一方位于另一个州，你应该在合同内写入一项条款规定哪个州的法律适用本合同。如果你没有，而合同又产生了纠纷的话，你很可能会面临一个全然不同的有关在本合同适用哪个州法的法律争执（这样成本更高）。所以应当在合同成立之初，双方都赞同时，对这一问题达成一致意见，从而避免这一令人头疼的事情。

2.7 包括补救措施和律师费

你可能需要订立一项条款规定将律师费补偿给胜诉方，特别是当你认为你很有可能就该合同向对方提起诉讼（而不是对方起诉你）的时候。没有这一条款，合同双方都必须各自支付律师费。

2.8 考虑调解和仲裁条款

在合同中写入一项条款，要求合同当事人在发生纠纷时进入调解或仲裁程序，或同时进入这两个程序，这样做是很有利的。调解是一个自愿的过程，在中立的第三方调解人的帮助下，合同双方都试图直接解决他们的问题。任何解决办法必须经双方同意。仲裁是一种更具对抗性的程序。仲裁员审理双方的争论并做出合同双方都必须遵守的决定。仲裁类似于审讯场景，但仲裁比法庭诉讼程序更快捷，成本更低。

2.9 考虑法律专业人士的帮助

如果平衡商业目标对你的企业成功与否至关重要，那么你需要拟一份商业合同来保护你的利益。学会如何拟一份商务合同是通往成功之路的第一步。然而，虽然你应该了解拟一份商业合同所需要的法律条款和程序，但是有时候在合同生效之前，你最好请一个律师来审查你的合同。务必向附近的商法律师寻求有关这方面的法律援助。

课文B 商务谈判

谈判是具有不同需求和目标的双方或多方当事人讨论问题，寻求彼此都能接受的解决方案的一个过程。在商业中，谈判就是在协议或合同准备过程中或在一笔商业交易的预备阶段去应对或与对方当事人商讨条件。

谈判技巧在非正式的日常互动和正式交易中都很重要，比如洽谈销售、租赁、服务、交货条款以及其他法律合同。

1. 商务谈判的重要性

有效的谈判对企业的成功有着重要的贡献，因为它们：

- 帮助你建立更好的商业关系。
- 提供长远的优质解决方案，而不是那些无法满足双方需求的短期的低质解决方案。
- 帮助你避免未来的问题和冲突。

谈判需要互惠互让。谈判旨在创建一个有礼貌的、建设性的、双赢的互动局面。最理想的成功的谈判是你能在价值不大的事情上做出让步，而给予对方看重的东西。无论双方的利益有何不同，你的方式都应该有助于友善关系的培养。

2. 谈判过程

每次谈判，你都必须做出选择，这些选择会影响你的业务最终是否能成功。要取得最好的谈判结果，你需要了解谈判过程所涉及的步骤。

2.1 策划谈判

在应对复杂的或高风险的谈判时，做再多的准备工作也不为过。策划好应对谈判主题的策略、你的语气以及沟通方式。

在策划谈判主题时：

- 在头脑中清晰地设定目标（包括你最低限度可接受的结果、预期的结果和你的理想的结果）。

- 确定你的下一步行动，如果谈判失败或某个特定的结果没有实现。
- 判定自己的需求、对方的需求以及背后的原因。
- 列出、排列并评估你的洽谈事项（然后再考虑你可能做出的让步）。
- 分析对方（包括他们的目标以及他们所需信息）。
- 研究市场并咨询同事和伙伴。
- 预演谈判。
- 写一份议程表，包括洽谈话题、参与者、地点和时间安排。

决定你的沟通方式时，要熟悉成功的谈判策略。用冷静和自信的语气、深思熟虑的回应方式以及你预设的谈判技巧来武装自己。

2.2 与对方进行谈判

- 介绍自己并清楚地陈述谈判议程。要表现得冷静自信。
- 提议——即第一次要约。对方也会要约。但是你不应该接受他们首次要约的条款。有证据表明，接受首次要约的人都不大满意并后悔自己的草率行为。
- 审查你是否理解了对方的提议。
- 记住你的目标。
- 讨论概念和想法。
- 考虑让步，做出让步并寻求对方的让步。
- 建议替代性方案并听取对方提供的建议。
- 转述对方的建议以明确并承认提议。
- 互惠互让。

2.3 结束谈判

花时间重新审视谈判目标。一旦你觉得你正在接近一个可以接受的谈判结果时：

- 寻求谈判结束信号；例如：
  ——越来越弱的反驳声音。
  ——对方疲惫的肢体语言。
  ——谈判立场趋同。
- 确定已达成清晰明了的协议，并已做出了让步。
- 使用“结束性”话语；例如
  ——“那项建议很有效。”
  ——“没问题。我在哪儿签名？”
- 尽可能快地以书面形式记录下谈判的协议。
- 及时跟进你允诺的责任。

3. 谈判技巧

有效的谈判技巧是指熟练的谈判者在谈判过程中为了给自己和对方创造价值或向对方索要有价物而使用的策略和技能。有效的谈判技巧包括识别谈判协议最佳替代方案、在谈判桌上有效地利用情绪、召开核心成员磋商会议、划定可能达成协议的区域以及其他的技巧，旨在实现综合性谈判结果而不是分散的或有争论的谈判结果。以下是一些有效的谈判技巧。

3.1　准备是关键

了解谈判对方的情况，这样你可以充分利用自己的优势和对方的弱点。如果对方很有经验，这意味着他过去的谈判记录包含的信息很有用。如果可能，你需要跟与这个人谈判过的同事交谈。你可以利用许多谈判者形成的谈判模式和某些风格，来增加你的优势。

如果你是买方，请确保你对即将成为谈判主题的产品或服务有全面深入的了解。如果对方意识到你对这些细节知之甚少，他们可能会把你作为其虚张声势的主要目标，或运用其他技能给你造成焦虑或不确定性因素。因此，你是否能够充分利用对方准备不足，并预测他们的下一步行动，心理因素的作用至关重要。

大多数谈判者在谈判开始前都有心理价位或目标。价格目标应该基于切合实际的期望，需要考虑到谈判过程中肯定会出现的各种制约因素。这些因素可能包括预算限制、经营导向、完成销售额的压力以及大量的其他外部因素。在谈判过程中，目标可能根据谈判余地以及对方采取的无可预知的措施而发生变化。只要最终目标切合实际，这就不应该成为妨碍你第一次报价或还价的因素。

在开始谈判前，确保对方有充分权力做出有约束力的允诺。你一定不想自己处于这样的境地，即当你认为你已经和对方达成了协议时，结果却发现达成的协议还需获得指挥链中某位高层人员的批准。

3.2　采用策略

这儿有一些适用于每次谈判的基本准则。通常第一次报价最重要，它是判断和比较所有后续报价的基准。不提出要求，你就永远得不到想要的东西，所以第一次报价要积极大胆。索价只是并通常是谈判过程中的可让步价。因此，不要担心你的报价会冒犯对方。只要你方报盘不荒唐，对方将继续谈判，希望能达成更好的价位。

作为买方，不要透露预算或其他谈判条件。卖方最喜欢运用的策略是重新调整产品规格、进度和其他限制性条件，以便向你销售符合你预算的劣质产品。因此，你想花钱买最好的产品，就需要采用某种策略，使你有可能花费比原计划更少的钱。

在不损害你谈判立场的情况下，经常做一些让步。如果你正在向买方提交一份价格建议书，务必考虑让对方在建议书内发现一些诱饵和额外的内容。例如，如果你正在投标一个项目，考虑包括一些可有可无的、对项目的成功并非至关重要的内容。还可以包括一些最后可有可无的备件。如果买方将这些内容去掉以降低整体成本的话，你并没有任何损失，但这可以帮助买方实现其价格目标。这些转移注意力的内容将有助于分散对方的注意力，使其不再苛责建议书中的主要内容。采用这一战略，必须视具体情况而定，并考虑其他竞标人正在采取的行动。如果你知道竞标成功的唯一途径是提供裸价，那么这一战略可能不合适。

观察线索，如身体运动、言语模式和对你的反应。如果你觉得谈判无进展或者对方一直坚持他们的谈判立场，那么你要做好暂停或取消谈判的准备。向对方表明你不愿在这些条件下继续谈判，并让对方纳闷儿你是否还会回来。如果他们“上钩”和我方达成了交易，他们会被迫采取行动。即使对方没有“上钩”，你也要有耐心。这对那些总是急于求成的人来说很难做到。但是你最不想做的事应该就是让对方觉得你顶着巨大压力，需要尽快结束谈判。

从合同的角度来看，反要约会自动拒绝所有先前的报价。一旦提出要约，你应该预计对方会接受还是拒绝你的要约，或提出反要约，使洽谈可以继续。如果对方拒绝你的报价并要求你重新提供更好的报价，一定不要“上当”。这等于是与你自己谈判，而你永远都不应该这样做。

3.3 找到优势

除了利用对方的弱点，还需要集中精力最大限度地利用你方的优势。如果你是某个特定产品的唯一供货源，你就有了巨大的全面性的优势。如果经济形势已经创造了一个你所销售的产品需求量大和供应量少的市场，这就给了你更多的议价权。如果你是经济低迷时期的买方，通常你会有货源充足而需求降低的优势。目前的住房情况就是一个典型的例子。当供给大大超过需求时，市场价格会大幅下降。

向对方展示你在谈判主题方面的专业知识，从而在谈判过程初期建立良好的基础。这样做可以在对方谈判人员建立自身信誉前震慑住他们，并使他们就范。在棘手的谈判中，扮演追赶对方的角色是很艰辛的，所以你最好要主动出击，使谈判过程朝你所期望的方向进展下去。

3.4 要约

要约提供的不仅仅是一美元。它必须包括所有的交易要素，通常包括正式协议的基本内容。如果报盘时没有确定所有细节，或许后来你会发现，你与对方并没有意思一致。交易的基础应包括报价（以适当的面额）、工作条款（即范围）、商品或服务的标识和数量、交货时间表、绩效激励措施（如果有的话）、明示保证（如果有的话）、条款和条件以及任何作为参考引用的文件。

以此条件交换彼条件——如以较低的价格换取宽松的时间表——是一种常见的策略。你应该随身携带这些谈判的筹码，直到你需要用它们来达成交易，并得到你想要的价格。虽然你通常主要关注的是价格，但你还应该经常记住自己交易的其他部分。不要被迫接受样板合同，其表现为“行业标准”或者“我们总是使用”等这样字眼的运用。一切事物，包括精美的印刷品都可以变更。如果对方拒绝修改烦冗的条款，那你可以考虑去别处交易。

3.5 争取双赢的解决方案

在整个谈判中，设法形成一个你认为对方可以接受的结果。这个结果未必只与价格有关，可能是多种因素的综合体。例如，交货期对于对方而言可能是最重要的，而产品质量却是你方是主要的驱动因素。

了解对方优先考虑的事情和清楚自己的首要目标同样重要，因此，要弄清楚如果你站在对方的立场，你会采取什么样的行动。在构建报价时，应该在不动摇自身总的谈判立场的情况下，尽力满足对方的一些优先事项。做好以“小”换“大”的心理准备，即在小事情上让步，以换取在大事情上的坚持。了解你的极限并知道自己在交易的各方面愿意谈判到何种程度。

当你有能力影响谈判进程，使其朝着对你方有利的方向进展时，你的目标应该是确保达成一笔好的交易，而不是提出合法但不合理的要求来榨取对方。如果你与同一当事人反复进行谈判的话，这一点尤其正确。最有效的谈判者是那些了解他们的企业，并且不让他们的个性以及非理性的行为干扰到谈判任务的专业人士。他们能使对方深信这是他们在那样的条件下能够达成的最好的交易。

3.6　达成交易

成功的谈判就像是讨价还价。它需要时间观念、创造力、敏锐的意识和预见对方下一步行动的能力。谈判还像是下国际象棋。走每一步棋不仅是在安排你的下一步行动，而且是在设计将来采取的多个行动。一般来说，你的动作幅度会逐渐变小，而你也可期望对方同样这样做。

Unit 10

Business Etiquette

Part One Dialogues

Sample Dialogue 1

Situation ▶ Sun Mei and a sales manager are discussing about a lunch meeting with the clients.

(A—Mr. Xu, the sales manager of Eastern Elevator Industry Company; B—Sun Mei, the executive secretary of Eastern Elevator Industry Company)

A: For our lunch meeting with the clients, do we have to make a reservation at the restaurant or do we must show up?

B: Usually for lunch, we don't have to reserve a table, they should allow walk-ins. But to be on the safe side, I'll order a table for half-past twelve. Will that suit your schedule?

A: I've arranged to meet them at the restaurant at twelve. Can you make the reservation a little earlier? If we start earlier, it will give us more time for a longer lunch.

B: Are you planning on treating the clients to a full-course meal?

A: Yes. We'll start with appetizers, follow with a soup and salad course, then main dishes of prime rib, and finish up with a delicious rich dessert of some sort.

B: That'll be pretty heavy for a mid-day meal, don't you think so?

A: As along as we stay away from anything alcoholic, we should be okay.

B: With your prime rib, you'd better hope nobody's vegetarian.

A: We can make some special arrangements if we need to. After all, it's the company who is paying the bill.

Sample Dialogue 2

Situation ▶ Liu Ting is talking with a foreign client at a cocktail party.

(A—Liu Ting, the secretary of ABC Frozen Foodstuffs Company; B—Black Hans, a client from the United States)

A: Good evening. Mr. Hans, it's a great pleasure to have you come to our cocktail party. I wish you could enjoy your time here.

B: Hello, Miss Liu. I'm happy to be invited here. How are you getting on in the company?

A: Well. So far so nice.

B: I'm happy to hear you say so.

A: Thank you, Mr. Hans! What would you like to drink?

B: A glass of punch would be fine, thank you.

A: Here you are.

B: Thank you. Do you like to drink some punch?

A: No. I'm afraid not. It's sweet, but I think it's pretty strong.

B: No. Not at all! It's just fruit juice and tasty.

A: Alright then. I'll have one glass.

B: Miss Liu, I went to your company's new office building this morning and it is very nice. How long have you been there?

A: Oh, about three months. We used to be in a much smaller place, but it got so crowded.

B: Then your company must be doing very well!

A: Oh, yes. In fact we've got more business than we can handle.

B: That's certainly good to hear. Let's take up this glass of punch and toast to your company's prosperity.

A: Thank you! Cheers!

Useful Expressions

1. Usually for lunch, we don't have to reserve a table, they should allow walk-ins.
   一般中午饭，我们不需要提前预订位子，他们应该能够接纳未预约的客人。
2. But to be on the safe side, I'll order a table for half-past twelve.
   但是为了保险起见，我去预订一张中午 12:30 的餐桌。
3. Are you planning on treating the clients to a full-course meal?
   你打算请客户吃一顿丰盛的午餐吗？
4. Yes. We'll start with appetizers, follow with a soup and salad course, then main dishes of prime rib, and finish up with a delicious rich dessert of some sort.

是的。我们先上些开胃甜品，接着是汤和沙拉，然后主菜是上等的排骨，最后是各种美味的餐后甜点。

5. That' ll be pretty heavy for a mid-day meal, don't you think so?
这样的午餐会不会太腻了？
6. Good evening. Mr. Hans, it's a great pleasure to have you come to our cocktail party.
晚上好。汉斯先生，承蒙您莅临本次鸡尾酒会，我们倍感荣幸。
7. I wish you could enjoy your time here.
希望您在这儿玩得开心。
8. Well. So far so nice.
哦，到现在为止还不错。
9. It's sweet, but I think it's pretty strong.
它很甜，但我认为它很烈。
10. Let's take up this glass of punch and toast to your company's prosperity.
让我们举起这杯酒，为了贵公司的兴旺，干杯！

Situational Dialogues

Using the Sample Dialogue as a model, try to create a new dialogue with your partner.

Situation 1 ▶ Deng Fang, the secretary of General Commercial Company, is consulting with Mr. Kent, the general manager of General Commercial Company, over arranging a dinner meeting with the clients.

Situation 2 ▶ Li Ying, the secretary of Beverage Industry Company, is talking at a cocktail party with Mr. Bred, one of her company's clients.

Part Two Text A

Business Etiquette

Etiquette is a code of behavior that delineates expectations for social behavior according to contemporary conventional norms within a society, social class, or group. In the business world, good business etiquette means that you act professionally and exercise proper manners when engaging with others in your profession.

Secretaries are important staff members in any organization. For secretaries at every level, especially those who are in contact with clients and other important outsiders, how they present themselves affects not only their reputation but also your company's image. Therefore, it is of great necessity for a secretary to master good business etiquette, which will make them stand out from others.

1. Benefits of Professional Business Etiquette

1.1 Image Enhancement

People judge you and your organization on how you carry yourself in social and professional situations. If you don't know the proper way to shake someone's hand or offer your business card, people might question your business skills as well. By observing proper etiquette, however, you suggest to fellow professionals that you're on their level.

1.2 Improved Workplace Relations

With its focus on respect for others, etiquette can pave the way for a collaborative and civilized corporate culture. Many basic business etiquette rules are actually common courtesies. Abiding by etiquette principles can eliminate some of the distractions associated with the workplace, such as gossip or personality clashes. It also ensures workplace relationships stay professional and that colleagues don't blur the line between work and personal life or allow their personal feelings to affect their workplace behavior.

1.3 Business Growth

Knowledge of business etiquette can open up several professional doors. Potential clients and associates will often judge you as much on your soft skills as they will judge your business savvy. Someone skilled in communication and comfortable in a wide range of professional situations will inspire trust more easily than someone who isn't. If you're always courteous and know how to handle yourself both in high-stakes meetings and at business lunches, you'll impress people with your versatility and people skills. If a client is looking for a public relations professional to represent his company, for example, he's going to favor someone who can make a positive impression on his behalf.

1.4 Build Rapport

Many core etiquette principles are designed to make others feel valued. For example, when introducing colleagues or associates, you should introduce the most important person first. When entering a meeting, you should greet each person individually. Though these gestures might seem small, they subtly indicate your respect for the other person. In addition, when everyone follows the same social customs, it ensures both personal and professional interactions get off on the right foot and can help you connect with everyone from new clients to coworkers.

2. Business Etiquette Guidelines

In business world, people form first impressions about others within seconds of meeting them—therefore, it is crucial to ensure you are properly prepared to present yourself as a professional. Business etiquette provides a framework for building successful professional relationships and showcasing your professional presence. Here are some foundational tips on what you need to know to behave properly when establishing relationships on various occasions.

2.1 Treating People

How you treat people says a lot about you.

• Learn names quickly. A good tip for remembering names is to use a person's name three times within your first conversation with them. Also, write names down and keep business cards. People know when you don't know their names and may interpret this as a sign that you don't value them.

- Don't make value judgments on people's importance in the workplace. Talk to the maintenance staff members and to the people who perform many of the administrative support functions and they deserve your respect.
- Self-assess: Think about how you treat your supervisor(s), peers, and subordinates. Would the differences in the relationships, if seen by others, cast you in an unfavorable light? If so, find where the imbalance exists, and start the process of reworking the relationship dynamic.
- What you share with others about your personal life is your choice, but be careful. Things can come back to haunt you. Don't ask others to share their personal lives with you. This makes many people uncomfortable in the work space.
- Respect people's personal space.

2.2 Communication

It's sometimes not what you say, but how you say it that counts.

- Return phone calls and emails within 24 hours — even if only to say that you will provide requested information at a later date.
- Ask before putting someone on speakerphone.
- Personalize your voice mail — there's nothing worse than just hearing a phone number on someone's voice mail and not knowing if you are leaving a message with the correct person.
- E-mails at work should be grammatically correct and free of spelling errors. They should not be treated like personal e-mail .
- When e-mailing, use the subject box, and make sure it directly relates to what you are writing. This ensures ease in finding it later and a potentially faster response.
- Never say in an e-mail anything you wouldn't say to someone's face.
- Underlining, italicizing, bolding, coloring, and changing font size can make a mild e-mail message seem overly strong or aggressive.

2.3 Business Meetings

Adherence to the proper etiquette for a business meeting establishes respect among meeting participants, helps the meeting begin and end on time, and fosters an atmosphere of cooperation.

• Arrival

Arrive to the location of the business meeting at least 15 minutes early. This allows you to find a seat and get situated before the meeting starts.

• Agenda

Call the chairperson to express any concerns about the agenda at least 48 hours prior to the meeting. The chairperson and concerned participant will then have time to determine if changes need to be made.

• Being Prepared

Come to the meeting with all of the materials and data which will be needed and an understanding of the meeting topic.

• Attire

Follow the attire rule laid down by the chairperson, which indicates what kind of attire is required for the meeting, either business casual or business formal.

• Speaking

Ask questions during the designated question period, and raise your hand to be recognized by the chairperson as having the floor. Do not interrupt someone while they are speaking or asking a question.

• Listening

You may find that many of the questions you have about a topic are answered by the content of the meeting. Listen attentively to the meeting and take notes.

• Nervous Habits

Avoid nervous habits such as tapping a pen on the table, making audible noises with your mouth, rustling papers or tapping your feet on the floor.

• Cell Phones and Laptops

Turn off your cell phone prior to the start of the meeting. If you are expecting an urgent call, then set your phone to vibrate and excuse yourself from the meeting if the call comes in. Unless laptop computers have been approved for the meeting, turn yours off and lower the screen so that you do not obstruct anyone's view.

2.4 Business Gift Giving

Gift-giving is such a thorny issue in business that most organizations have explicit rules governing the practice. Thus, it is vital to know the etiquette of giving business gifts to prevent any misunderstanding. Here are a few important elements of business gift-giving.

- Professional gifts can be quite varied, from food to wine to small conveniences (such as a business-card holder or a pen) to office items (such as a picture frame or a computer accessory).
- When selecting a gift, be careful to abide by your company's policy concerning gifts. A bit of research and thought can make the gift-selection process a whole lot easier.
- Should you decide to give a business gift, make certain that it's not too personal. Be careful with humorous gifts as well. If you aren't sure that the recipient will be pleasantly amused, don't send it.
- Extravagant gift-giving is both bad strategy and in poor taste. Others may not share your love of lavish gifts and may be embarrassed by them — or, worse, resent you for going overboard.
- Giving a material gift isn't the only way to go, even in business. The gift of your time for volunteer work or for helping a colleague's or client's company charity might be appreciated more than a material item.

2.5 Business Reception

At a business reception, minding your manners is never more important than during work events. Not only can a faux pas cause you embarrassment, it can leave a bad impression on people who may be important to your career. Unlike more formal events like presentations, dinners and banquets, a business reception is a casual affair where people from all levels of employment and all departments are usually encouraged to mingle and relax together. Here are some guidelines for you to follow at a business reception.

• Punctuality

Punctuality is more important at a business gathering than a personal one. A late entrance can be remembered and may even be seen as indicative of irresponsibility or disrespect for the time of your colleagues.

• Timing

Being a host of a business reception, you should plan for the business reception to be between two to three hours. That's long enough to give people time to feel appreciated and get to know one another, yet short enough that it won't exhaust everyone. You should shake everyone's hand and greet guests as they arrive. All guests should greet the host upon arrival. They should approach the host when leaving to express their thanks and say goodbye.

• Curb Gossip

When gathering with colleagues, bosses and other professionals for a business reception, it's inevitable that talking about the company will come up. Keep all shop talk casual, though. Do not confide in a new acquaintance and resist the temptation to gossip about others within the company or badmouth the business itself.

• Polite Conversation

In addition to avoiding gossip and negativity, it's important to be a conscientious conversationalist in many ways. Political, religious and deeply personal issues should also be avoided. It's a faux pas to ask about someone's marital status, sexual orientation or work history when you've just met them in a professional setting. Safe topics include current events that aren't too serious and industry news. A polite compliment and expressing a willingness to help someone professionally are great ways to strengthen an initial conversation as long as they are sincere. If you're talking in a group, attempt to include everyone in the conversation and ask others' opinions more often than you share your own.

• Colleague Cues

An employee attending a business reception often leaves a first impression on many colleagues. Set the tone for conversations you have by being considerate of the other person. Practice active listening and allow others to lead conversations. Use proper posture and make direct eye contact with everyone you meet. Indicate that you are listening by paraphrasing what the other person is saying when they are obviously passionate about making a point.

• Mingling

Business receptions are ideal times to network and make new friends among your colleagues. The art of mingling requires constant consideration for your fellow guests. If someone is by herself, it's polite to go to introduce yourself by your first and last name, then ask her full name if she doesn't automatically give it. Address her formally unless she sets the tone by using your first name, then it's safe to assume you are on a first-name basis. The only exception would be if it's someone in a much higher position in the company, in which case the lines may be blurred on how to properly address him. Share your position within the company right from the start so that there are no embarrassing conversation errors.

• Drinking Concerns

If refreshments are being offered, take a snack or beverage in your left hand and keep it with you; the right hand should be free for handshakes. It's always a wise idea to avoid drinking alcohol at business receptions. If you do plan on drinking, set your limit ahead of time and stick to it. Having too much to drink and embarrassing yourself in a business setting can have lasting consequences and give you a bad reputation within the company.

2.6 Business Attire

When you first enter or are in the business world, you must know how to dress appropriately for any given situation. What you wear for an interview or career fair is likely to differ from your day-to-day business attire. Most businesses provide their employees with dress code policies to give guidance on what type of clothing is allowed and prohibited on professional and casual dress days. Some guidelines for business attire are listed as follows.

• Business Formal

When you dress in business formal attire, you are dressing to impress. Business formal attire is an upgrade from your normal day-to-day professional outfits. Dressy evening events and award ceremonies may call for business formal dress. Men wear a dark colored suit over a dress shirt with a silk tie. Silk or linen pocket squares are also a requirement for men. Dress shoes and matching dark pants complete the outfit. Formal business attire for women is a suit with a skirt while wearing pantyhose and closed toe pumps.

• Business Professional

When you dress business professional, you are wearing generally conservative clothing to portray yourself in a professional manner. Business professional is similar to business formal, but does not necessarily mean you have to break out your best shoes and suit. Careers that may require business professional dress on a daily basis include finance, accounting and organizations that have a strict dress code policy. Women can wear a skirt or pants suit with heels while men may wear a blazer or suit jacket, button down shirt, suit pants, a tie and dress shoes.

• Business Casual

When the dress code for your company is business casual, it simply means you do not need to wear a suit. However, it does not call for casual attire such as jeans and T-shirts. Women typically wear a collared shirt or sweater with dress pants and dress shoes or boots. Conservative dresses and skirts are also acceptable attire. A man's option for business casual includes a polo shirt, collared shirt or sweater. Khaki or dress pants along with dress shoes make up his business casual outfit. He does not need to wear a tie.

New Words

etiquette [eti'ket] *n.* 礼仪，礼节
contemporary [kən'tempərəri] *adj.* 当代的，现代的
conventional [kən'venʃənl] *adj.* 传统的，依照惯例的，约定的
reputation [ˌrepju'teiʃən] *n.* 名气，名声，信誉，声望
enhance [in'hɑːns] *vt.* 加强，提高
observe [əb'zəːv] *vt.* 遵守
collaborative [kə'læbərətiv] *adj.* 协作的，合作的
civilized ['sivilaizd] *adj.* 文明的，有礼貌的，有教养的
eliminate [i'limineit] *vt.* 淘汰，排除，消除
distraction [dis'trækʃən] *n.* 注意力分散，分散注意力的事物
clash [klæʃ] vi. 交锋，争论，不合 *n.* 冲突，不协调
blur [bləː] *vt.*（使）变模糊，（使）难以区分
savvy ['sævi] *n.* 悟性，机智，理解 *adj.* 有见识的，懂实际知识的
inspire [in'spaiə] *vt.* 激励，鼓舞，赋予灵感
versatility [ˌvəːsə'tiləti] *n.* 多才多艺，多用途
favor ['feivə] *vt.* 支持，赞成
subtly ['sʌbtli] *adv.* 敏锐地，巧妙地
framework ['freimwəːk] *n.* 框架，体系，结构
showcase ['ʃəukeis] *n.* 玻璃陈列柜，显示优点的东西 *vt.* 使展现，显示，在玻璃橱窗陈列
foundational [faun'deiʃənəl] *adj.* 基本的，基础的
interpret [in'təːprit] *v.* 解释，理解
deserve [di'zəːv] *v.* 值得，应得，应受
self-assess [self-ə'ses] vi. 自我评估
subordinate [sə'bɔːdinit] [sə'bɔːdineit] *adj.* 下级的，次要的，附属的 *n.* 部属，部下，下级 *vt.* 使……居下位，使服从，使从属
dynamic [dai'næmik] *adj.* 动态的，充满活力的 *n.* 动态，动力学，活力，动力
haunt [hɔːnt] *v.* 经常去，出没于，困扰
count [kaunt] *v.* 重要，有价值
personalize ['pəːsənəlaiz] *vt.* 使（某事物）针对个人，带有个人感情，个性化
underline [ˌʌndə'lain] *vt.* 在……下面画线，加强，强调
italicize [i'tælisaiz] *vt.* 用斜体字排字，在字下画横线
font [fɔnt] *n.* 字体，字形
foster ['fɔstə] *v.* 培养，促进，抚育
attire [ə'taiə] *n.* 服装，衣服
designate ['dezigneit] *vt.* 指定，标明，选派
audible ['ɔːdəbl] *adj.* 听得见的
rustle ['rʌsl] *adj.* 发出沙沙的声音
vibrate [vai'breit] *v.*（使）振动，颤动，摆动
obstruct [əb'strʌkt] *v.* 阻碍，妨碍
thorny ['θɔːni] *adj.* 棘手的，多刺的，痛苦的
accessory [æk'sesəri] *n.* 附件；（衣服的）配饰，妇女饰品
extravagant [iks'trævəgənt] *adj.* 奢侈的，浪费的
lavish ['læviʃ] *adj.* 过分慷慨的，浪费的

resent [ri'zent] *vt.* 怨恨，愤恨，厌恶
charity ['tʃæriti] *n.* 慈善(行为),施舍,捐助
embarrassment [im'bærəsmənt] *n.* 难堪，窘迫
mingle ['miŋgl] *v.* 混合，混淆，与……交往
punctuality [ˌpʌŋktju'æliti] *n.* 准时
indicative [in'dikətiv] *adj.* 指示的，暗示的
irresponsibility ['iriˌspɔnsə'biləti] *n.* 不负责任
disrespect ['disris'pekt] *n.* 失礼，无礼 *vt.* 不尊敬，不尊重
exhaust [ig'zɔːst] *vt.* 用尽，耗尽
curb [kəːb] *n.* 限制，抑制 *vt.* 制止，束缚
inevitable [in'evitəbl] *adj.* 不可避免的，必然发生的
badmouth ['bædmauθ] *v.* 诽谤，说坏话
negativity [negə'tiviti] *n.* 否定性，消极性
conscientious [ˌkɔnʃi'enʃəs] *adj.* 认真的，谨慎的，负责的
compliment ['kɔmplimənt] *n.* 称赞，恭维 *vt.* 恭维，称赞
willingness ['wiliŋnis] *n.* 乐意，愿意
cue [kjuː] *n.* 暗示，提示，信号
exception [ik'sepʃən] *n.* 例外，除外
upgrade ['ʌpgreid] *vt.* 提升，升级，提高档次 *n.* 升级，上坡
outfit ['autfit] *n.* 全套装备，一套服装 *vt.* 装备，配置设备，供给服装
conservative [kən'səːvətiv] *adj.* 保守的;(式样等)不时新的
portray [pɔː'trei] *vt.* 描写，描绘
heels [hiːls] *n.* 高跟鞋
blazer ['bleizə] *n.* 运动夹克，男式便上装
Khaki ['kɑːki] *n.* 卡其布；土黄色

Phrases and Expressions

business etiquette 商务礼仪
social class 社会阶层，社会地位
stand out from 从……中脱颖而出
business card 名片
pave the way for 为……铺平道路，为……做好准备
make a positive impression 留下一个好印象
on one's behalf 代表，为了
social customs 社会习俗
get off on the right foot 一开头就很顺利
cast sb. in an unfavorable light 对某人不利
subject box 主题框
to one's face 当着某人的面
adhere to 坚持
have the floor 有发言权
go overboard 过分爱好；狂热追求；爱走极端
business reception 商务招待会

faux pas 失礼，失言
be indicative of 表示；暗示
shop talk 谈工作；行话
confide in 信任，信赖
resist the temptation 抵制诱惑
marital status 婚姻状况
sexual orientation 性取向；性定位
set the tone for 为……确定基调
be considerate of 体谅……；替……着想
be passionate about 对……充满热情
make a point 发表论点；重视；特别注意
be on a first-name basis 相互直呼其名
right from the start 从一开始就
plan on 打算
in any given situation 在任何特定情况下
career fair 招聘会
business formal 商务正装
dressy evening event 讲究穿着的晚会
award ceremony 颁奖典礼
panty hose 女式连袜裤
closed toe pumps 不露脚趾的轻舞鞋
business profession 商务职业装
dress code 着装规定
pant suit 长裤西服装；裤装
button down suit 领尖有纽扣的西装
dress shoe 晚会鞋，礼服鞋
business casual 商务便装
a polo shirt 马球衫

Notes

1 It's sometimes not what you say, but how you say it that counts.

本句中，句子主干为"it is + 被强调部分 + that"强调句结构，其中被强调部分为主语 not what you say, but how you say it。

在该结构中，被强调部分可以是主语、宾语、表语或状语。请看下例：

It was not until she took off her dark glasses that I realized she was a famous film star.

直到她摘下墨镜，我才意识到她是一位电影明星。

另外，句中"not... but..."意为"不是……而是……"常构成平行结构，连接两个并列的成分。请看下例：

She is not playing computer games but eating chocolate.

她不是在玩电脑游戏，而是在吃巧克力。

2 Gift-giving is such a thorny issue in business that most organizations have explicit rules governing the practice.

本句中，主干为"such... that ..."结构，该结构引导结果状语从句。

在英语中，so... that... 与 such... that... 都能引导结果状语从句，表示"如此……以致……"，但后者常用于"such + a (n) + *adj.* + *n.* + that"或"such + *adj.* + *n.* (*pl.*) + that…"结构中。请看下例：

There are many such good books that I can't decide which one to choose.

有这么多的好书，我无法决定选择哪一本。

另外，本句中 governing the practice 是现在分词短语在句中作后置定语，修饰和限定先行词 explicit rules。请看下例：

The girl standing under the tree is really charming.

站在树下的那个女孩真的很迷人。

3 Should you decide to give a business gift, make certain that it's not too personal.

本句中，Should you decide to give a business gift 为省略了 if 的虚拟条件句。

该句型常省略 if, 将条件句中 were, had 或 should 放在句首构成倒装。请看下例：

Should you be interested in our offer, please contact us.

你若对我们的报价感兴趣，请与我们联系。

Had you not helped us, we should have canceled this transaction.

假如没有你的帮助，这笔生意早就告吹了。

4 Address her formally unless she sets the tone by using your first name, then it's safe to assume you are on a first-name basis.

本句中，连词 unless 引导条件状语从句，意为"除非，如果不"。it's safe to assume 常是习惯表达，意为"可以有把握地设想或假定"。请看下例：

It is also safe to assume that if the United States undertakes such a policy, other states will follow suit.

还可以有把握地推测，如果美国实行这样一项政策，其他国家也会效法。

另外，句中 on a first-name basis 为固定短语，意为"相互直呼其名"。请看下例：

I know that Mr. Toland and Mr. Vinson were on first name basis.

我知道托兰先生和文森先生曾是互相直呼名字的好朋友。

5 Most businesses provide their employees with dress code policies to give guidance on what type of clothing is allowed and prohibited on professional and casual dress days.

本句中，主干为 Most businesses provide their employees with dress code policies，而 to give guidance on... casual dress days 是动词不定式短语作后置定语，修饰和限定先行词 dress code policies。另外，句中介词 on 意为"关于"，what 引导名词性从句，作介词 on 的宾语。请看下例：

He was annoyed by what the woman bunged in.

他对女士的插嘴感到恼火。

另外，句中 provide... with... 为固定短语，意为"对……提供……"，与 provide... for 意思相当。请看下例：

The present conflict may provide fresh impetus for peace talk.

目前的冲突可能会给和谈提供新的推动力。

We are here to provide the public with a service.

我们来这里是为公众服务。

Exercises

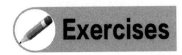

EX. 1 Answer the following questions.

1. What is etiquette according Text A?
2. What does good business etiquette mean in the business world?
3. What are the benefits of professional business etiquette according to Text A?
4. List at least three rules of etiquette on how to treat people?
5. Why is it necessary to use the subject box when emailing?
6. According to business meeting etiquette, how should a person ask questions during the meeting?
7. Why is extravagant gift-giving not advisable according to business gift-giving etiquette ?
8. What are safe topics and unsafe topics when you've just met some people at a business reception?
9. Why is it not advisable to have too much drink at a business reception?
10. What careers may require business professional dress on a daily basis according to Text A?

EX. 2 Complete the following sentences with appropriate words or expressions in the box.

subordinate	pave the way for	confide in	eliminate	subtly
conventional	stand out from	collaborative	compliment	foster

1. Delegates signed a treaty to reduce the number of ________ weapons in Europe.
2. You need to identify the skills and accomplishments that make you ________ other people in your industry.
3. This is the highest ________ that I could receive and I thank you for that.
4. We can never ________ financial crises, but we can reduce their likelihood and severity.
5. My colleagues and I are happy to have a ________ work with you.
6. Social-cultural attitudes and values reinforce women's ________ place in society.
7. And more broadly, we need to ________ cooperation and respect among all nations and people.
8. We hope that the recent progress can ________ a peaceful settlement of the conflict.
9. Her version of events is ________ different from what actually happened.
10. If you're reluctant to seek treatment, ________ a trusted friend or loved one.

EX. 3 Translate the following sentences into English.

1. 当然，不是每个人清楚在与公司老板、同事以及其他客户交往时如何运用适当商务礼仪。(business etiquette)

2. 年轻人之间的关系受严格的社会习俗的制约。(social customs)
3. 在我发言时，我还想提出两点意见供思考。(have the floor)
4. 你可以跟同事开玩笑，但切忌不要玩得太过火了。(go overboard)
5. 你的雇员是否明白在商务招待会上举止恰当是非常重要的。(at a business reception)
6. 我们必须通过礼貌，穿着，守时和知识表现出外在职业形象。(punctuality)
7. 商务便装要想被政界和法律界所接受仍需假以时日。(business casual)
8. 你的面试服装应该符合公司的着装规范，或更上一层楼。(dress code)
9. 选择商务礼物时你应该谨慎地考虑客户的喜好和需求。(be considerate of)
10. 营销部主任费尽心机使其项目有一个良好的开端。(get off on the right foot)

EX. 4 **Translate the following passage into Chinese.**

Celebrating a co-worker's birthday or lunch with the team to mark the end of a successful project are at-work social functions. Your behavior can be more informal on these occasions. The idea is to let your hair down a little and enjoy the company of your co-workers and leave your workday life behind for a while. However, it does not mean that you can crack off-color jokes, overeat or demean anyone in the group. You are still expected to behave in a business-like manner.

After-hours functions include the company holiday party, company picnics, company-sponsored trips, the ballgame or dinner with clients. Here your behavior can change somewhat depending on the locale. For example, good business social behavior at the holiday party or at client dinners means not over-drinking and making an effort to remember that the event is really a business event; your demeanor should, at all times, reflect that understanding. Similarly, the company picnic is more informal, so a more informal dress is appropriate, as is more informality in your interactions with co-workers. Just remember that it is still a business event nonetheless, and that you want to be remembered for your social graces.

Part Three Text B

Business Meal Etiquette

How you conduct yourself at the table can either positively or negatively influence a business decision. And it should come as no surprise that dining, unless done well, could be disastrous to your reputation. It is for these reasons that any professionals should learn the basic business meal etiquette.

1. Invitation

Business invitations can be informal or formal. Although invitations have traditionally been sent through the mail, informal invitations such as emails and phone invitations are becoming more acceptable.

1.1 Invitation Timing

For most informal occasions, it's best to invite guests three to four weeks in advance. If you choose to invite your guests by phone, remind them again in writing two weeks before the gathering.

Here are some additional guidelines to follow:

- Six to eight months before an important seminar to which out-of-town executives are invited.
- Four to six months before an important dinner to which out-of-town guests are invited.
- Three to five weeks before a luncheon.
- Four weeks before an evening reception.
- Two to four weeks before a breakfast for a large group.
- Two to four weeks before a cocktail party.
- Two to three weeks before a tea party.

1.2 Invitation Format

On the business invitation, you will find:

- Company logo or symbol (at the top or bottom of the invitation),
- Names of the host,
- Invitation phrase (any of the following, depending on your company and the occasion),

"you are cordially invited to"

"requests the pleasure of your company at"

"requests your presence at"

"invites you to"

"requests the honor of your presence"

- Nature of the party — State whether the event is for breakfast, luncheon, or dinner, a cocktail party or some other occasion.
- Purpose of the party — Such as to introduce someone or a new product, to honor a retiree, or to celebrate an occasion or another festive event.
- Date and time — The date and time of the event completely written out. Never abbreviate days of the week. The most formal style is to write, "Friday, the twenty-seventh of July at six-thirty o'clock" The least formal is "Friday, July 27, at 6:00 p.m."
- Place — The address of where the event will be held is next. A map is typically included with the invitation if your house or the country club is difficult to find or if your guests haven't been there before.
- Where to RSVP — The RSVP address or phone number is in the bottom left-hand corner of the invitation.
- Special instructions — Across from the RSVP address are any special instructions such as attire, parking instructions, where the event will be held in case of rain, and so on.

Formal business invitations are most commonly engraved or printed in black, navy, dark gray, or brown ink on white or off-white high-quality paper. A company can use any color of paper, as long as it upholds and promotes the company's image.

Preprinted invitations work well for most informal dinners and parties. For a casual gathering, there is no need to have invitations printed or engraved.

2. Arriving

Good dining etiquette and the impression you make on your business lunch companions starts when you first arrive at the restaurant.

2.1 Don't Be late

It's appropriate that this is the first rule of dining etiquette. Arriving even five or ten minutes late leaves a bad impression; any later than that sends a clear message of carelessness and thoughtlessness.

2.2 Dress Appropriately

Avoid errors on the side of dressing up. Call the restaurant to see if they have a dress code.

When you arrive at the restaurant and your host hasn't arrived, etiquette dictates that you wait in the lobby or waiting area for him or her. Don't go to the table and wait there.

If you are the host, wait for your guest in the lobby. If some of your guests have already arrived, you should wait in the lobby only until the time the reservation is made for. Then proceed to the table and have the maitre or waiter escort the late guests in.

3. Table Manners

Dinning etiquette affects almost every aspect of dining and dinning rules apply before you ever take your seat and continue after you excuse yourself from the table. Table manners rules are not complicated, but will help you make a great impression at your business meal.

3.1 Seating Etiquette

Your host may have seating arrangements in mind, so you should allow him to direct you to your seat. As the host, you should suggest the seating arrangements.

In a restaurant, the guest of honor should sit in the best seat at the table. Usually that is one with the back of the chair to the wall. Once the guest of honor's seat is determined, the host should sit to her left. Other people are then offered seats around the table.

3.2 Napkin Etiquette

At informal meals, place the napkin in your lap immediately upon seating. During formal occasions, before unfolding the napkin, wait for the hostess to remove her napkin from the table and unfold it in her lap.

3.3 Food Service Etiquette

During service of a formal dinner, the food is brought to each diner at the table; the server presents the platter or bowl on the diner's left. At a more casual meal, either the host dishes the food onto guests' plates for them to pass around the table or the diners help themselves to the food and pass it to others as necessary.

3.4 Table Setting

Deciding which knife, fork, or spoon to use is made easier by the outside-in table manners rule — using utensils on the outside first and working your way inward. The table setting will be discussed in greater detail as follows.

- Forks — Both forks are placed on the left of the plate. The fork furthest from the plate is for salad. The fork next to the plate is for the dinner. (Please Note: At more formal meals where the salad is served after the main course, the order of placement is reversed.)

Fork tines may be placed downward, in the continental style, or upward, in the American style.

- Dinner Plate — The dinner plate is placed on the table when the main course is served and is not on the table when the guests sit down.
- Large plates, such as the dinner plate and luncheon plate, are laid about one inch in from the edge of the table.
- Salad Plate — The salad plate is placed to the left of the forks.

Small plates, such as the salad plate, fish plate, and dessert plate, are laid about two inches in from the edge of the table.

- Dinner knife — The dinner knife is placed on the right side, and directly next to and one inch away from, the plate. The blade should face the plate. If the main course requires a steak knife, it may be substituted for the dinner knife.
- Spoons — The soup spoon is on the far right of the outside knife.
- Bread Plate with Butter Knife–A small bread plate is placed above the forks, above and to the left of the service plate. The butter spreader is laid on the bread-and-butter plate.
- Glassware — Usually one wine glass is used along with a water goblet. If the table setting is uncrowded, there is room to arrange glassware in any way you like, such as in a straight line parallel with the edge of the table or a diagonal line angled toward the table's edge.
- Water Goblets — The water glass is placed in a position closest to the hand, approximately one inch above the tip of the dinner knife.
- Wine Glasses — At least one wine glass should sit to the right and possibly above the water glass.
- Napkins — Place the napkin in the place setting's center, or left of the last fork.
- Coffee Cups — Place a cup and saucer to the right of the place setting. The coffee spoon goes to the right of the saucer.

Place approximately one inch beyond the outermost piece of flatware. The top edge of the saucer is aligned with the top rim of the plate or bowl.

Cup handles are faced in the four o'clock position for easy access.

- Desert Spoon and Fork — At an informal meal, when two utensils are provided for dessert, the utensils are laid on the table or presented on the dessert plate.

The dessert spoon (or dessert knife) is laid on the table above the dinner plate in a horizontal position, handle facing right.

The dessert fork is laid beneath the dessert spoon (or dessert knife), handle facing left.

The dessert utensils may also be presented on the dessert plate in the same way as formal service.

- Salt and Pepper — Since more people use salt than pepper (and most people are right-handed), the salt shaker is placed to the right of the pepper shaker, in a position closer to the right hand.

The placement of the pepper shaker is to the left of the salt shaker, and for added definition it is angled slightly above the salt shaker.

They are placed above the cover or between two place settings.

3.5 When to Start Eating

At a small table of only two to four people, wait until everyone else has been served before starting to eat. At a formal or business meal, you should either wait until everyone is served to start or begin when the host asks you to.

3.6 Handling Utensils

The continental table manners style prevails at all meals, formal and informal, because it is a natural, non-disruptive way to eat.

- Hold your fork in your left hand, tines downward.
- Hold your knife in your right hand, an inch or two above the plate.
- Extend your index finger along the top of the blade.
- Use your fork to spear and lift food to your mouth.
- If your knife is not needed, it remains on the table.
- At informal meals the dinner fork may be held tines upward.

3.7 Passing the Food

Pass to the right. One diner either holds the dish as the next diner takes some food, or he hands it to the person, who then serves herself. Any heavy or awkward dishes are put on the table with each pass. Special rules apply to passing salt and pepper and passing bread and butter.

3.8 Resting Utensils

When you pause to take a sip of your beverage or to speak with someone, rest your utensils by placing your knife and fork on your plate near the center, slightly angled in an inverted V and with the tips of the knife and fork pointing toward each other.

3.9 Meals End

At a formal affair, plates are removed by a professional staff. But as most informal meals are served without help, the hostess clears the plates, often with the help of a guest or two. At a family meal, members clear their own plates.

3.10 Leaving the Dining Room

To signal dinner is concluded, the hostess catches the eye of the host, lays her napkin on the table, and suggests that everyone go into another room for coffee and after-dinner drinks. The hostess rises from her chair.

When it's time to leave, rather than detain one's host with a lengthy good-bye, make the departure brief but cordial.

4. Business Meal Follow Up

4.1 Thank-You Note

A note sent by the guest serves as a thank-you for the meal and an enjoyable time, as well as a confirmation of any decisions that were made. The host should also write, telling the guest how nice it was to dine with him or her and briefly recapping any business details. A follow-up phone call by either party could be made instead, but a note has two advantages: It doesn't interrupt the other person's day, and it comes across as warmer and more gracious.

A sample thank-you letter for a breakfast or lunch meeting:

Dear Kathy,

Thank you for arranging our breakfast meeting this morning! I appreciated your being so well prepared and giving your helpful comments and suggestions for content. I'm thrilled to be working with you and Robin. Together we'll have a very successful June seminar. Thank you for asking me to be the featured speaker.

Very truly yours,

Elizabeth Winters (Professional Speaker)

4.2 Reciprocating with an Invitation

Inviting someone to a business lunch, dinner, or breakfast does not always mean they are obligated to reciprocate.

You are not expected to repay an invitation to a strictly-business meal (especially one charged to an expense account), no matter who invited you — a customer, a client, or your boss. But you may certainly do so if you have continuing business together.

A client who is entertained by a salesperson or supplier is not expected to return the invitation, even if his or her spouse or family was invited.

Do return social invitations from coworkers and other business associates.

New Words

disastrous [di'zɑːstrəs] *adj.* 灾难性的，损失惨重

gathering ['gæðəriŋ] *n.* 聚会，采集，集会

luncheon ['lʌntʃən] *n.* 午宴，午餐会

phrase [freiz] *n.* 成语，短语；叙述，措词

cordially ['kɔːdjəli] *adv.* 热诚地，诚挚地

retiree [riˌtaiə'riː] *n.* 退休者

festive ['festiv] *adj.* 喜庆的，欢乐的，节日的

abbreviate [ə'briːvieit] *vt.* 缩略，使简短；使用缩写词

engrave [in'greiv] *vt.*（使）铭记，雕刻，印刷

navy ['neivi] *n.* 藏青色，深蓝色

off-white [ɔf-wait] *n.* 灰白色；米色

preprint ['pri:'print] *vt.* 预先印好
companion [kəm'pænjən] *n.* 同伴；志趣相投的人
thoughtlessness ['θɔ:tlis] *n.* 不体贴，欠考虑
dictate [dik'teit] *vt.* 规定；决定
lobby ['lɔbi] *n.* 大厅
maitre ['mɛtrə] *n.* 餐厅领班
escort [is'kɔ:t] *vt.* 护送；陪伴
lap [læp] *n.* 膝部；（衣服的）下摆
unfold [ʌn'fəuld] *v.* 展开，打开；展现
platter ['plætə] *n.* 大浅盘；一盘食物
dish [diʃ] *vt.* 使成碟状；装盘
utensil [ju'tensl] *n.* 器具；用具
blade [bleid] *n.* 刀刃，刀锋
spoon [spu:n] *n.* 匙；调羹
glassware ['glɑ:swɛə] *n.* 玻璃器具类
goblet ['gɔblit] *n.* 高脚杯；酒杯
diagonal [dai'ægənl] *n.* 斜线，对角线
saucer ['sɔ:sə] *n.* 茶杯托，茶碟
rim [rim] *n.* 轮缘，边，缘
horizontal [ˌhɔri'zɔntl] *adj.* 水平的，地平线的
pepper ['pepə] *n.* 辣椒，胡椒
continental [ˌkɔnti'nentl] *adj.* 大陆的；欧洲大陆的
prevail [pri'veil] *vi.* 流行，盛行
non-disruptive ['nɔn-dis'rʌptiv] *adj.* 非破坏性的
tine [tain] *n.* 齿；叉；鹿角尖
spear [spiə] *vt.* 刺，戳
inverted [in'və:tid] *adj.* 反向的；倒转的
detain [di'tein] *vt.* 扣留；耽搁，延误
confirmation [ˌkɔnfə'meiʃən] *n.* 确认；证实
recap [ri:'kæp] *v.* 扼要重述，概括
thrill [θril] *vt.*（使）激动；感到紧张
reciprocate [ri'siprəkeit] *v.* 互换，交换；报答
outermost ['autəməust] *adj.* 最外面的，离中心最远的

Phrases and Expressions

business meal 商务餐宴
an evening reception 晚宴招待会
a cocktail party 鸡尾酒会
business invitation 商务邀请
dress up 打扮，穿上特殊服装
take one's seat 就座，落座
seating etiquette 入座礼仪
main course 主菜，大菜
substitute for 替换，用……代替
service plate 餐盘
butter spreader 奶油刮刀
parallel with 与……平行
align with 与……结盟
salt shaker 盐瓶
pepper shaker 胡椒瓶
index finger 食指
take a sip of 呷一口，喝一口
come across 碰到；遇到；无意中发现；被理解
a featured speaker 演讲嘉宾
be obligated to 对……负有责任或义务；必须

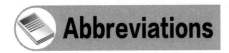

Abbreviations

RSVP (Répondez s'il vous plaît) 请答复

Exercises

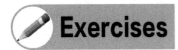

EX. 5 **Answer the following questions.**

1. When should you send out the invitations if you want to invite out-of-town executives to attend an important seminar?
2. How are formal business invitations commonly engraved or printed?
3. What is the first rule of dining etiquette according to Text B?
4. What is the seating etiquette in a restaurant?
5. What is the napkin etiquette at formal meals according to Text B?
6. What rule can make it easier for us decide which knife, fork, or spoon to use ?
7. When should you start eating at a formal or business meal?
8. Why does the continental table manners style prevail at all meals?
9. When and how do you rest your utensils at a formal meal according to Text B?
10. Why is a thank-you-note necessary after a business meal?

Part Four Extended Reading

Text	Notes
Cocktail Party Etiquette	
Cocktail parties, client receptions[1], and networking hours can be wonderful career-developing opportunities for you. You get to know others — and they get to know you — all while in a relaxed environment. But don't make the mistake of "letting your hair down"[2] simply because you have a drink in your hand! These functions are still business in nature[3] and best used for making new connections, finding resources, nurturing[4] existing relationships, and staying on the inside track[5], NOT partying till the cows come home[6]!	[1] 接待客户 [2] 放松自己 [3] 实际上；本质上 [4] *vt.* 养育；滋长 [5] 保持处于有利地位 [6] 无限期地

1. General Cocktail Party Etiquette

1.1 Circulate[7]

- Your company is expecting you to walk around in order to connect with clients, prospects, board members, competitors, vendors — to build bridges, deepen[8] relationships, gather intelligence, and find new business. Even when it's a purely internal event, this is your chance to put faces on that org chart[9] and get the skinny[10] on clients, projects, openings, etc.
- If you enter the room and don't immediately see someone you know, try to make eye contact with a friendly face or head toward an already-formed group of people who look like they're having fun.
- Don't clump[11]! It's okay to hang out with[12] your friends for one drink or a few appetizers[13], but then it's time to disperse[14] and find new people to talk with.
- The best places to stand are either by a food table or in the center of the room. Food tables attract foot traffic so they're great places to find people to engage in conversation. Food also provides good conversation starters[15] ("Have you tried that?" "Do you think the green sauce goes with that?"). And everyone moves through the center of the room during an event making it another good place to connect, disengage[16], and connect again.

1.2 Respect Boundaries[17]

- Use a filter[18] when you talk. Don't let company secrets slip out[19] in your conversation or share something off-color[20] or controversial[21]. You don't want to be next week's "hot topic"!
- If you're not on a first-name basis [22]with someone between 9 & 5, you're not after 5:00 either.
- Don't monopolize[23] any one individual. 10-15 minutes per person is a good amount of time for small talk.

1.3 Don't Overindulge[24]

- Limit your alcohol intake[25] to 1 or 2 drinks. If you don't drink alcohol, don't feel pressured to[26] do so. Choose a soft drink or water instead.
- Don't pile food onto your appetizer plate. Better to make a few trips back to the food table to replenish[27], than to advertise you're starving[28] and the frig is empty at home.

One Final Tip: Go with the attitude that you're the host of the party, even when you're the guest. Keep an eye out for[29] people who need help with their coats, finding their name badge[30], or locating a colleague. Doing what you can to make the party a success will shine a nice spotlight on [31]you.

[7] *v.* 来回走动
[8] *vt.* 变深，加深
[9] 组织结构或框架
[10] 获取内部消息
[11] *v.* 使成簇；扎堆
[12] 和某人混在一起；和某人出去
[13] *n.* 开胃菜
[14] *v.*（使）分散，（使）散开；分散
[15] 开场白；谈话开场白
[16] *v.* 解除；分开，使脱离
[17] *n.* 边界；分界线
[18] *n.* 过滤器；筛选
[19] 无意中说出，泄露；悄悄溜走
[20] *adj.* 下流的；近于淫猥的
[21] *adj.* 有争议的
[22] 直呼其名的
[23] *vt.* 独占，垄断
[24] *v.* 过度放纵
[25] *n.* 摄入量
[26] 被迫做某事
[27] *vt.* 补充；重新装满
[28] *adj.* 挨饿的
[29] 留心，注意
[30] 胸牌；姓名牌
[31] 使注意到；（使）暴露；照亮

2. Cocktail Dress Code Etiquette	
Our cocktail dress code etiquette comes into it's full glory[32] when we receive an invitation stating cocktail attire[33]. It is one of those exciting moments when we are given the opportunity of looking our most glamorous[34]!	[32] *n.* 光荣；壮丽 [33] *n.* 服装，衣服 [34] *adj.* 迷人的；富有魅力的
So in this part, my guidance concerning cocktail dress code etiquette can be extended to smart social events where you are expected to dress well but not too formally.	
2.1 What Should You Wear to a Cocktail Party?	
Cocktail dress code etiquette is a way of stating the dress code that is suitable for the evening; more formal than casual clothes and less formal than evening wear i.e. black tie.	
Cocktail Attire can also be stipulated[35] for dinner parties and drinks parties so when purchasing an outfit for this type of occasion, try and work some versatility[36] into your choice so you can be prepared for most events that may fall into this category[37].	[35] *v.* 规定，约定 [36] *n.* 多才多艺；多用途 [37] 属于这一类
Traditional cocktail dress code etiquette states that a dress's length is to the knee, but nowadays you can go for something a little shorter if you wish. Short, strapless[38] styles can look great on young ladies.	[38] *adj.* 无吊带的
Just remember to keep it dressy[39] and elegant, but not too formal. The appropriateness tends to be judged more on its sumptuousness[40] rather than length so you should lean towards sensual fabrics[41] like silk and crepe[42] in good strong colors.	[39] *adj.* 衣着考究的 [40] *n.* 奢侈，豪华 [41] 性感的面料 [42] *n.* 绉纱，绉绸
Your choice of fabric and style should also be appropriate to the season, for example, choose wool and wool blends in the winter, and satin, silk and fine-gauge knits for spring or summer.	
If you are attending a Cocktail Party with your husband/partner then you should ensure you co-ordinate[43] the level of formality[44] of your outfits with his.	[43] *v.* 使……协调；统筹 [44] *n.* 礼节；程序；拘谨
2.2 Formal Cocktail Parties Attire	
The level of formality for cocktail attire can also alter dependent on the location, reason and season. For example, a pre-opera cocktail party would be more formal than an after work event.	
A good indication as to the formality of the occasion is the type of invitation you receive — if it came by phone or e-mail it is more likely to be a casual affair. If it's a formal invite, especially from a charity[45] or association, then you should consider it dressy.	[45] *n.* 慈善；慈善机构
The events most fun to dress for are weekend cocktail parties! Anything ranging from a shift dress with dressy shoes, to skinny cigarette trousers worn with a silk camisole[46].	[46] *n.* 女式背心

If you are pregnant and invited to a cocktail party you will want to ensure you look blooming[47]. Tiffany Rose have a stunning[48] range of dresses for every occasion. And of course you will need to RSVP in the most appropriate manner, depending on the formality of the invite that you receive.	[47] *adj.* 盛开的；妙龄的 [48] *adj.* 令人震惊的；极好的，出色的
2.3 After Work Cocktail Parties If you are attending a cocktail party straight from work, try taking a smaller handbag for the evening, some sparkly[49] jewellery and some evening shoes to change into. Teamed with a black wool dress, this can transform[50] your day to evening look with minimal effort. In summer you may wish to change into a spaghetti-strap dress[51] with strappy sandals[52]. If it's a summer afternoon party then a simple A-Line Sun Dress[53] is appropriate; for a summer evening event you may wish to choose more of an elegant ensemble[54]. Once you are happy with your cocktail dress code etiquette, you can be confident that you look good and can now concentrate on mingling with[55] the other guests, ensuring you are a charming guest and great conversationalist.	[49] *adv.* 闪耀的 [50] *vt.* 改变；转换 [51] 吊带裙 [52] 系带凉鞋 [53] A字裙 [54] *n.* 全套服装；总效果 [55] 与……混合；参加，加入

参考译文

课文A 商务礼仪

礼仪是一种行为标准，它阐明一个社会群体、社会阶层或社会团体内依据当代习俗标准进行社交的行为规范。在商务领域中，良好的商务礼仪意味着在工作中与他人交往时行为专业，举止适当。

在任何组织中，秘书都是重要职员。对各级秘书来说，特别是那些接触客户和其他重要外部人员的秘书，他们的表现不仅影响到自身的名声，而且影响所在公司的形象。因此，秘书有必要掌握良好的商务礼仪，使自己脱颖而出。

1. 专业商务礼仪的益处

1.1 改善形象

你在社交和工作场合的行为举止将影响他人对你以及你所在组织的判断。如果你不知道该如何正确地握手或出示名片，人们可能也会质疑你的业务技能。相反，通过遵守适当的礼仪，你可向职业同行们表明你和他们的业务水平相当。

1.2 改善工作关系

由于强调尊重他人，礼仪为创建合作文明的企业文化奠定了基础。事实上，许多基本的商务礼仪是一些共同遵守的礼节。遵守礼仪准则可以消除一些与工作场所有关的干扰因素，如闲话或个性冲突。它还确保工作关系职业化，避免同事因模糊工作和个人生活之间的界线而让其个人情感影响工作场所行为。

1.3 增长业务

商务礼仪知识有助于打开多扇职业大门。潜在的客户和同事通常会根据你的软技能来判断你以及你的业务头脑。擅长在各种职业场合中沟通的人要比那些不擅长的人更容易让人产生信任感。如果你始终有礼貌，并知道如何在一些重要的会议和商务餐会上举止得当，你的多才多艺以及交际技能会给他人留下深刻印象。例如，如果一位客户正在寻找一名能代表他公司的公关专业人士，那么他将青睐能代表他给他人留下良好印象的某个人。

1.4 建立友好关系

许多核心礼仪准则都是为了给予他人受重视的感觉。例如，介绍同事时，你应该首先介绍最重要的人。参加会议时，你应该分别招呼每个人。虽然这些举措看起来不重要，但它们能很微妙地表示你对对方的尊重。另外，当每个人都遵循相同的社会习俗时，它能确保人际交往和职场交流从一开始就进展顺利，并且有助于你与所有人交往，包括新客户和同事。

2. 商务礼仪准则

在商界，人们在见面的几秒钟内就能形成对对方的第一印象，因此，确保做好充分的准备，以专业人士的身份出现，这一点至关重要。商务礼仪为建立成功的职业关系，以及展示你的职业风采提供了一个框架。有关在不同场合下建立关系时，如何能举止得当，这里提供了一些基本的技巧。

2.1 待人

你如何待人透露了你的很多信息。

- 快速记住名字。记住名字的要诀是在你和他们进行第一次对话时，三次使用这个人的名字。此外，还要写下名字并保存名片。人们了解到你不知道他们名字这种情况后，可能会由此认为你不重视他们。
- 不要根据他人在工作场所中的重要性来做主观评断。你有必要跟维修人员以及承担行政支持性工作的职员交谈。他们值得你尊重。
- 自我评估：想想你是如何对待你的上司、同事以及下属。你与他们的关系存在的差异，如果被别人发现，是否会对你不利？如果是这样的话，找到差异存在之处，并开始改善这种动态关系。
- 你可以选择与他人分享有关你个人生活的信息，但一定要谨慎。因为，有些事情可能会来困扰你。所以，也不要要求别人与你分享他们的个人生活。这会让很多职场人士不舒服。
- 尊重他人的个人空间。

2.2 沟通

有时，不是你说话的内容，而是你说话的方式，这至关重要。

- 务必在24小时内回复电话和邮件——即使只告诉对方你将晚些时候提供所需信息。

- 在用免提通话之前，务必征求对方同意。
- 个性化语音留言——没有一种情况比在某人的语音留言中只听到电话号码却不知你是否正在给合适的人留言这种情况更糟糕了。
- 工作性质的电子邮件语法和拼写都应该准确无误。它们不应该被视为个人电子邮件。
- 发送邮件时，使用“主题”框，并务必使它与你的邮件内容直接相关。这确保你以后能够轻松地找到邮件并做出可能更快的回复。
- 千万不要在邮件中说一些你当着某人面时不会说的事情。
- 下画线、斜体、粗体、着色、改变字体的大小都会使一封“温和的”电子邮件变成一封言辞过于激烈或咄咄逼人的邮件。

2.3　商务会议

遵循得体的商务会议礼仪可以使与会人员之间建立尊重，有助于会议准时开始和结束，并营造合作的氛围。

• 到场

至少提前 15 分钟到达商务会议的会场。这样你可以找一个座位坐下来等待会议开始。

• 议程

至少在会议前的 48 小时内，致电会议主席，表示对会议议程的关注。这样会议主席和有关的与会人员将有时间决定是否需要更改会议议程。

• 准备

参加会议时，带上会议所需的所有材料和资料，并了解会议主题。

• 着装

务必遵循会议主席规定的着装规则。该规则规定了会议所需的着装类型，即商务休闲装或商务正装。

• 发言

务必在指定的提问时间内发问，并举手，等会议主席确认你有发言权。当别人在发言或提问时，不要打断他们。

• 听

你可能会发现，你有关某个话题的很多问题，其答案就在会议内容中。所以，务必认真听会议内容并记笔记。

• 紧张的习惯

避免一些紧张的习惯，如在桌子上轻轻地敲笔、嘴里发出声响、让纸张发出沙沙声或在地板上跺脚。

• 手机和笔记本电脑

会议开始前，关掉手机。如果你正在等一个紧急电话，那么请将手机铃声设置为振动，而且接电话时，应请求准允，到会场外接听。除非会议准许使用笔记本电脑，否则关机，并放低屏幕，以免挡住他人的视线。

2.4　商务送礼

送礼在商务活动中是一个非常棘手的问题，大多数公司都有明确的规定来管理这种做法。因此，知晓商务送礼的礼仪，避免任何误解，这一点很重要。这里提出有关商务送礼的几个要点。

- 商务礼品可以是各式各样的，包括从食物到酒、小的用具（如名片夹或钢笔）再到办公物品（如相框或电脑配件）等各种礼品。
- 挑选礼物时，一定要遵守公司内有关送礼方面的政策。进行一些调查、花一点心思可以使礼品选择过程更容易。
- 如果你决定赠送商务礼品，一定要确保它不要太私人化。此外，赠送幽默礼品时，要格外小心。如果你不太确定一件礼品是否会使接收礼品的人感到愉快，就不要赠送它。
- 送奢侈的礼品是个糟糕的策略，而且不得体。别人可能并不像你那样热衷于奢侈的礼品，还可能会因此感到尴尬。或者，更糟的是，他们会厌恶你这种极端的做法。
- 赠送物质性的礼物不是唯一的选择，即使是在商务领域。挤出时间为同事或客户公司的慈善机构做一些志愿者工作，这个礼物可能会比物质礼品更可贵。

2.5　商务招待会

在商务招待会上注意你的举止与在工作活动中同等重要。失礼不仅使你尴尬，还可能使你在他人心目中留下坏印象，而这些人可能对你的职业生涯很重要。不同于更为正式的活动，如演讲、筵席和宴会等，商务招待会是非正式的社交活动，通常鼓励各部门各级职员聚在一起放松。以下是你在商务接待会需要遵循的一些准则。

• 守时

守时在商务聚会上比在私人聚会上更重要。别人可能会记住你迟到这一行为，并且由此认为你不负责任或不尊重同事的时间。

• 安排好时间

如果你是商务招待会的举办人，你应该将招待会的时长计划在二到三小时之内。这样的时长足够让招待会上的客人感受到你的盛情，有足够的时间相互结识，却不会过于劳累。当他们到达时，你应该和每位客人握手打招呼。所有客人在到达时应当问候主人，在离开时，向主人表示感谢，并说再见。

• 克制讲闲话

当与同事、老板和其他专业人员一起参加商务招待会时，你们的话题会不可避免地谈及到公司。然而，谈及公事时一定要随意轻松。不要信任刚认识的人，并且克制自己，不去讲公司其他职员的流言蜚语或诽谤所在的公司。

• 礼貌交谈

除了避免闲话和消极言论以外，在诸多话题中，成为谨慎的健谈者，这一点也很重要。同时，还要避免谈及政治、宗教和极私人的话题。在职业场合中，刚遇见对方就问及对方的婚姻状况、性取向或工作经历，这是非常失礼的行为。保险的话题包括不太严肃的热门事件以及行业新闻。礼貌地赞美他人并表示愿意在工作上给予帮助，这些方式都能在很大程度上增强初次交谈的效果，只要你的赞美和意愿是真诚的。如果你正在一群人中说话，尽量让所有人都参与交谈，而且在多数情况下，让别人陈述他们的看法，而不是一味地讲述自己的观点。

• 给同事留下印象

出席商务招待会的员式通常会给许多同事留下第一印象。确定谈话基调时，应多考虑对方的立场。积极倾听，让对方来引导话题内容。保持适当的姿势，并和你遇到的每个人进行直接的眼神接触。当他们在慷慨陈词时,应当释义他们所说的话,以此表明你正在倾听。

• 融入

商务宴请是与同事沟通并结识新朋友的最佳时机。融入他人的艺术需要不断地体谅同来的客人。如果有人独自一人在招待会上，走过去以全名介绍自己，然后问求对方的全名（如果她没有主动给你的话），这样做是礼貌的。以全名称呼对方，除非在交谈中，她直呼你的名字，从而定下谈话基调，否则你不能想当然地认为你们可以在交谈中相互直呼其名。唯一例外的情况是当你与担任公司较高职位的人交谈时。在这种情况下，如何才算是准确地称呼对方可能会难以界定。所以，应当从一开始就表明你在公司里的职位，这样就不会在交谈中产生令人尴尬的错误。

• 饮酒问题

如果有点心提供，你应当一直用你的左手拿着点心或饮料，以便右手能随时与他人握手。通常，在商务宴请上不饮酒是明智的。如果打算饮酒，你一定要提前设置饮酒限量，并遵守。在商务活动中饮酒过量，使自己尴尬，这会在公司里对你产生永久性的不良后果，并损害你的名声。

2.6 商务着装

当首次涉足或已身处商界时，你必须知道如何在特定的场所适当地着装。参加面试或招聘会时，你的服装很可能不同于日常商务装。大多数企业制定了着装规范政策，就员工在职业装和便装日如何着装提供了指南。有关商务着装准则列举如下。

• 商务正装

穿商务正装，你会给人留下深刻印象。商务正装是高档的日常职业装。正式的晚宴和颁奖典礼要求着商务正装。男士身穿深色的西装，里面着一件西装衬衫，系上一条丝绸领带，并戴上丝绸或亚麻装饰方巾，最后再配以礼服鞋和配套的深色裤子。女士则身穿裙子，外面搭一件外套，下面穿连裤袜和不露脚趾的鞋。

• 商务职业装

穿商务职业装意味着你通常穿着保守的衣服，塑造着专业的形象。商务职业装类似于商务正装，但并不意味着你一定要穿最好的鞋和外套。在日常工作中需要着商务职业装的职业包括财务、会计和有严格着装规定的机构。女性可以穿裙子或长裤套装，再配以高跟鞋，而男性可以穿休闲西装或西装外套、领尖有纽扣的衬衫、西装裤，再配以领带和皮鞋。

• 商务便装

当所在公司的着装规范是商务便装时，这就意味着你不需要穿西装。然而，它并不是要求你穿如牛仔裤和 T 恤之类的休闲装。女性通常穿带领的衬衫或毛衣，配以时装裤、时装鞋或靴子。保守的衣服和裙子也是可以接受的。男性商务便装的选择包括 POLO 衫，带领的衬衫或毛衣。他们的商务休闲装通常是卡其布裤子或时装裤，再配以时装鞋，而无须系领带。

课文B 商务餐宴礼仪

你在餐桌上的行为举止可能对一个商业决策产生积极或消极的影响。如果表现糟糕，这将对你的名声产生灾难性的影响，这一点不足为奇。正是因为这些原因，所有的职场人士都应该学习基本的商务餐宴礼仪。

1. 邀请

商务邀请可以是非正式的或正式的。虽然人们传统上通过邮件发送邀请函，但非正式的邀请，如电子邮件和电话邀请，正变得越来越受欢迎。

1.1 邀请时间

在大多数非正式的场合下，最好是提前三到四周邀请客人。如果您选择通过电话邀请客人，一定要在聚会前的两周内写信提醒客人。

下面是一些需要遵循的其他准则：

- 邀请外地高管参加重要的研讨会，需提前六到八个月发出邀请。
- 邀请外地的客人参加重要的宴会，需提前四到六个月发出邀请。
- 邀请客人参加正式的午宴，需提前三到五周发出邀请。
- 邀请客人参加晚宴，需提前四周发出邀请。
- 邀请客人参加集体早餐，需提前二到四周发出邀请。
- 邀请客人参加鸡尾酒会，需提前二到四周发出邀请。
- 邀请客人参加茶会，需提前二到三周发出邀请。

1.2 邀请函格式

在商务邀请上，你会发现：

- 公司标志或符号（在邀请函的顶部或底部）。
- 主人的名字。
- 邀请语（以下都是邀请语，具体取决于你的公司和场合）。
  "诚挚地邀请您参加"
  "恭候光临"
  "敬请光临"
  "邀请您参加"
  "敬请您赏光参加"
- 聚会的性质——注明此次社交活动是早餐、午餐、晚餐、鸡尾酒会还是其他社交场合。
- 聚会的目的——如介绍新人、发布新产品、对某位退休人表示敬意、庆祝一个盛典或其他节日活动。
- 日期和时间——活动的日期和时间必须完整写出。不能缩写星期数。最正式的书写格式如，"Friday, the twenty-seventh of July at six-thirty o'clock"，而最不正式的格式为"Friday, July 27, at 6:00 p.m."。
- 地点——接下来是活动举行的具体地址。如果你的房子或者乡村俱乐部很难找或者你的客人以前没有到过那里的话，你通常要在邀请函中附一张地图。
- 如何回复邀请——回复邀请的地址或电话号码在邀请函左下角。

• 特别说明——特别说明写在 RSVP 地址的下方，如有关着装、停车、下雨情况下活动举行的地点等说明。

人们通常用黑色、深蓝色、深灰色或棕色的油墨将商务邀请函印在白色或灰白色的优质纸张上。公司可以使用任何颜色的纸，只要它能保持和提升该公司的形象。

预先印好的邀请函适用于大多数非正式的餐宴和聚会。但如果是一次很随意的聚会，则没必要印邀请函。

2. 到达

务必遵循良好的用餐礼仪。你到达餐厅的那一刻，其他共进午餐的人就会对你形成某种印象。

2.1 不要迟到

这应当是用餐礼仪的第一条准则。即使迟到五分钟或十分钟，也会给他人留下一个坏印象；如果迟到超过十分钟，则表明你粗心且自私。

2.2 着装得体

避免在着装方面犯错。打电话给餐厅，了解他们是否有着装规定。

当你到达餐厅，而主人还没到，这时，根据礼仪，你应该在大厅或等候厅等。不要去餐桌等。

如果你是主人，应该在大厅等你的客人。如果一部分客人已到，你应该在大厅里等到预订好的餐宴开始时间，然后再去餐桌，并让领班或服务员为晚到的客人引路。

3. 餐桌礼仪

用餐礼仪几乎影响到用餐的各个方面。在你就座前以及中途离开后又继续用餐时，用餐礼仪都适用。餐桌礼仪规则并不复杂，但有助于你在商务餐宴上给他人留下深刻印象。

3.1 座次礼仪

主人或许对座位安排已有考虑，所以你应该让他引你去座位上。作为主人，你应该提示座位安排。

在餐厅，主客应该坐餐桌最好的座位。通常这个座位上的椅背对着墙。一旦主客的座位确定，主人就应该坐在她的左边。然后，其他人则在桌子周围依次就座。

3.2 餐巾礼仪

在非正式的餐宴上，就座后，应当即刻把餐巾放在膝上。但在正式场合下，需要等女主人从餐桌上拿下餐巾并展开放在她的膝上时，你才能展开自己的餐巾。

3.3 餐饮服务礼仪

在正式餐宴的服务过程中，侍者必须将食物端给餐桌上的每一位用餐者，并从用餐者的左边端上盘子或碗。在较随意的餐宴上，或者由主人将食物盛在客人的餐盘里，顺着餐桌传下去供用餐者享用；或者由用餐者取食物，并在必要时，给他人递送食物。

3.4 餐具摆放

由外而内的餐具使用规则，可使用餐者对刀、叉或汤匙的使用变得简单易行，即先使用摆放在外部的餐具，然后再向内逐次使用。以下是对餐具摆放的具体说明。

- 叉——两个叉子都在主菜盘的左边。距主菜盘最远的叉子是吃沙拉用的，在主菜盘旁边的叉子是吃主菜用的。（请注意：在比较正式的餐宴上，沙拉通常在主菜后上桌，因此摆放顺序相反。）
  叉齿或按照欧洲大陆式用餐礼仪朝下；或按照美式用餐礼仪朝上。
- 餐盘——客人就座时，餐盘并没有摆放到餐桌上，而只有在主菜上桌时，餐盘才摆上来。
- 大盘子，如 晚餐和午餐盘，常放在距桌边一英寸处。
- 沙拉盘——沙拉盘放在餐叉左侧。
  小盘子，如沙拉盘、鱼盘和点心盘，则放在距桌边两英寸处。
- 餐刀——餐刀放在右侧，距餐盘一英寸处，直接挨着餐盘。刀刃应该对着餐盘。如果主菜需要牛排刀，则可用牛排刀代替餐刀。
- 餐匙——汤匙放在外侧餐刀的最右边。
- 面包盘和黄油刀——小的面包盘放在餐叉的上方，餐盘的左上方。黄油刮刀放在面包盘上面。
- 玻璃杯——通常酒杯和水杯一起使用。如果餐具摆放空间有余，可按照你喜欢的方式摆放杯子，如与桌边平行摆成一条直线或与桌边呈对角线摆放。
- 水杯——水杯放在离手最近的位置，在餐刀上方约一英寸处。
- 酒杯——在右边至少要放一只酒杯，而且很可能就放在水杯的上方。
- 餐巾——将餐巾放在餐具的中心位置，或小餐叉的左侧。
- 咖啡杯——将咖啡杯和垫盘放在餐具的右侧。咖啡匙则搁在垫盘的右边。
  将咖啡杯和垫盘摆在距最外侧餐具约一英寸处，而且垫盘的上边缘与主餐盘或碗的顶部边缘对齐。
  杯柄指向四点钟位置，以便取用。
- 甜点勺和叉——在非正式的餐宴上，当提供两种甜点餐具时，餐具可摆在桌上或甜点盘上。
  甜品勺（或甜点刀）放在餐盘正上方的水平位置上，匙柄向右。
  甜点叉 摆在甜品勺（或甜品刀）的下面，叉柄向左。
  在正式的场合下，甜品餐具也可以同样的方式摆在点心盘上。
- 盐和胡椒——由于食盐者比用胡椒的人多（而且大多数人是用右手的），所以盐瓶放在胡椒瓶的右侧，摆在靠近右手的位置。
  胡椒瓶则放在盐瓶的左边，再具体一点来说，即摆在盐瓶上方斜一点的位置上。
  盐瓶和胡椒瓶摆在一套餐具的上方或两套餐具之间。

3.5 用餐时间

在一张只有两到四人的小餐桌上，你必须等到其他所有人的饭菜都端上来后，才可开始用餐。但在正式的或商务餐宴上，你应该等到所有人都开始用餐时或主人请你用餐时，方可用餐。

3.6 使用餐具

欧式用餐方式盛行于所有的正式和非正式餐宴，因为它一种自然的、有序的用餐方式。

- 左手拿叉，叉齿向下。
- 右手拿刀，距主盘一到两英寸。
- 食指沿着刀刃的顶部伸直。
- 用餐叉叉取食物并送入口中。
- 如果不用刀，则将它放在餐桌上。
- 在非正式餐宴上，叉齿可向上。

3.7 传递食物

应向右传递食物。用餐者或者端着菜让下一位客人取用，或者将这道菜递给她，由她自助取食。所有笨重的菜应放在桌上，供每位客人取食。有关如何递盐、胡椒、面包和黄油等都有专门的规定。

3.8 搁放餐具

当你停下来喝饮料或与别人交谈时，你应该放下餐具，将刀叉稍微倾斜，呈倒转的“V”字形，放在靠主盘中心的位置上，并使刀叉顶部相向。

3.9 用餐结束

在正式的餐宴上，盘子由专门人员清理。但是，在没有他人帮忙，自己上菜的非正式餐宴上，女主人会清理盘子，通常由一到两位客人帮忙。当家庭聚餐时，用餐者需要自己清理盘子。

3.10 离开餐厅

在示意餐宴结束时，女主人与男主人进行眼神交流，把餐巾放在桌子上，建议大家到另一个房间去喝咖啡和餐后饮料，并且从椅子上站起来。

在离开时，客人应该让离别简短而亲切，而不是用冗长的告别耽搁主人。

4. 商务餐宴的后续事宜

4.1 感谢信

客人写信是为了感谢主人提供的盛宴和愉快时光，同时确认餐宴上做出的任何决定。主人也应该写信告诉客人很高兴能和他或她一起用餐，并简要概括所有的业务细节。餐宴后，双方也可相互致电，但写信有两大优点：它不会打断别人的日常安排，而且看上去似乎更温暖、更亲切。

早餐或午餐会的感谢信范本：

亲爱的凯茜：

谢谢您安排我们今天上午的早餐会！我非常感激你的精心准备以及你就内容方面提出的有用评论和建议。很高兴能与你和罗宾一起工作。我们一起会有一个非常成功的六月研讨会。另外，谢谢你邀请我做演讲嘉宾。

诚挚地，

伊丽莎白·温特丝（职业演说家）

4.2 回请

邀请某人共进商务午餐、晚餐或早餐并不总是意味着他们必须回请。

你没有必要对一个纯粹公事性质的餐宴回请（尤其是可报销的餐宴），不管是谁邀请你——无论是你的顾客、客户或你的老板。但是如果你们有持续的生意往来，你当然可以回请。

受销售人员或供应商款待的客户没有必要回请，即使是他的配偶或家人也受到了邀请。

然而，你一定要回报同事和其他商业伙伴的社交邀请。

质检5